The Story of Ross

The Story of Ross

by
Pat Hughes & Heather Hurley

with a contribution by
Lawrence Hurley

Logaston Press

LOGASTON PRESS
Little Logaston Woonton Almeley
Herefordshire HR3 6QH
logastonpress.co.uk

First published 1999
This revised edition 2009
Copyright © Pat Hughes & Heather Hurley 2009

ISBN 978 1 906663 25 4

Typeset by Logaston Press
and printed and bound in Great Britain
by Bell & Bain Ltd.

Contents

Acknowledgments

There are many people and organisations who have helped with information, illustrations and their time in the production of this book whom we wish to thank. In particular staff of Hereford and Ross libraries, Hereford Museum and Art Gallery and Herefordshire Record Office, Margaret Bickerton, Cliff Blanchet of Palace Pound, Morris Bricknell, Dean and Chapter of Hereford Cathedral, Paul Deneen of John Kyrle High School, Fred Druce, John Eisel, Andrew Foley, Geoff Gartside, Dr Kate Harris of Longleat, Michael Hill, Joe Hillaby, Ken Hoverd, Peter King, Annette Leech, Hilary Leeds, Robin Lloyd, Giles Mason, the Paul Mellon Centre, Owen Meredith, Roger Mills of Welsh Water, staff of Monmouth Museum, Pip Morgan, Virginia Morgan, Martin Morris, Jim Murray of the Friends Meeting House, Elizabeth Okell, Okell & Stewart, John Oliver Bishop of Hereford, PGL at Alton Court, Eve Porter, John Powell, Mary Powell, Jonathan Preece, Public Record Office (now The National Archives) at Kew, Bob Purvis, Keith Ray, Nicholas Redman of Whitbread's archives, Mrs. B.M. Rhys, Shawcross & Co., Dave Skipworth, Ian Standing and the staff of Ross Heritage Centre, Roger Stirrup former Rector of Ross, Sue Tanner of Merton House, the *Ross Gazette*, Ross Old Books and Prints, Ross Town Council, the Royal Hotel, and Jim Tonkin. In addition we would like to thank all those owners and occupiers of buildings in Ross who have allowed us to look, peer and take photographs.

Introduction

Heather Hurley and Pat Hughes met while researching the history of Ross for the exhibition in the Market House Heritage Centre, which opened in 1997. A wealth of new material was uncovered but much was surplus to requirements, so prompted by local booksellers and those interested in local history, the pair continued to work together to produce *The Story of Ross* first published in 1999.

In order to write the book, yet further research was necessary. The early history was researched by Lawrence Hurley, the records at Longleat were examined by Pat Hughes and the contents of the Rectory Box were investigated by Heather Hurley. All of this material, together with that held at the Herefordshire Record Office, existing histories of the town and many other sources were thoroughly studied before putting pen to paper.

Since the first edition of *The Story of Ross* a number of changes, improvements and projects need to be noted: excavations at the Prospect 'have unearthed evidence of the medieval Bishop's Palace and an underlying Roman sacred site', the Town Council moved into the Corn Exchange, a Flood Alleviation Scheme was installed and Wilton Castle was restored and made open to the public. The old Alton Court Brewery building has been redeveloped and its records forming the Whitbread Archive together with the documents in the Rectory Box have been deposited at the record office.

Heather Hurley
Hoarwithy 2009

1   Early Beginnings

The distinctive red sandstone of Ross-on-Wye's market house is the perfect symbol of its geological heritage. The lowlands of south Herefordshire, which stretch to the Welsh border in the west, the Malvern Hills in the east, the Forest of Dean to the south and the Shropshire Hills to the north, are almost exclusively formed from this rock. As for the serene landscape and fertility of the land in this corner of the county, this was created simply because the area around what is now Ross-on-Wye was largely spared from the immense forces of glacial drift during the ice ages. That is what gives the landscape 'a more mellow appearance', as Trevor Rowley calls it, than other parts of the county.[1]

It is not until the Mesolithic period that evidence is found of the earliest human activity in the vicinity of Ross. Flints dating from this period were found on Chase Hill, just above the town. This site was later to become an important hill fort in the Iron Age. Although little evidence has been found, these were not the first humans to have occupied south Herefordshire. Even by the standards of the icy Palaeolithic Age (roughly 26,000-8,000BC), the area was sparsely populated and no evidence of mankind has been found that dates back

The entrance to Arthur's Cave above the Wye

1

further than the Upper Palaeolithic (10,000-8,000BC). Almost all the evidence comes from cave dwellings, although Dr. Stanford points out that the repeated ice flows of the Lower and Middle Palaeolithic Ages would have obliterated any evidence of life before then.[2] The nearest excavated cave dwelling to Ross is King Arthur's Cave on the Doward, some six miles south of the town. Sited 100 metres above the River Wye, the cave consists of two chambers, the larger of which is 12 metres long. Taylor's excavations in 1925-27 found a hearth and a collection of Palaeolithic flints. Remains of mammoth, woolly rhinoceros, hyena and various other animals were also found. Although the mammoth is dated at 34-38,000 years old according to a

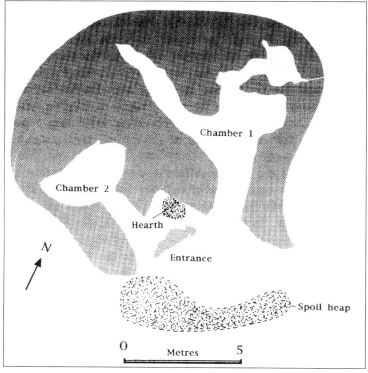

A plan of Arthur's Cave

1995 survey, a further archaeological report in 1997 dated some broken deer bones to the Upper Palaeolithic and suggested that hunters had snapped the bones in order to eat the marrow.[3] The cave would have been occupied by hunters who followed their prey northwards as the climate improved, although it is impossible to tell whether the site was occupied permanently throughout the period. The hearth is near the front of the cave, which corresponds with the theory that early hunters only occupied the entrance areas.

King Arthur's Cave was not the only Palaeolithic dwelling in the area. A 'rock shelter' said to be 'one of the biggest such shelters in southern Britain'[4] near the Seven Sisters Rock has also been excavated. To date, archaeologists have only found Mesolithic remains, but it is

Aerial view of the Doward

Artist's impression of Arthur's Cave when in use

likely the site was used earlier. Other caves and rock shelters exist in the cliffs and hillsides above the Wye, but the only other Palaeolithic remnant to be found in the immediate area is a hand-axe discovered at Welsh Newton just a few miles north-west of King Arthur's Cave. A further hand-axe was found at Sarnesfield in north-west Herefordshire, intriguingly discovered in a lowland area quite near the surface.[5]

The climate rapidly changed at the beginning of the Mesolithic Age (a phase known as the Boreal period – 8,300-7,500BC), introducing warm and dry summers and cold winters. King Arthur's Cave remained in use, and Walters mentions that the evidence suggests 'intensive occupation' of the site up until 4,000BC,[6] whilst mesolithic finds at the Seven Sisters Rock shelter include a hearth and flints.[7] But the improving climate allowed the human hunters to reduce their reliance on the rock shelters and caves and venture to Chase Hill, Great Howle, Huntsham Hill and Hangerbury Hill. It may be, too, that the human population was expanding, generating a need for families to find new homes, be they temporary or semi-permanent, and for the hunting territory to be ever expanded.

Neolithic man (4,000-2,000BC) generally makes himself much more visible than his ancestors to the archaeologist by, most obviously, erecting huge stone and earth tombs and, less obviously, adopting a more settled way of life with villages and the planting of crops. Huntsham Hill has proven a good source of Neolithic finds, prompting Walters to say that there was 'a strong Neolithic presence'.[8] Other local Neolithic sites include Walford, Great

The Queen Stone

Howle and, once again, the Doward. The 1995 survey of King Arthur's Cave suggested that it was now used as a burial chamber.[9]

Despite the increasing evidence of human occupation, the area was still only lightly populated in the period leading up to the Bronze Age (*c*.2,000-700BC). This period, with the introduction of metalworking, also saw other cultural changes taking place, with smaller barrows and cists replacing the large tombs, and the appearance of enigmatic standing stones. The date of erection of these stones is nigh on impossible to ascertain, as no other remains are found with them, even in the packing at their base, but they are generally believed to date to the Bronze Age. The Queen Stone, just below Huntsham Hill, is set within one of the many loops of the Wye near Symonds Yat. It stands 2.1 metres high, with a further 2.4 metres below ground level. Formed out of local sandstone, it has a series of sharply cut grooves running down to ground level; it is unknown whether these were created by natural weathering or by man. The stone is one of four in the Forest of Dean area, a suggestion being that they marked trading centres and were used as the focus for various festivals.[10]

Several finds around Ross confirm that the area was now permanently occupied, the most interesting being a finger-decorated urn at Pontshill near Weston-under-Penyard, about 4 miles to the east of the town. There could well have been a cemetery nearby and the urn is thought to have held cremated remains. Various bronze weapons have also been found near Ross. These include a flanged axe, rapier and spearhead at Aston Ingham, (about 5 miles east of Ross), a palstave (a type of axe-head) at Weston-under-Penyard and a late Bronze Age spearhead near Walford (3 miles south of Ross). A find of Bronze Age metalwork was also uncovered as a result of ploughing at Foy, 2.5 miles north of Ross, in 1791. According to a report compiled seven years later, the metalwork included 'a sort of blade, resembling a hatchet'.[11] More recently, in July 1999, the *Hereford Times* reported on the discovery of a Bronze Age mound on the Doward, indicating that the site had already been in continuous use for several thousand years.[12] As significant finds of both flint and Bronze Age copper alloy metalwork have been found at Weston-under-Penyard, and Aston Ingham there is considerable local evidence for continuous human interaction with and then occupation of the landscape around Ross over several thousand years. Although in use from the Neolithic period, Chase Hill immediately above Ross was not to come into its own as a permanently settled site until several centuries later.

2 Iron Age to the Norman Conquest

At over 650ft high, Chase Hill occupies a commanding position over the River Wye and surrounding lowlands; the perfect site for an Iron Age hill fort. It is just one of many such forts in south Herefordshire, with others at Gaer Cop in the parish of Hentland and, not surprisingly, the Doward, just up the hill from King Arthur's Cave. Although Chase Hill had been used in the Bronze Age and Mesolithic period, evidence suggests that it was only intensively occupied from the 5th or 4th century BC when the earthwork defences were extended, utilising the steep slopes on its northern side. At its peak, the Chase Hill fort covered 19 acres, and around 1,400 people are thought to have lived in the settlement that was laid out on a grid system with rectangular houses and storage blocks.[1] Stanford surmises that the construction or adaptation of many hill forts in the area is linked to the growth of

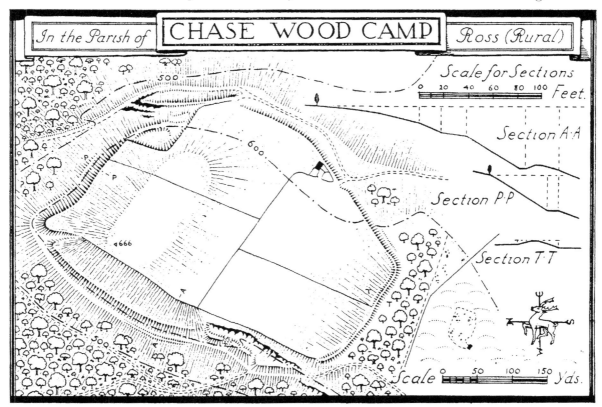

the pottery industry in the Malvern Hills which brought new settlers to the area.[2] Several different kinds of pottery from the Malvern Hills area have been found, with many different identifying marks suggesting that it was an industry making items in bulk. Examples of Malvern Hills pottery have been found throughout Herefordshire and in the Cotswolds, with Stanford claiming that the market in Herefordshire was largely filled with the pottery from around 330BC.

There is a certain amount of confusion about the tribe to which the people of Chase Hill belonged. Historians are forced to rely on Tacitus (a Roman writing in the 1st century AD, whose only contact with Britain was that he married the Roman governor's daughter), various other selections of Roman documentary evidence and finds of Celtic coins. Whilst it is known that the tribe to the west of the Wye were the Silures and that occupying what is now Gloucestershire were the Dobunni, Tacitus mentions another tribe in the vicinity — the Decangi.[3] Stanford believes the Decangi occupied central Herefordshire,[4] but Walters says that the Chase Hill residents were sufficiently distanced from the possible Decangi camps to the north to more logically form an entity with those occupying settlements in the Forest of Dean. He claims, romantically, that the Dean people were a separate tribe, part of 'a foreign land',[5] but if they were they must have at least had commercial links with the Dobunni, if not actually being a part of the tribe.

Chase Hill remained in occupation throughout the Iron Age and, prior to the Roman invasion, it is thought that the tribe based there controlled the land where the Roman settlement and possible military fort of Ariconium was founded in c.50AD. Ariconium, located

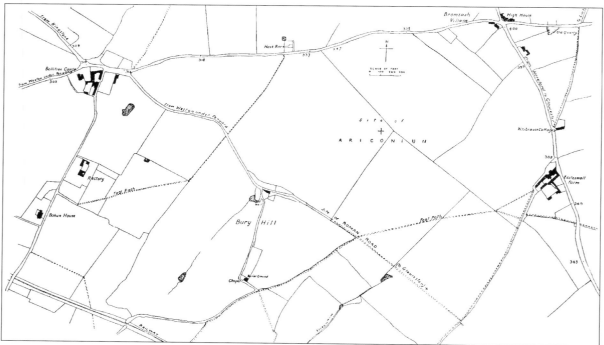

Sketch map showing the site of Ariconium

6

Finds from Ariconium

near Weston-under-Penyard, was a modest administrative centre and iron-working site for the 10th Legion which was pushing west under the leadership of Ostorius Scapula. Around the time of Ariconium's foundation the Romans were pursuing Caractacus, the legendary British warrior who had resisted the invaders since 43AD, though where he fought his final battle and was caught in 51AD remains a mystery. Tacitus describes it as: 'On one side were steep hills ... and at his [Caractacus'] front there was a river without easy crossings.'[6] Some claim this refers to the slopes of the Doward and the River Wye.

No evidence of a military presence at Ariconium was found until an aerial photographic survey was carried out by the Dean Archaeological Group in 1989 when two small 'fortlets' were discovered. These two sites overlapped each other so they cannot have been contemporary, and were situated to the north of the iron-working site, next to the Roman road leading to Lydney. When excavated, large deposits of iron ore slag were also found, showing that this site was also used for iron-working. Evidence of iron-working in the early Roman period has also been found at Great Howle, Aston Ingham, Symonds Yat and at various sites in the Forest of Dean. Finds of native pottery in the vicinity showed that the Britons were closely involved, working in tandem with the invaders. Walters points out that the natives would have received certain benefits for their help, citing the imported, better-quality Samian pottery found in civilian dwellings at Ariconium as an example.[7]

Ariconium remained in use as an iron-working site until the 3rd century AD. In fact, there is evidence of a boom in the mid-2nd century when additional sites came into use nearby. Large deposits of slag have been found at Whitchurch, 5 miles west of Ross, and evidence has also been found at Tretire and Peterstow. (Extensive slag remains were found at Peterstow as recently as July 1999, as identified by Sarah Skelton.) Ariconium itself also expanded in the 2nd century with more furnaces and smithing areas opening up. What appears to have been a guest house block and stabling area was also built for travellers passing through, and Ariconium gained a listing in the *Antonine Itinerary XIII* compiled around 150AD to aid the journeying of the empire's military and civilian officials, as the first stopping off point after

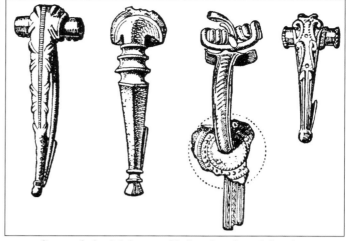

Some of the 20 bronze fibulae found at Ariconium

Gloucester on the road to Monmouth. The Romans had built an extensive road system in the area, including the Dean Road from Lydney to Ariconium and a road linking the Forest

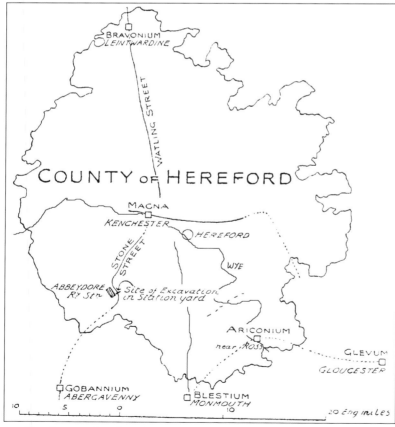

Sketch map showing the pattern of Roman roads in Herefordshire

of Dean with the Roman base at Gloucester. A minor Roman route is also thought to have forded the river at Red Rail in Hoarwithy (4 miles north of Ross) and at Goodrich. The ancient ford crossing over the Wye at Wilton was also most likely to have been used, both for the journey west and for those travelling north. The concentration of activity at Ariconium is shown by a 84ft by 72ft section of the site excavated by N.P. Bridgewater in 1963. Walters notes that in this relatively small area, the archaeologist found six smelting furnaces, smithing hearths, a covered charcoal store and samples of coal dating from before 125AD until the end of the 2nd century.[8]

The 2nd century also saw the construction of the Roman villa at Huntsham, below the old Neolithic settlement. Three main buildings were excavated by Bridgewater between 1959 and 1970, leading to the conclusion that it was mainly an agricultural site and maintained a 'very modest degree of luxury' according to Elizabeth Taylor. The site consisted of a main nine-roomed building, a smaller five-roomed house and an aisled barn containing a corn drier. After her own investigation, Elizabeth Taylor also suggested that a water mill was built to the north of the site which would have been a 'considerable investment'.[9] Walters surmises that the villa was probably occupied by tenant farmers who may have also have been responsible for the iron-working sites at Whitchurch.[10]

Roman altar found at Tretire

The golden age of iron-working in the area seemed to come to an abrupt halt at the beginning of the 3rd century, with both Whitchurch and Ariconium closing down. Walters says this could have been due to depletion of the iron ore or the lack of military activity in the area,[11] for the flashpoints were now far away up in Scotland and iron ore could be extracted from sites further north. By the 4th century, Ariconium was fading fast even as a stopping off point, and no coins have been found dating later than the 360s. Lack of any evidence concerning farming activity suggests that the former bustling iron-working centre became something of an industrial wasteland. Economic decline may not be as exciting a theory as Rev. T.D. Fosbroke's claim in his *Wye Tour* guide of 1833 that Ariconium was destroyed by Vikings in 918,[12] but archaeological evidence speaks louder than words. By the start of the 5th century the Romans were having second thoughts about their empire, besieged as they were on all sides by hordes of 'barbarians'. Britain was eventually abandoned.

It is not known exactly when Ross became a settlement, though it had obtained the status of a small village at the time of Domesday in 1086 (see chapter 3). Since there is no reference to Ross, or any settlement there, during the Roman occupation, it is reasonable to assume that the area either around St. Mary's Church or further down at Brookend began being settled at some point during the Saxon period. The lack of any major archaeological data concerning the town means it is impossible to say which part of the town was settled first, though this may change once analysis of finds at recent excavations near the Prospect has occurred. As the Domesday entry mentions a priest, it may be that the area around the current church was that first chosen, though there is no evidence of an earlier church on the site of St. Mary's. This site would also have been more naturally defensible in a period threatened by Danish and Viking raids, though, again, no evidence has been found for any defences on the sides not protected by the bluff.

Llanfrother Farm

There is also a lack of evidence from religious charters and the *Anglo Saxon Chronicle* — none refer to a place called Ross or a settlement in the vicinity. The See of Hereford was not founded until 676, but Christianity had reached the area well before the Romans left. The 6th century saint Dubricius had close links to the area, and legend has it that he was born in Ergyng, a small British 'kingdom' whose territory stretched from the Black Mountains to the Wye and possibly at its fullest extent as far as the Malvern Hills, in amazing circumstances. The story goes that Peipiau, king of Ergyng was incensed when he saw that his daughter, Efryddal, was pregnant. He ordered that she be put into a sack and thrown into the Wye. Somehow she survived and was washed up on a sandbank. Peipiau ordered that she be burnt on a pyre but it would not light and the next morning she was found with her baby — Dubricius. In later life, Dubricius founded a seminary at Hentland where the *Liber Landavensis* says he had 2,000 brethren.[13] The site is thought to be at Llanfrother, on a hill between Hentland and Hoarwithy. Dubricius was also granted land by King Peipiau for a monastery at Welsh Bicknor, (around 4 miles south of Ross) and a house at Llandinabo (6.5 miles north-west of Ross). Churches at Hentland, Whitchurch and Ballingham are still dedicated to the saint.

The Saxon invaders reached the Wye by the 590s, when the city of Hereford was founded. Early incomers included the Hwicce and the Magonsaetans, but the whole area east of the Wye was gradually absorbed into the kingdom of Mercia under King Penda. This left Archenfield, the rump of Ergyng, on the west side of the Wye, acting as an English controlled buffer between the Welsh and English. This did not stop the Saxons raiding the area in *c*.745.[14] The *Book of Llandaff* reports 'frequent day and night encounters' across the River Wye and that King Ithel of Mercia was forced to make a series of gestures to the people of Ergyng in order to retain their loyalty after the raids. This episode suggests that

Ergyng was an important political battleground for the English and the Welsh. The *Book of Llandaff* also mentions a 'rare plague' which depopulated the area.[15]

If settled at this point (and it is unknown whether it was), Ross would surely have been involved in this upheaval, situated as it is, just over the river from Archenfield. It would also have been near to the border when King Offa of Mercia built his famous dyke in *c*.784. This was a frontier between the English and the Welsh, using the Wye and man-made dykes to create a border running from the mouth of the Wye in the south to the Dee estuary in the north. Whether it was built purely as a political boundary or as a barrier is open to interpretation, and it also raises questions as to the status of Archenfield. No remains of the dyke exist between Hereford and Monmouth and it was previously assumed that the river acted as the border. If this was the case, then Archenfield would have been on the Welsh 'side', though a client state to Mercia. It could be that the dyke never existed at all in south Herefordshire as Archenfield was felt to be sufficient protection, or because special arrangements existed between Archenfield and Mercia.

During the 9th century Viking raiders launched incursions into the area via the Severn and Wye rivers. King Burgred, king of Mercia in the mid-9th century, was involved in constant battles between 866 and 874, when he fled to Rome. By 877, the Vikings were in a position to install Ceolwulf as king. In 914, the Vikings returned, and according to the *Anglo Saxon Chronicle*,[16] they ravaged Archenfield and took Cyfeilog, the bishop of the area, as prisoner. This prompted the Saxons of Hereford and Gloucester to join together to fend off the Danes, a campaign which ended in victory, reputedly partly through the use of surprise. Legend has it that the decisive battle took place at Kill Dane Field near Ariconium. Walters pours cold water on this theory, saying the site is 'rather too open for a surprise attack', though the area may well have been covered by woodland at the time of the battle. Walters also suggests that a possible route the invaders would have taken was to land at Lydney harbour and then take the old Roman road through to Ariconium and then on to Ross and Archenfield.[17]

A meeting which could well have affected people living around Ross was held in Hereford in *c*.926. The resulting document is known as the Ordinance Concerning the Dunsaete, Dunsaete being a name given to people of mixed Welsh and Saxon background who lived on both sides of the Wye, thus falling on both sides of the border. Elizabeth Taylor records that the Ordinance officially made the river in south Herefordshire the English-Welsh border.[18] The Ordinance effectively set a series of laws concerning cross-border activities such as cattle stealing. The unstable nature of the border area is emphasised by the raids of the mid-11th century, just prior to the Norman invasion. Under the Welsh prince Gruffydd ap Llewellyn, joint Welsh and Danish forces frequently made raids into Archenfield in the 1040s. In 1055 they reached as far as Hereford, and Domesday mentions the area as being laid to waste. The decisive battle may have taken place at Bloody Meadows near Holme Lacy, where a mass horse grave has been found, possibly representing the remains of the defeated cavalry of the Norman Count of Vexin, then responsible for Hereford's defence.[19]

Any people who may have settled at Ross by this time, or in the preceding centuries, would have been at the crossroads of all this activity. They would also have come under the influence of several different cultures. This helped create a separate border identity which, to some extent, remains today. Stanford notes that, despite the new cultures of the invaders being imposed on the natives, 'below the political and religious veneer, some British communities survived to integrate slowly and form the border's own culture.'[20]

The foundation of Ross remains a mystery. Perhaps the answer remains hidden below ground, waiting to be excavated at some time in the future. All we know for sure is that by the time William the Conqueror's officials came to Ross, there was a small settlement tucked up against the Wye which had somehow emerged out of all the Anglo-Welsh rivalry, and survived.

3   Growth and Trade in the Town

The Domesday Book entry for Ross, made in 1086, states:

> In Ross are 7 hides paying geld. In demesne is 1 plough and there could be 2 more. There are 18 villeins and 6 borders and a priest with 23 ploughs. There are 3 slaves and a mill rendering 6s 8d and 16 acres of meadow. The woodland is in the King's preserve. The villeins pay 18s as revenue.

Domesday Book entry for Ross (courtesy of the NA)

The bishop's manor of Ross covered a huge area, including parts of Walford, Penyard and Upton Bishop and was only later divided for convenience into the two parts of Ross Borough and Ross Foreign, the lands outside the borough. Much of the land was forested and most of the group of 24 men, with their wives and children, the three serfs or slaves and the priest, would have been concentrated in the area now known as the town. In fact, it seems most likely that there were two centres for this little community; the one near the mill on the Rudhall brook at the foot of the hill, where the town mill stood for centuries; the other round a church of some sort served by the priest in the Domesday entry, and established on the promontory overlooking the River Wye. Some time during the next 50 years, a third unit, the market, was added to these entities, linking the two and stimulating the growth of the town.

On Whit Sunday 1138, when he attended High Mass in Hereford Cathedral, King Stephen issued two charters, granting to Bishop Robert de Bethune the right to hold markets in Ross and Ledbury.[1] The Ross charter may not imply the origins of the borough, for it is likely that markets were already established in both towns. The final phrase in the charter, 'I ordain that men going or coming may have my peace', indicates the unrest of the time and was probably an attempt on the bishop's part to safeguard the lives and property of his tenants in the difficult and troubled times of Stephen's reign.[2]

Even if the granting to Bishop Robert de Bethune of a market charter for Ross in 1138 does not signify the founding of a market there, it does provide a formal acknowledgement of the importance of the market to the town's overlord. Markets produced stall-holders who paid rents, and tolls could be levied on the produce brought into the town. They also stimulated the wider economy, bringing in more trade from the surrounding countryside whilst focusing commercial activity on the borough.

This nineteenth-century engraving of Ross from Wilton Bridge shows the proximity of Wilton to the town.
(Hereford City Library, Pilley Collection 183)

The establishment nearly a hundred years later of a midsummer fair, just down the road at the river crossing at Wilton, must have been something of a blow to the Bishop of Hereford. On 7th March 1231, Henry de Longo Campo, of Wilton Castle, was granted a charter by Henry III to hold the fair, on the eve, the feast-day and the day following the feast of St. John the Baptist, the 24th of June. Such a fair would bring in merchants and dealers from a wide area, but although it might benefit the townspeople of Ross by filling the inns and bringing in passing trade, it added nothing directly to the bishop's revenues.[3] It therefore seems likely that the charter for another fair, this time at Ross, granted by the king to the Bishop of Hereford ten years later, was the direct result of an appeal by the bishop. This fair also was to be held in summer, on 20th July — a month after the one at Wilton — on the eve, day and the morrow of the feast of St. Margaret.[4] The charter also made provision for a Thursday market. St. Margaret's Fair was later known as the Wool Fair and a Saturday market has now been added to the Thursday one.[5] The charter was repeated in 1355, at the request of the Bishop of Hereford.[6]

As was the case in a number of other towns, the market was sited in a wedge-shaped space at the junction of two roads. Other Herefordshire towns, like Hereford and Ledbury, have similar triangular market places, but then so do towns in the east of the country.[7] The form may therefore have less to do with any regional significance than with the unplanned nature of the market and the layout of the road system. The site of the market, roughly equidistant from the church at the high point of Ross, and the mill down by the brook, was crucial to the town's development, encouraging building in the vicinity and effectively filling the gap between the community at the mill and that nearer the church.

The market must also have stimulated trade, for the town continued to grow apace. In the last years of the thirteenth century, a series of surveys of the episcopal estates was made and later bound up in red leather as the *Red Book of the Bishops of Hereford*. This contains a rent roll, dated 1277 to 1285, for Ross which suggests that there were something like 100 houses in Ross Borough alone, and around 500 inhabitants.[8]

The second page of the Rent Roll for Ross from the Red Book of the Bishops of Hereford. The entry for the miller comes nearly halfway down the page. (HRO HD O/L28)

Since the Bishop of Hereford was the overlord of the manor of Ross the rents from the town were due to him. Within the town the main streets were laid out in 'burgage plots', each held by a 'burgess' and attached to these were not only certain dues but also privileges. The system of burgage tenure enjoyed by the inhabitants of Ross Borough, meant that the bishop merely received a money payment of 12d a year from his burgesses for their landholdings. He could not claim personal services from them, nor were they bound to remain within his estates, like their counterparts in the country. They might marry when and where they wished, or move from the town to another, more profitable area. Ross Borough, therefore, achieved a different status to Ross Foreign.[9]

The 1277 rent roll lists the tenants of the manors of Ross Borough and Ross Foreign and records the payments for burgages, together with those who paid for shops, cottages or land within the town.[10] Unlike the equivalent list for Ledbury, it does not enter the tenants under individual streets and cannot therefore provide a basis for a detailed study of the town. Nevertheless, there are certain markers that offer clues to the layout and provide a comparison with later documentary material.

The first of these is the separate listing, at the end of the roll, of the permanent stalls or shops in the town. Although some merchants may have had 'lock-up shops', most would have lived at or near their business premises, and the stalls would have been sited immediately outside the dwelling house, projecting into the street. By matching the names of the stall-owners with the names of the burgage holders, it can be seen that almost all the stalls appear as a cluster, round the market place and up the street, now known as High Street, but, in the mediaeval period, part of the market.

The second fixed point is the burgage of 'Robert the priest's man', whose position in the list implies his proximity to the church. He probably lived near the junction of High Street and Church Street. The remaining 23 burgages would then cover the west end of the High Street and, possibly, Edde Cross Street.

The town mill at Ross, rebuilt many times, was still in use until the 1980s but has now closed. The stone building housing the latest mill survives at what was once the edge of the town and marks the third fixed position in the list. If the mediaeval mill was on the site of its successor, this point must mark the dwelling of the miller, Walter, who paid for three burgage plots. There are 24 tenants listed before him in the roll and 25 between him and those identified as shopkeepers. This is roughly the equivalent of the number of properties marked between New Street and the Town Mill on the Ordnance Survey maps made during the 1880s, but it is likely that some of the plots had become subdivided over the centuries. The 50 tenants were probably spread between the present New Street, down Broad Street and Brookend, into Brampton Street. It therefore seems extremely likely that, by 1277, the town had taken on its present form, that the main streets had been set out in burgage plots and that shops had been established.

Further evidence that the main streets of Ross were laid out in burgage plots comes from later title deeds, in which a number of properties between Brookend and the end of High Street, near the church, are actually described as burgages, indicating their mediaeval origins.[11] Mediaeval burgage plots were set out to a standard size, which was laid down by charter, and, although no charter now exists for the town, the regularity of many of the plots can be recognised from the nineteenth century ordnance map, even after 700 years.

The module on which these measurements are based is more difficult to calculate, although there is some slight indication that, as in Ledbury, some of the frontages measured 22 feet.[12] Few title deeds for Ross contain measurements and even in the thirteenth century rent roll subdivision had already started to take place, some tenants managing on a quarter of a burgage, while affluent townsfolk could afford to spread their houses over two or three plots. Later divisions, amalgamations and the creation of side alleys to give access to work

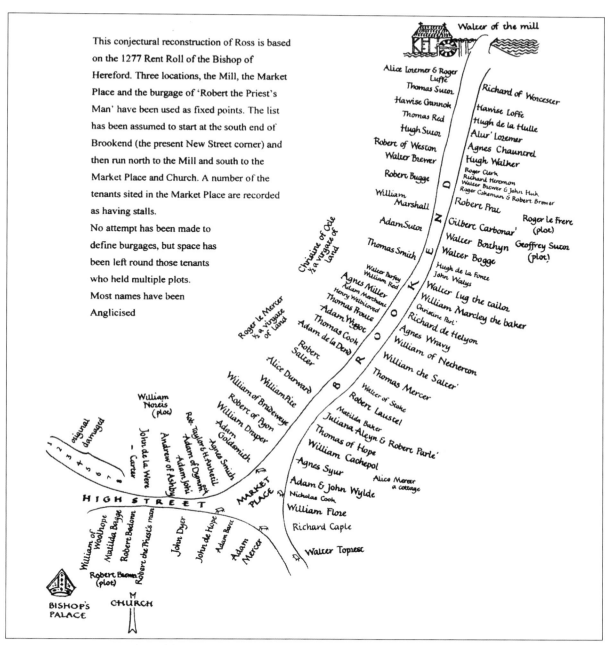

This conjectural reconstruction of Ross is based on the 1277 Rent Roll of the Bishop of Hereford. Three locations, the Mill, the Market Place and the burgage of 'Robert the Priest's Man' have been used as fixed points. The list has been assumed to start at the south end of Brookend (the present New Street corner) and then run north to the Mill and south to the Market Place and Church. A number of the tenants sited in the Market Place are recorded as having stalls.

No attempt has been made to define burgages, but space has been left round those tenants who held multiple plots.

Most names have been Anglicised

Walter of the mill

Alice Loremer & Roger Luffe
Thomas Sutor
Hawise Gannok
Thomas Red
Hugh Sutor
Robert of Weston
Walter Brewer
Robert Bugge
William Marshall
Adam Sutor
Thomas Smith

Richard of Worcester
Hawise Loffe
Hugh de la Hulle
Alur' Loremer
Agnes Chauncrel
Hugh Walker
Roger Clerk
Richard Heremon
Walter Brewer & John Huk
Roger Cokeman & Robert Brewer
Robert Frat
Gilbert Carbonar'
Walter Borthyn
Walter Bogge
Hugh de la Fonte
John Walys
Roger le Frere (plot)
Geoffrey Sutor (plot)

Christine of Cole ½ a virgate of land

Walter Parfey
William Red
Agnes Miller
Adam Merchant
Henry Welbiloved
Thomas Rouce
Adam Wygot
Thomas Cook
Adam de la Dene
Robert Salter

Walter Lug the tailor
William Marcley the baker
Christine Part
Richard de Helyon
Agnes Wravy
William of Nethercon
William the Salter
Thomas Mercer
Walter of Stoke
Robert Laustel
Matilda Baker
Juliana Aleyn & Robert Parle'
Thomas of Hope
William Cachepol
Alice Mercer a cottage

Roger le Mercer ½ a virgate of land

Alice Durward
William Pie
William of Brideweye
Robert of Pyon
William Draper
Adam Goldsmith
Agnes Smith
Rob. Taylor & H. Aukeill
Adam of Dymok
Adam Johi.
Andrew of Ashby
John de la Were
Carter

William Noreis (plot)

Agnes Syur
Adam & John Wylde
Nicholas Cook
William Flore
Richard Caple
Walter Topvesc

HIGH STREET

MARKET PLACE

William of Woolhope
Matilda Bagge
Robert Bedom
Robert the Priest's man
John Dyer
John de Hope
Adam Barre
Adam Mercer

Robert Brown (plot)

BISHOP'S PALACE

CHURCH

1 2 3 4 5 6 7

original damaged

rooms, cottages and stables at the rear of the plot have also distorted the picture of the mediaeval town plan.

This having been said, the map of the town made in 1823 for the collection of the parish poor rate indicates these early plots clearly enough.[13] From the mill they ran up both sides of Brookend Street as far as the Market Place, with the rear boundaries of the plots all neatly aligned. The curve of the Market Place created problems with the back of the plots and, on the north side of the Market Place, the burgages seem to run out in a jigsaw of oddly

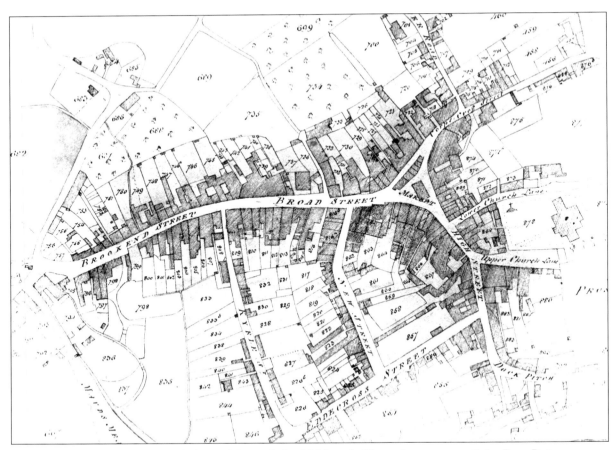

Section from a map of the parish, made in 1823 to facilitate the payment of the Poor Rate.
This part shows the core of the town. (Courtesy of Miss E. Okell)

shaped parcels of land. New Street, built up in the seventeenth and eighteenth centuries, now runs behind this area, but its older name, Back Lane, indicates that at one time it acted as a service road for the back of the Market Place.

The south side of the High Street rose steeply and here the length of the plots is, of necessity, drastically curtailed. It is even possible that this part was not originally laid out for housing at all, since the parish church and the Bishop's Palace occupied the high ground behind the street. Alternatively, this may have been the large plot, charged at 1s 4d, which is listed just beyond the burgage belonging to the priest's man. The west side of Edde Cross Street can hardly have been laid out in typical burgages due to the way the ground drops away towards the river.[14]

The street names of Ross have been discussed at length, notably in a series of articles and letters published in the *Ross Gazette* in 1891.[15] There has been much conjecture, but little hard evidence regarding the origins of some of the names, like Edde Cross Street or Copse Cross Street. Perhaps the earliest list of street names is found in a rent roll of 1648, although individual streets have been found in earlier documents.[16]

Underhill, Thomas Tudor c.1820. (Monmouth Art Gallery)

The High Street — in sixteenth century Latin documents, 'alta vico' — is associated with a whole list of names for it not only included the Market Place, but also a row of shops — Underhill — otherwise known as Under Hell, Behind Hell or Upon Hell. The many variants on this last name seem to come from the Saxon 'helle', meaning a dark place, and imply that the encroachment took place while such words were still in common use. Alternative names for the lane were Butchers Row and Middle Row (chapter 6). It is probable that some part of this Row was, at one time, called 'the Ladyes wash Rowe', part of the Market Place where William Fisher illegally left timber in 1678.[17] The Market Place itself was used as the Bull Ring, but the account for 'mending ye bullring at Ross' found in the Bailiffs' account for 1655, appears with entries for Ross Foreign.[18]

The stretch of road, now part of High Street, from St. Mary's Street to the top of the hill leading to the river, was, in 1648, known as Wilton Gate Street and later in the eighteenth century as Townsend.[19] Some sixteenth and seventeenth century deeds refer to the whole of this part of the street from the Market Place to Edde Cross Street as 'the street between Corne Market Street and Wiltons Gate' but the exact location of 'Wilton's Gate' has not been established.[20]

Behind the High Street / Brookend line lay Edde Cross Street, which joined Wilton Gate to the New or One Mill at the lower end of the town. It has been suggested that the street derives its name from a stone cross, and,

Wilton Gate, later called Townsend, and now part of the High Street

19

in fact, the base of a mediaeval cross, now lost, has been discovered in the area. However, the earliest known document, dated 1339, refers to a 'curtilage' — a courtyard — in the 'street called Edecroft.' This name is repeated in various sixteenth century documents and in the seventeenth century glebe terrier for the parish, and probably reflects ancient usage.[21]

Deeds for property in the street are confusing, for, in the seventeenth and eighteenth centuries, it seems to have been called indiscriminately, Edde Cross Street, Back Lane, New Street or Merton Street. Part of the explanation may lie in the nature of Back Lane or New Street, which, by the mid-1640s, linked Edde Cross Street with the High Street.[22] It is likely that this started its life as an unnamed track crossing the disused Bell Forge site (see below) and that the corner plots at the junction with Edde Cross Street were described as being part of the older street, a description that persisted. Nevertheless, even this attempt at rationalisation may be a simplification. Seventeenth and eighteenth century charity papers for property stretching between New Street and High Street persistently refer to New Street as Edde Cross Street, rather than Back Lane.[23] As if this is not sufficiently complicated, there also seems to have been an attempt in the nineteenth century to replace the mediaeval title of Edde Cross Street proper, with the name Merton Street, after the large house in the street. There is even anecdotal evidence that Merton Street is the older name!

Associated with New Street/Back Lane was the area called the Bell Forge, about which there is very little information, but which seems to have had mediaeval origins. The impres-

The shop of W.E. Hill, on the site of the Upper Bell Forge, in 1925/6. Mr. Hill (William Enoch) wears the apron. His son Geoffrey William stands beside him. The name of the boy is not known. (Courtesy of Mr. Michael Hill of Cheam, Surrey)

The sites of the Upper and Lower Bell Forge in 1999

sion given in later deeds is that of a large site spanning the present street. Originally it probably ran back as far as Edde Cross Street.[24] The earliest known reference to it is in 1625, when the dish or glass market was to be placed 'belowe the Bellforge', but if, as the name implies, church bells were being made in Ross, it likely that the forge flourished before the Reformation and had disappeared before the beginning of the seventeenth century.[25] Bellmaking had, apparently, ceased in Ross before the seventeenth century. The sanctus bell in the church, the earliest of the surviving bells, cast in 1635, bears the initials, IP, John Pennington of Monmouth. The inventory of church plate, made in 1553, lists five bells in the Ross steeple but there are no records to suggest where they were cast.[26]

Back Lane had become established across the site before 1648, when it formed the boundary between Brookend at the north or lower end of the town and High Street towards the Market Place. The two parts of the site were then known as the Upper and Lower Bell Forge.[27] At the end of the century the site was owned by a glover, William Mann, who lived at the Upper Bellforge in the late seventeenth century, while George Mann, also a glover, lived at the Lower Bellforge.[28] There are echoes of the earlier trade when the site was sold to Samuel Prosser of Hereford, brassfounder in 1779.[29]

The name, Broad Street, was a nineteenth century creation — it appears on the parish map of 1823, but has not been found earlier. It stretches between New Street and Kyrle Street which, until it was renamed, was part of Brookend.

The surnames in the thirteenth century rent roll in the *Red Book of the Bishops of Hereford*, provide some clue to the trades carried on in the town. The food trade was represented by two cooks, two bakers and two men called salters; the cloth trade by three weavers, a dyer, a fuller and a draper, with two tailors to make up the cloth. The leather trade, important in later centuries, was indicated by three shoemakers. There was a merchant, a goldsmith,

The remains of the sluice gates near the bottom of the bridge at the bottom of Brookend

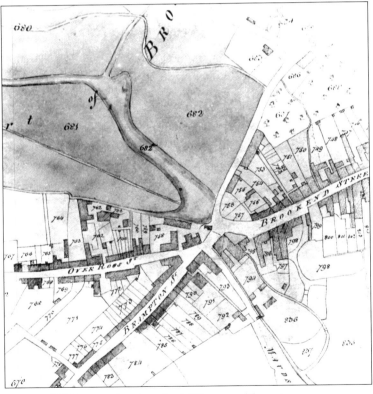

1823 map showing the Mill area with watercourses.
(Courtesy of Miss E. Okell)

and a mercer, each with a shop in the Market Place. There was also a farrier, William Marescall. There must, however, have been many other trades carried out by those whose surname reflected their nickname or place of origin, rather than their source of livelihood — for example, the second baker was William Marcleye. Admittedly, by the end of the thirteenth century surnames are not a secure guide to occupations, as can be seen from the roll itself. Here, Agnes Miller was the previous miller's widow and therefore had no direct connection with the milling trade.[30]

Within the mediaeval town, the largest industrial complex was the mill. The *Red Book* lists Walter of the Mill as paying for three burgages, almost certainly on the site of the present nineteenth century mill buildings. The mill ceased to operate in 1947 and the large millpond on the opposite side of the road has been filled in and is now a car park, but the brook and the sluice gates can still be seen above the bridge.[31]

The importance of the mill can be judged by its worth to the bishop's estate. In the 1277 bishop's rent roll the total value of the manor of Ross was assessed at £54 16s 2½d, of which £20 6s was the rent from the mill. Within the complex there were three mills in operation — two corn mills and a fulling mill.[32]

The low-lying ground near the Rudhall brook was seamed with water courses, some of which supplied the mill and all of which had to be kept clear. Seventeenth century records concern the obstruction of the channels to the mill as when John Merrick was 'presented' for (charged with) 'continuing his encroachment on the water course at the Three Mills' and for placing 'rubbish and other obstructions in the water course at Three Mills.'[33]

The mills in Ross have already been mentioned as a source of income for the manor. In the 1620s a Rent Roll for Ross Foreign stated that: 'The 2 Mills and the Tuck Mill in Ross are now lett at 34li per annum but are thought to be worth 40li.'[34]

These mills on the Rudhall brook, at the junction of Brookend with Brampton Street, were later known as the Town Mill. Since the term 'mill' in this case referred to the sets of millstones or machinery rather than the building, the premises were sometimes described as Two Mills, i.e. the two grist mills, and sometimes as Three Mills, which included the tuck, or fulling mill attached.[35] The millers there were flourishing tradesmen in their own right. Moses Hanks was the miller in 1627 and he was followed in 1646 by Richard Harris.[36] The upkeep of the mill and machinery involved a heavy outlay and there are a number of mentions of Harris in the manor documents. In 1655 the mills needed repair and he was allowed £3 to buy timber.[37] In 1656 there was a breach in the mill pool wall which had to be made good, while in 1676 he was presented for allowing the 'Bridge at ye Millpond head and ye causeway from Philip Osbornes house to ye mill & ye streete before ye milldoore be out of repayre.'[38] The prevalence of flooding in the area would have made such causeways and the wooden bridge, mentioned previously, a necessity.

Richard Harris lived in one of the houses at the lower end of Brookend on the opposite side to the mill itself. There he had a parlour, with a chamber behind, and another over it, a hall and a kitchen. It was comfortably, if modestly furnished, with plenty of brass pots and pewter dishes and candlesticks. There was a well-furnished bed in the chamber over the parlour, and beds in the parlour and the other chamber. The kitchen and hall were the main living rooms.[39]

The importance to the landlord of the mill and of the dues paid by the customers, is further emphasised by the establishment of a 'new mill' at Ross sometime before 1418.[40] This 'new mill' retained its name until the early eighteenth century, when it became known as 'One Mill' and is described in a lease of 1705 as 'the New Mill otherwise the

The Mill Pond with the Railway Inn and the Mill behind, c.1900.
(Fred Druce Collection)

The Mill building

One Mill'. The same property can be traced back to 1666.[41] It can therefore be identified with the mill, which, until the nineteenth century, lay on the Rudhall brook nearer the junction with the River Wye.

The millponds also doubled as fishponds, and the right to catch eels in the one at Ross formed part of a deal to maintain the dam and floodgates of the millpond made in 1461 with Thomas Martyn and Walter Seny.[42] It is not stated to which of the mills this contract refers, but it is likely to have been the larger, main town mill, which had a huge pond, draining a large low-lying area. The pond serving the New Mill, or One Mill, was a much smaller affair, hardly likely to provide sufficient fish to warrant the outlay on the facilities.

Yet another mill was in operation by the end of the seventeenth century, and may, of course, have been built many years before that. It was later known as the Chace Mill, but seems to have started life as Chest's Mill. A deed of 1693 describes it as:

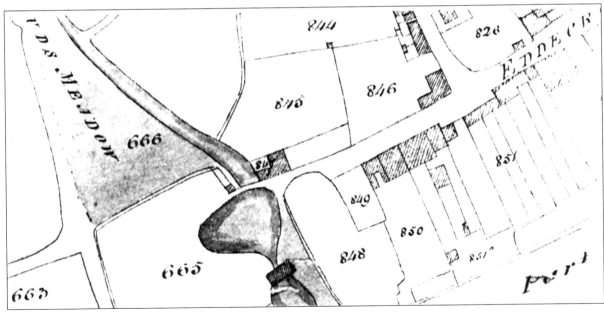

1823 map showing the position of the 'New' Mill or One Mill. (Courtesy of Miss E. Okell)

The probate inventory for Richard Harris, the miller

All that Water Grist Mill called Chest's Mill Scituate lyeing and being in the parish of Rosse ... with all houses barnes buildings Orchards Waters Water-courses Wares bancks Stancks Dams Millponds Floodgates Streams of Water ... sometime tenure of John Griffiths.[43]

It is known that the Forest of Dean was a centre for iron working from Roman times, but it is clear that the trade continued to prosper during the middle ages. The bishop's manor of Ross Foreign included large areas of woodland within the parishes of Weston-under-Penyard, Walford and Upton Bishop. Within this area were a number of pits and forges. No value can be put on these for at the time of the Red Book, the bishop kept them in his own hands, and exploited them for his own direct profit.[44]

No doubt as a direct consequence of the local iron industry, there were several craftsmen working in metal in Ross in the late 1200s. Apart from Thomas the Smith, who may merely be the local blacksmith, a lorimer — a maker of bridles and bits — and a nailer appear in the rent roll. Another trade depending on the iron industry was that of charcoal burner. Giles Carbonar' must have processed the fuel so necessary for the heating of the furnaces. The essential woods are listed along with the pits and forges.

The probate inventory for Richard Harris, the miller

1823 map showing the position of Chest's or Chace Mill. (Courtesy of Miss E. Okell)

At a later date, in the sixteenth century, Ross was a centre for the industry. Camden wrote in his Britannia: 'Rosse, made a free Burrough by King Henry the Third, now well knowne by reason of iron smiths.'[45]

Among the Talbot papers there is a report of an incident that took place between two rival groups of iron founders.[46] One group was from the Earl of Shrewsbury's 'Furnace at Billmelene' and one from the works of Sir Herbert Croft, and each had visited the town to buy provisions and stabled their horses at an inn. After one of Shrewsbury's men, who was drunk, had had a fight with one of the grooms at the inn, he and his mates were set upon, as they started for home, by Sir Herbert's men, who attacked them with a pike. They retaliated, firing off a 'Birdynge peece by Chance' and injuring one of the attacking party. Such an occurrence can hardly have been unusual between men, primed by drink and carrying offensive weapons, but in this case it was rumoured that a child had been killed. The report, sent to the Earl of Shrewsbury in November 1603, sought to establish that there had been 'noe hurte or damage to the infant by any shott' and the child's father, Christopher Fox, was among those who signed the paper. Christopher Fox appears to have managed the local iron workings for the Earl of Shrewsbury.[47] Although there is little detail within the report, and the name of the inn is not mentioned, the brief statement conjures up a vivid picture of a section of society in Ross at that time. It depicts the busy inn, with stabling and grooms to accommodate the horses belonging to the foundrymen, the noise, the rivalry and the hard drinking before the men returned to their scattered forges in the surrounding area. It is unfortunate that the relationship between Christopher Fox and the foundrymen is not stated. He seems to have been at pains to attest their innocence!

By the sixteenth century Ross had become famous for another craft, that of leather working. While Gilbert Talbot, son of the Earl of Shrewsbury, was living at Goodrich Castle in 1576, he wrote to his father:

> According to my riches and the country I dwell in, and not to my desire, I send your Lordship a New Year's gift – a Monmouth cap and a rundlet of perry: and I must require pardon to name another homely thing, a pair of Ross boots, which, if they be fit for your Lordship, you may have as many as you wish to appoint ...[48]

There may have been some measure of 'tongue in cheek' about Gilbert's suggestion of the boots, but it is also the case that, in 1632, the constable of Goodrich Castle, Richard Tyler, supplied his patron and overlord, the Countess of Kent, with kid gloves and kid skins.

> One dozen and a half of kiddleather gloves sent up to her honour
> More for 2 ditto and a half of gloves and 6 kiddskins sent to her honour.[49]

There were numerous tanneries established in the low, well watered, area of Brookend.

Caps, perhaps in the same style as the Monmouth cap offered to the Earl of Shrewsbury, were also made at Ross. In 1576, Ross was listed among many towns whose poor cappers were to benefit from any excess profits made by the 'searchers' for the capping industry — the officials responsible for maintaining standards.[50]

In 1559 the manors of Ross Borough and Ross Foreign ceased to belong to the bishop. Certain church assets had reverted to diocesan control when the monasteries were disbanded, a situation that did not please the government. In order to redress the balance — and to supply the Crown with some much needed income — Elizabeth I decreed that when a bishopric became vacant, a commission should be set up to decide how much of these extra profits the diocese should keep. Along with Canterbury, Ely, London and Chichester, Hereford was one of the dioceses which lost land to the Crown. Officially property was only taken to the value of the newly acquired assets, but it is clear that it was land with potential that went to the Crown, while the bishops retained rectories and tithes which would have a fixed value.[51]

By this date the value of the manor of Ross Borough had outstripped that of Ross Foreign, with a rent roll of £30 1s 11¾d. Ross Foreign was valued at £22 3s 9¾d.[52] Initially the Crown kept the manors in its own hands, appointing stewards to run them. John Scudamore was steward in 1578, but in 1588 the queen granted the manor of Ross Foreign to Edward Downing and Henry Best, who, in their turn assigned their interest to the queen's favourite, Robert, Earl of Essex. At the request of the earl, all the Crown lands in Ross and Walford were granted to Gelly Meyrick and Henry Lindley, but when Essex fell from favour and was executed in 1601, the two manors were, once again, divided, Ross Foreign going to Thomas Crompton and Ross Borough to Sir Henry Lindley.[53] After the death of

Elizabeth I in 1603, Essex's widow bought both manors for £7,000. She passed them to her son, the third Earl of Essex, and he left them to his sister, Lady Frances Devereux, the Marchioness of Hertford, who, after the restoration of the monarchy in 1660, became the Duchess of Somerset. Finally, both manors came into the hand of Lord Weymouth, who became Marquis of Bath. He was the Duchess of Somerset's grand-daughter's husband! Many of the seventeenth and eighteenth century records of both manors are now among the family archives at Longleat.

4   Woodlands and Manors

The bishop's tenants in the manor of Ross Foreign had none of the security or freedom enjoyed by those who lived in the town. The customary tenant of the rural manor was bound to remain on his lord's land. He also owed certain services to the bishop in addition to the rent he paid for his properties. For example, as well as the 4s 3d he paid to the bishop for his virgate of land, John Babbe had to give the manorial market dues of 'tol and tak'. He also had to pay 'merchet', a marriage fine, if he gave his daughter in marriage.[1]

Other tenants paid the whole of their rent in services. Hugh de Budel held

> 1 messuage and 3 acres of land for which he ought to work one day a week from Michaelmas to Lammas Day and the total of works in August are 43 works worth 2½d. And he ought to work one day each week from Lammas Day to Michaelmas. Total works in Autumn 9 works worth 9d in cash.

Ralph de Surpirie

Misericord from the choir of Hereford Cathedral — the carving is said to indicate marital discord! (Courtesy of the Dean and Chapter of Hereford Cathedral)

holds 1 messuage and 3 acres of land and ought to work 43 works before Autumn which are worth 21d and 9 works in Autumn which are worth 9d.

Some of these 'works' involved ploughing the lord's land or carrying his goods, but whatever they actually involved, they came at the busiest time of year, when the tenant would be occupied with his own harvest on which the very existence of his family would depend during the winter. It is possible that the '9 works in Autumn' might be commuted for a cash payment.

In the thirteenth century the total rents from the manor of Ross Foreign came to £26

6s 6½d, but this was only the beginning of the bishop's profits from his manor. None of this covered the woodlands, which he kept in his own hands, and which therefore do not feature in the rent roll. The diocese is known to have owned woods at Bishop's Wood, Chase Wood and Penyard, and at Tedgewood, in Upton Bishop. These lands, having been forest before 1154, were exempt from the 1225 edict of Henry III which ruled that all land afforested since that date must be cleared. Enquiries and perambulations made on behalf of the jurors of Gloucestershire at the time of the 1225 edict, to establish the limits of ancient forest, found that these lands were regarded as part of the Forest of Dean. They stated that: 'The Bishop of Hereford has his Chace by ancient title in a certain wood called Lax Penyard within the Forest aforesaid.'[2]

The bishop's title to the land was ancient, but ambiguous! Until 1300 the land was part of the king's forest and subject to forest law. Moreover, the king's hunting grounds, in his 'forest of Penyard', marched with the bishop's land in Penyard, which was part of his fee of Ross. In 1228 the king decreed that foresters should make a perambulation of Ross and Penyard to establish the boundaries between the bishops' territory and his own.[3] By 1300 it appears that the Herefordshire lands were no longer included in the forest and rulings against deforestation no longer applied. Penyard Forest became Penyard Park although both the Chase and Bishop's Wood retained an element of woodland. These tracts of land were farmed for their timber, for high quality timber for houses, boats and furniture, for coppice wood, for fences and rafters, and, above all, for fuel.

It was the woodland, in particular, that gave the manors their value and it is understandable that many of the official orders concern the regulation of woodland. A hierarchy of officials, stewards, bailiffs and foresters was set up to ensure the efficient management of the estate resources. In 1276, Bishop Cantilupe had reason to deplore the mismanagement of past years and called upon his steward to look into the appointments of bailiffs for Whitborne and Ross. Rules were formulated concerning the estate and the management of the accounts, so as to prevent any further loss to the diocesan revenues.[4]

In spite of the precautions taken, the profits from woodland were always at risk; the culprits ranged from those who went beyond their customary rights, taking more firewood than they were due, to systematic plundering. The constable of Goodrich Castle was

This stained glass portrait of Bishop Cantilupe, part of the east window of Ross church, dates from 1430, when it was given by Bishop Spofford to the Bishop's Chapel at Stretton Sugwas. It was brought to Ross when that chapel was destroyed in the eighteenth century and re-assembled and re-leaded in 1873

among those guilty of filching firewood and, in 1344, was commanded by his overlord, Aymer de Valence, Earl of Pembroke, not to take more from the Bishop's Wood than was allowed by ancestral custom.

There are a number of references to those who 'despoiled' the bishop's woodland. In 1316 the bishop complained that 'persons' forcibly entered his woods at Ross, felled trees growing there and carried them away.[5] In 1345 there is mention of 'persons' who entered various properties of the void bishopric and felled trees, fished and hunted, while in 1383 the clergy of the Deanery of Ross and the Forest were required to publish the excommunication of the despoilers of the bishop's woods at Ross.[6]

There were other more serious offences. In 1268, judges were appointed to determine cases of trespass by persons who burnt and carried away goods on the bishop's manors, including Ross, while in 1329 the bishop complained that Reginald, son of Henry de Grey, of Wilton Castle, backed by a band of local men, broke his manor of Ross, carried away his goods and assaulted his servants.[7]

Another threat came from the marauding band which, in the early 1300s, while the bishop was safely away at York, raided the manors of Ross and Upton and drove away 120 oxen and 240 sheep. Other animals and quantities of wheat, oats and other produce were also taken. Knowing that the bishop was away and supervision was lax, the raiders were in no hurry and completed their foray by spending 15 days charcoal burning in the forests. The damage was estimated at £240. The scale of the enterprise and the presence of illicit charcoal-burners suggests that, like the earlier incident, this attack was instigated by a rival landlord, seeking to redress an injury, rather than a band of outlaws.[8]

It seems undeniable that some of these occurrences were directed against the bishop in his capacity as landlord. Certainly in the 1320s, the 'Prior of Hereford', who had been granted the lands of the Bishop of Hereford, temporarily forfeit to the Crown, complained that he was assaulted at both Ross and Hereford and prevented from executing his office. No doubt the decisions made by his court had proved unpopular.[9]

Although the bishop's woodland provided him with revenue, it was also a source for game and was preserved accordingly. Hunting was a popular pastime, even among bishops and their entourage, and since the king also owned forest land near Ross, where hunting took place, there was ample opportunity for clashes of interest. Even after the perambulation of 1228 had established the boundaries between the two estates, problems continued. In 1247, the bishop found his land forfeit to the crown after an incident when huntsmen strayed over the boundary and a hind was taken in the king's woodland. A pardon was subsequently granted and the land restored.[10]

The 'marauding band', already mentioned, who entered various properties belonging to the void bishopric in 1344, and who fished and hunted, were, no doubt, representative of other poachers, but their depredations were hardly on the scale of Walter Moton, Bishop John de Trillek's own employee. A bizarre episode took place in 1354 when Moton, the bishop's warden, robbed his master of 500 hares, 1,000 rabbits, 1,000 partridges and 200 pheasants, to the value of £1,000. The jury found him guilty of trespass and fined him £4. He also took £20 worth of fish for which an additional £4 fine was levied. In April that year the bishop's register recorded that Moton 'submitted himself to the bishop on all points', confessing his crimes and formally resigning the office of warden![11] This was not the first time Moton had been in trouble and it is somewhat surprising to find him in such a position of trust. In 1337 John Inge had complained that Walter Moton, with a number of others, had broken into his park at Penyard Regis and cut down and removed some of his trees.[12]

Misericord from the choir of Hereford Cathedral — a boar hunt. (Courtesy of the Dean and Chapter of Hereford Cathedral)

At a later period the woodland was mainly cropped for timber and fuel. Parts of it were leased out to tenants such as Thomas Brynde, who, in 1614, rented 180 acres in Bishop's Wood and the 'new mill within the said wood', paying £15 per annum for the woodland and £6 for the mill.[13] The same mill, designated as a 'grist mill in Bishop's Wood' was let to William Farmer for £3 in 1646.[14]

Fuel was required not only by the domestic consumers, but also in large quantities for the forges and furnaces situated in the bishop's woodland. Giles Carbonar's charcoal making would have been carried out near to the iron-making sites, wherever they were — for these early sites are now lost.[15] Prior to the introduction, about 1500, of new technology which used water-powered blast furnaces to smelt the ore, 'malleable iron', that is iron fit for the smith to use, had been produced direct from the ore. This process, in use from the Roman period, left behind only a residue of cinders and has provided little datable evidence, especially as no power source was needed and the various forges might be of short duration and marked only by the cinders typical of the process.

This, no doubt, is the reason why the mediaeval iron industry has received little attention. There are many references to iron-making at an 'early' date, but little direct evidence of mediaeval activity. The various authorities leap straight from the Roman iron-makers to the better documented ironmasters of the late sixteenth century and early seventeenth centuries. In his *History of the British Iron and Steel Industry*, Schubert states that in 1597:

> The iron-works [in Ross] must have been considerable, since they are the only item in the valuation of the manor of Ross foreign which was valued as 'well worth per annum £66 13s 4d'.[16]

But he goes on to suggest that the works were set up shortly after 1588.

There are numerous references to these sixteenth and early seventeenth century iron workings. There was a site at Old Forge, Whitchurch, below Goodrich Castle, another nearby

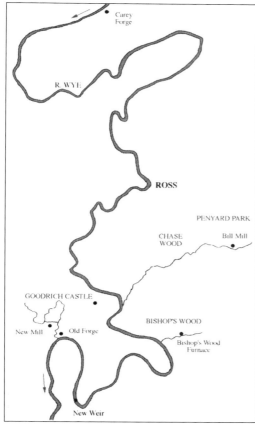

Map showing iron working sites

at New Mill, one at Carey Mill and one at Bill Mills, on the edge of Penyard Park, the 'Billmelene', mentioned in the last chapter, where the Earl of Shrewsbury's workmen were based.[17] The forge at New Wear, which flourished in the eighteenth century, was in operation before 1589, when rioters, apparently with official backing, demolished the weir.[18] All these sites were situated either on tributaries of the Wye or on the Wye itself and depended on water power to drive the blast furnaces. Slag from this type of working has been found at Bill Mills.[19]

Manorial papers contain regular entries concerning later iron-making in the seventeenth century. In 1628, the Earl of St. Andrews and the Earl and Countess of Essex leased to William Baildon, gent, 'all that furnace & furnace place called the lower furnace scituate in a place called Byshopps Wood for 21 yeares from Michaelmas last.' The rent per annum was £4. In 1646, John Vaughan held, for the same rent, what is likely to be the same furnace in Bishop's Wood, 'set by the hands of Walter Kirle, Esq.', who was steward to the manor. John Vaughan still had the furnace the following year, but was paying £5.[20] The ironmasters were expected to maintain the furnace and to hand it back in good repair when they surrendered the lease. Sir John Kyrle, who leased a mill and forge in nearby Goodrich from the Earl of Kent, found himself in trouble with the earl's steward because of 'one great wheel at the Forge called the chaffery wheele out of reparacions and most of the chimneys.'[21]

The furnaces at Bishop's Wood were on the Bishop's Brook, right on the border of Ross manor and on the Herefordshire/Gloucestershire boundary. They appear on Isaac Taylor's 1786 map of Herefordshire, as two mills and a dam, with the label 'Bishop's Wood furnace'. One of these mills was the grist mill already mentioned, the other would have powered the bellows and hammers for the forge. The dam, pool and some masonry can still be seen, half buried in the woodland.

Sometime shortly before 1668, the furnaces at Bishop's Wood became part of the Foley industrial complex. Thomas Foley of Witley Court, Worcestershire had amassed a group of ironworkings, furnaces and forges in south Staffordshire, Shropshire and north Worcestershire, which he managed with the help of his sons. The Bishop's Wood furnace supplied pig iron, which was shipped down the Wye to Bristol and up the Severn to the Stour valley iron mills.

Isaac Taylor's map of 1786 showing Bishopwood Furnace

An inventory for the furnace, made in 1675, lists among the assets on the site, 'Sow' — pig iron — worth £2,340, charcoal worth £113.12s, 'myne', the actual iron ore, was listed at £35, cinders were worth £25, coal sacks valued at £12, coal baskets and cinder baskets at £1 3s. Tools — the 'Bellows, Ringers [crowbars] & other Implements' were worth £30. There was a hearth stone, still at the quarry, valued at £1 and two sets of beams and weights — a large one worth £5 and a smaller one to weigh pigs at the furnace at £1.[22]

Huge amounts of charcoal were required to fuel the furnaces and a contract survives, from 1683, between the King's Surveyor General 'of his Majesties Woods on this side Trent' and Paul Foley for supplying 8,000 short cords from the Forest of Dean. A cord was a measure of cut wood and tended to vary between localities. In this particular contract the billets — that is the individual pieces of wood — were to be 2 feet 2 inches long, and each whole cord was to be 8 feet 4 inches long and 4 feet 6 inches in height from the ground, although how these dimensions fitted together is something of a mystery. The making of the charcoal took place where the timber was felled, and Paul Foley's workmen were granted access to the woodland 'to convert Cordewode into Charcoale upon the Ground where the same shall have binne groweing, and to Digge Turfes, make Cabbins and have and Enjoy All usuall necessaries there for that purpose.'[23] The wood available from the Foleys' holdings in Bishop's Wood itself does not seem to have been adequate at this time for 'farmers coppice neare Bishopwood Furnace' only yielded 1,316 cords of wood.[24]

By 1748, the works at Bishop's Wood were extensive; the bellows alone were worth £40. There was a casting room, a store for charcoal, 'a Stocktaker's Storeroom', a clerk's house and a house for the ironfounder. However, the Foleys were about to relinquish the site and, by 1768, Mr. Walter Mynd was the tenant.[25] Mynd sold his lease to the brothers John and William Partridge, who were, at the time, two of the most prominent ironmasters in the area. Although the family came from Ross, the brothers settled in Monmouth.[26] Even as late as 1805 it is recorded that 'great quantities of iron ore, brought from Lancashire, are smelted' at 'Bishop's Wood furnace.'[27]

The nineteenth century, however, was to see the industry in decline. The increase in steam power and the decline in the use of charcoal in the production of iron were two of the factors that concentrated iron-working in the north of England, where coal fuelled huge new furnaces and mills. The woods above the Wye valley returned to their rural peace, and Ross gradually ceased to be a centre for the smiths and nailers who depended on the industry.

5   The Palace and the Church

The fact that Domesday Book lists a priest among the inhabitants of Ross assumes the existence of a pre-Norman church of some kind. The position of the church, at the south end of Ross, on high ground above the river and overlooking an ancient river crossing, suggests that there may have been an important Saxon church on the site, as there was at Bromsgrove and Dodderhill in Worcestershire where there are similar features. Other indications are the size of the parish and the presence of an episcopal 'palace'.[1]

Aerial photographs of the site show very clearly, despite the disruption of the nineteenth century road, the relationship of the high plateau on which church and palace stood to the rest of the town. The high ground slopes away gently towards the town, and more sharply towards the river meadows. This steep descent was called, in later times, the Bishop's Court Bank.

Any evidence for the Saxon church, if indeed it exists, or for the palace, lies buried under the much disturbed layers of the church and churchyard. The earliest stonework of the present church building, the chancel, the nave and the transepts, dates from about 1280, soon after the institution of the first recorded rector, William Daubeny, in 1277.[2] The church has been much restored and little of the fabric from even this building is evident. The window splays in the chancel and aisles and the thirteenth century chancel arch are examples. The nave arcades were raised in 1743 using the old, original materials. The tower was built in the early fourteenth century and the church was dedicated in 1316. Later in the century the north porch was added and the chancel was extended.[3]

Aerial photograph of the Prospect showing the site of the Bishop's Palace and the way the ground slopes away towards the river meadows. (Courtesy of Ian Ashpole)

Interior of the church before the restoration of 1878 from
Photographic View Album of Ross and District *(Lawrence and Fowler)*

Not long after its dedication, in 1324, Ross church was the scene of a disturbance during the visitation of Bishop Adam de Orleton. William de Irby, the excommunicated Prior of St. Guthlac's, in Hereford, interrupted the bishop as he was saying mass on St. George's Day and 'violently assailed me ... disturbing the service and my Visitation ... in derogation of God's love and to the great scandal of Christians'.[4]

Towards the end of the thirteenth century wealthy parishioners made bequests to the church to found chantries where masses would be said for the repose of the founder's soul. Special chapels were erected, often over the benefactor's tomb, and these were endowed with lands, tenements, rents or money, which provided a stipend for a priest to celebrate the mass.[5] As property usually formed the endowment of a chantry it was necessary to obtain a 'licence to alienate' the premises from the Crown. In Ross the earliest record of a licence dates from 1307 when 'Master John de Ros' donated a messuage and 74 acres of land to provide for a chantry, dedicated to the Blessed Virgin Mary, where 'divine service' would be said for the souls of Master Ros and his family.[6]

John de Ros was probably the third son of Robert de Ros, first baron of Helmsley or Hamlake, who was known to have made a pilgrimage in 1276 to St. Edmund of Pontigny. John held the living at Ross prior to 1307, subsequently becoming a canon of Hereford, archdeacon of Salop, a papal chaplain and finally Bishop of Carlisle. He died in 1332.[7]

A second chantry was connected with the Fraternity of St. Thomas the Martyr, and the brothers apparently ran a hospice in the town. This chantry was endowed with 12 messuages, 11 shops and 40 acres of land. The founders must have considered the property sufficient to fund adequate incomes for the two foundations, but, during the lean years following the Black Death, Bishop Gilbert of Hereford was forced to amalgamate the two endowments and provide one chantry priest to serve both.[8] The resulting foundation was sometimes referred to by one title, sometimes by the other, occasionally by both.[9]

Records of the post-Reformation redistribution of chantry property in Ross list 11 messuages in the town which are described as belonging to the chantry of St. Mary and some of these must have been the ones originally given to the brotherhood.[10] In addition, two messuages in the area of the church were given to the priest 'in that chantry or service': one, perhaps the messuage left by John de Ros, was in the churchyard and would later become the Church House, and one was in Church Lane. It was probably the latter that housed the hospice and brethren of St. Thomas and may have even have been refounded in the post-Reformation period as Rudhall's Almshouses. There was a third chantry, dedicated to St. George, also with a resident priest. He had a house in Ross and a garden in Edde Cross Street. This last chantry was also associated with that of St. Margaret and was, apparently, situated at the east end of the church. Yet another chantry was recorded by Bishop Trefnant in 1402, as dedicated to St. Calewe.[11]

The relics of these endowments remain; it is thought that John de Ros's foundation used what was later called the Rudhall Chapel at the east end of the south aisle.[12] There is piscina — a stone basin for washing the communion vessels — in the south wall. The recess has a trefoiled head and ball-flower ornament contemporary with the founding of the chantry.

One of the piscinae in the church

There are five other piscinae, indicating the positions of altars where masses were said, in the east wall of the north aisle, in the chancel, and at the level of the rood loft. No doubt two of these were dedicated to St. Thomas and St. George. Another is claimed for a chantry of St. Margaret. Yet another piscina is in the early sixteenth century chapel, now known as the Markye Chapel.[13]

Even in the thirteenth century the church was surrounded by trees, in this case, ash trees. In 1290 the Vicar of Ross received a pardon for tampering with these trees, cutting down nine of them. This apparently, was the rector's prerogative.[14] The parish was unusual in having both a rector and a vicar. At Ross the office of rector was a sinecure, but he received the bulk of the tithes. The vicar, appointed by the rector, was required to provide for the parochial duties of Weston-under-Penyard and

*Mezzotint from William Farrer's painting
of the church and Prospect in 1832*

Brampton Abbots in addition to those at Ross. Much later, in 1537, Thomas Cromwell wrote that Edward Fynche, Rector of Ross from 1521 to 1539 was 'sick and not likely to escape'. He was also a 'Dr. of Physicke' and a 'residencer' of Salisbury, and left his duties in Herefordshire to the vicar.[15]

By the seventeenth century, it seems that the vicars were men of status and the parsonage house was of some size. The earliest glebe terrier, undated, but made during the 1630s, when Philip Price was the vicar, describes the parson's house as having a hall, two parlours and a kitchen, with 16 chambers and 'houses for offices'.[16]

The terminology used for this house is ambiguous. The parson is another name for the rector, although, in fact, the vicar seems to have lived in the parsonage house. Fosbroke states:

> The Church of Ross was surrounded by the Bishop's Palace in the Prospect, the Rector's in the meadow below, and the Vicar's at the other end of the church.

He then goes on to say:

> The Vicarage, now the rectory, still subsists. The Parsonage, a small building, was taken down in 1793.[17]

This seems to imply that the present house, built in the 1950s, is on the site of the vicarage, and that the original parsonage house or rectory, despite its officially higher status, was a much smaller building, perhaps because it was so little used. It has always been

Artist's impression of the Rectory

38

claimed that it was the house near the present rectory site that was pulled down and rebuilt in the 1790s, but this now looks less likely. The original rectory seems to have been nearer the Prospect.

The seventeenth century parishioners of Ross were largely fortunate in their parish clergy. The Rev. Philip Price, who was vicar from 1615–1661, was renowned both for his care of his flock during the plague year of 1637 and for his stand against the Directory for Worship which supplanted the Book of Common Prayer as the official service book in 1645. In 1646 he was turned out of his living and replaced by a series of ministers more in sympathy with the teaching approved by Parliament. The first of these was the Rev. John Tombs, a man of some erudition who had Baptist leanings and who, after the Restoration, became a Baptist minister in Bewdley.[18] He was followed by the Rev. John Skinner and by Jonathan Smith who later became a minister of the Ross Congregationalists. Little is known of these last two men, and what is known has been gleaned from their opponents.[19]

Although Philip Price was restored to his living in 1661, he died almost immediately. His successor, John Newton, was instituted as vicar of Ross the same year. Also in 1661 he was made Doctor of Divinity and became chaplain to Charles II. A strong upholder of the monarchy, he had supported himself by his mathematical skills during the Commonwealth and was author of a number of books on mathematics and astronomy. Once established in Ross he took a great interest in the local grammar school. Wood, writing at the end of the seventeenth century, described him as a 'learned but capricious and humourous person', a phrase that suggests he had a riotous sense of humour![20]

He was also a man of great character and generosity. Not only did he pursue an enlightened policy with regard to his nonconformist parishioners (see chapter 8), but he made strenuous efforts to end the centuries old anomaly of the system whereby the great tithes, those charged on cattle, grain and hay, were paid to the rector and the small tithes — on goods of lesser value like wool, pigs, lambs and chickens — to the vicar. In this he was not motivated by a desire for personal gain, but was concerned for the pastoral oversight of the parish of Ross and its chapelries. As a result of his efforts, not only Ross, but Brampton and Weston became rectories and the tithes were divided between the three.

The entry in the Parish register, made at the time of his death, claims that:

> He did (at his own great charge, as well as ye contribucon of others) reunite ye greater Tyths and by Act of Parliament settle them upon the Church and yt upon the expiracon of ye Lease by wch the Tyths were sett out ye Chappellarys of Brampton and Weston shall become Parochiall & distinct.[21]

The Act became law in 1671 and was commemorated in the front of the 1671 parish register, thus

> This Act was procured by the pains and care
> of John Newton DD & Vicar of this Place

Remember me, O my God, concerning this and wipe not out
my good deeds that I have done for the house of my God, and
for the offices thereof, and spare me according to the
greatness of thy mercy   Nehemiah 13: 14, 22

To my successors at Ross,
Brampton and Weston

If you chance to find
Glebe and Tythes to your minde
Procur'd without yor cost
Be good to the Poor
As God gives you store
And then, my Labours not lost.[22]

*Page from the Ross parish register recording the change
in status of Ross parish. (Courtesy the Rector,
Ross parish church)*

The lease of the tithes did not expire until 1675 and John Newton enjoyed his new status as rector until his death four years later.[23]

He was succeeded first by Thomas Brom, later by Dr. Whiting and then, in 1712, by Robert Morgan, whose efforts went into the repair of the church fabric. There are three entries in the parish registers concerning this activity. In 1721, we are told: 'This year the spire was rebuilt, (ie) abt 16 yards of it. And also three of ye Pinacles.'[24][25]

In 1725 the middle aisle was 'cieled', and in 1728, galleries were added and decoration applied: 'This year ye western galleries (on each side of ye organ gallery) were built. The Chapiters of ye Pillars were also gilt.' The major work on the side aisles, when the roofs were raised, took place in 1743 under Morgan's successor.

Nearby, on the site of the Royal Hotel, the bishop had, by 1166 built himself a residence which he used when he visited the neighbourhood. Although this was hardly what would today be classed as a palace, it was much more than just a stopping place for the great man and his entourage, and was classed as a defended house. It was a large, sprawling structure, with a great hall where the bishop could hold court, and plenty of out-buildings. Fosbroke, writing in 1822, claimed that the palace was:

For the most part a timber building, and had a large gateway and Porter's Lodge annexed
to it at the principal entrance, which was between the Pounds House and the Prospect;

the Pounds House itself was part of the outbuildings; some ruins of the mansion were remaining till the close of the seventeenth century, and suggested the plan of a building with wings, fronting the north and west, having a large hall and a room eastward, more perfect than the rest, with remains in that room, of wood and stone sculpture, partly painted and gilt.[26]

Here the bishop entertained his principal tenants and his fellow magnates. Close Rolls dated 1232 and 1256 imply that Henry III visited Bishop Cantilupe at his Ross manor in those years.[27] Here also came Bishop Swinfield as part of his progress through his diocese during Lent, in March 1289. Accounts survive for that year and give some idea of the progress of the bishop's visit.[28]

It started with the coming of the messengers who heralded his arrival. They were presumably sent, not only to announce that he was on his way, but also to deliver summonses to those who must appear before him. Carters followed, carrying the bishop's personal baggage, which would include furnishings and bedding to make the place habitable. 3d was expended in cleaning the houses in readiness for the bishop's stay.

As was the case with any great landowner, when the bishop travelled his household travelled with

The church in the late nineteenth century showing the pinnacles and the vulnerable top of the slender spire, rebuilt in 1721, 1852, 1911 and 1952. From Photographic View Album of Ross and District *(Laurence and Fowler)*

him. Hillaby, writing of Bishop Swinfield's visit to Ledbury at a similar date, lists the members of his household who travelled with him. He divides them into three categories; first, the 40 or so attendants with the squires at their head. These would be followed by the bishop's chief servants, the clerk of the chapel, the chief carter, the larderer, the porter, the stable groom, the butler, the chamberlain, the farrier, the head huntsmen, the messenger and the falconer. Next came the kitchen staff, the cook and the baker and their helpers and associates and finally the lowest group of page boys, and kitchen, stable and kennel attendants. Hillaby notes that it

Conjectural reconstruction of the Bishop's Palace

was not 'merely the duties of office, but also the problems of provisioning that kept the bishop constantly on the road.'[29]

The quantities of hay delivered indicate the numbers of horses that had to be fed. Not all those who attended the Bishop's Court would expect to be entertained, but the increasing amount of food which was brought in shows that the number of visitors to the palace rose to a peak on the Thursday when there was a great feast, although, since it was Lent, meat was forbidden. The normal kitchen staff was inadequate to deal with the numbers and extra water carriers had to be employed to carry water for the palace at a cost of 5d.[30] The accounts show that there was wine and beer in abundance and huge quantities of food. During his three day stay the bishop's household ate more than 20 salmon, 35 eels and four lampreys. Some of the freshwater fish came from the bishop's own great fish pond, probably in the region of the Chase, where John of Longford and his colleagues were paid 8d for their activities 'at the great fishpool'. From the distant sea there were cod and plaice and large numbers of herrings, all probably dried or salted. On the Saturday, Bishop Swinfield moved back to Hereford, where he dined in his palace on Palm Sunday.[31]

Two other buildings were noted by Fosbroke; both of them appear to have survived longer than the palace itself. One was the prison.

There was also a prison belonging to the Bishops; it stood near the corner of Mr. Amos Jones house, now occupied by Mr. Merrick, a wool-stapler; it was a small stone building; the stonework of it but little above ground, and the upper part was timber; being greatly decayed and dangerous, it was pulled down altogether between three and four score years ago.'[32]

This was the bishop's own prison for delinquent clergy within the palace. In 1280 two of the clerics so imprisoned, Ralph and Nicholas, escaped. John de Arderne, their gaoler,

42

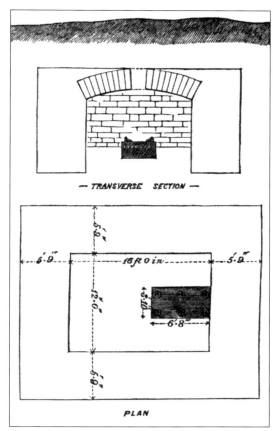

— TRANSVERSE SECTION —

PLAN

Bishop's Prison from J. Webb,
Civil War in Herefordshire

was required to give a bond of indemnity to Bishop Cantilupe and promised greater care in the future![33] In 1411, after the bishops had ceased to use the palace, the prison was apparently used by the town. In that year 'evildoers' broke into the gaol, dragged out Philip Singer, who was awaiting his trial for homicide, and killed him in the street. This must have taken place in the present St. Mary's Street.[34] When the Royal Hotel was built in 1837, the bishop's prison was discovered, complete with the iron rings for shackling the prisoners.[35]

Cellars belonging to parts of the Bishop's Palace were found on the site of the present Royal Hotel, but a recent visit found no certain evidence.[36]

The other building that survived was the dovecote. Fosbroke records: 'South of this, in the inclosure, was a dovecot of curious appearance.'[37]

No description of this 'curious appearance' has been found but it would appear that it was this dovecote, a 'Pigeon house being near the Church yard of Rosse and that parcell of land and pasture adioyning to the Churchyard', that was let to Herbert Westfaling Esq. in 1612.[38]

In April 1356, after the disaster of the Black Death, the need for drastic economies meant that bishops ceased to use the palace at Ross, and indeed, also abandoned their houses at Ledbury, Bromyard, Colwall, and Bishop's Frome.[39] The palace fell into disuse and, about 1540, Leland described it thus:

> The convict prison for the Bysshope of Hereford was at Rosse now at Hereford and the palace at the veri west end of the paroche churche yarde of Rosse now in clene ruynes.[40]

After Ross manor passed into secular hands in 1599 the Bishop's Palace and Court was held by the lords of the manor, first by the Earls of Essex and then by the Marchioness of Hertford, who later became the Duchess of Somerset. They let the property that had comprised the Bishop's Palace and demesne to various tenants. As has been said, the pigeon house and the adjoining pasture went to Henry Westfaling, a local gentleman. In 1629, the wife of Samuel Killing surrendered into the lord of the manor's hands a messuage, garden and close, of approximately an acre, together with another piece of land in Ross Foreign, both adjoining the churchyard. This property was then given to John Fisher, and passed down his family.[41]

In 1684, the messuage, close and garden were leased to William Fisher, together with one acre adjoining the palace and one parcel of land adjoining the churchyard and one 'lying within the beast market'. In 1707 he was granted a licence to sublet to Richard Ball.[42]

The beast-market is first mentioned in a description of land in the area in 1612. The same land passed into the Cowles family in 1613 and, in 1649, was described as adjoining the Fisher property:

> the Pounds & Garden, stables & Pinfold near the Beastmarket on the East … Lands then occupied by Jno Fisher- Rees Berkeley - & a piece called the Bishops Court on the West & the Pinfold lying Eastward from the House; under the churchyard wall.[43]

This plot clearly contained the house which became the Pounds Inn, which stood just to the west of the pound, while, it seems, the Fisher property lay to the east. In fact, careful comparison of the records suggests that the Pound Inn and its ancillary buildings and gardens covered most of John Cowles' land. A later abstract of title for the Royal Hotel states that the hotel, its outbuildings and its approach road, 'were built on the site of an Ancient Inn called the Pounds Inn.'[44]

There was a pound on the site by 1647, when, in a document entitled, 'Mr. Kyrles Accompt', Walter Kyrle Esq., on behalf of the lord of the manor, recorded charges for making, or, more probably, rebuilding it.[45] In 1670 and 71, the Ross churchwardens were presented at the manor court for not repairing the wall between the churchyard and the pound and forfeited 20s.4[6] In due course, the combination of the pound and the inn, named after it, would supplant the old and obsolete name of the 'Bishop's Court'. The area was

Effigy of Lady Mary Cheek in Ross church. Although she outlived him and twice married again, she is shown beside her husband, John Rudhall. The two are holding hands

known by this later name as early as 1648 when Lady Mary Cheek (or Chalke) appears on the rent roll as lessee of the Pounds. The name appears again in 1689, when a petition requested that 'the pig-market was removed from a certain place called ye pounds.'[47] It is possible that Lady Mary's house may, as Fosbroke suggests, have once been part of the Bishop's Palace and later became the Pounds Inn, the fate of many large old-fashioned houses.[48]

Joseph Cowles, son of John, married Sarah Fisher, daughter of William Fisher, the Quaker, and heir to John Fisher. The link between the two families seems to have created considerable confusion over the adjacent property held by each, particularly as William Fisher became innkeeper of the Pounds. This confusion is typified in the abstract of title to the ground, made when the Royal Hotel was planned in 1833, which enquired whether the 'mess[uage] is or is not the Pound House'.[49]

The same abstract also deals with other property in the area designated for the Royal Hotel. William Fisher, senior, sub-let another part of the Bishop's Court from John Kyrle, and left it to his son Nicholas. This part was described as 'the said piece of land called Bishop's Court, the said garden and the said piece of land called Bishop's Court Bank'.

This last piece of land was the steep slope to the west, now transformed by excavations for the nineteenth century Wilton Road, but the bank also sloped towards the north and there is evidence within the Royal Hotel car park of considerable changes in ground level. The flatter, upper ground of the Bishop's Court became the Prospect, leased to John Kyrle, in 1696, from Lord Weymouth, the lord of the manor. The lease contains the intriguing and baffling proviso that Kyrle was to 'keep in repair 3 Keys and 3 Towers' — were these buildings the remains of the old palace? The ground was laid out by Kyrle as a pleasure garden with trees, walks, and a fountain that also supplied water to the townspeople of Ross. He then let the land, three years later, to William Fisher, for £5 per annum, with 'Liberty for JK to build plant trees and cut walks for the Public to use Gratis' — and with the possibility that Lord Weymouth might 'make a woolmarket' there.[50]

It is clear that the property contained more than the garden now called the Prospect. The same abstract, quoting a deed of 1755, refers to three houses built within the area by Nicholas Fisher, described as grandfather of the present

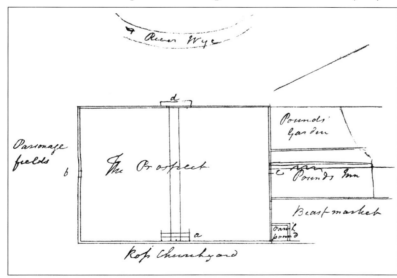

Plan taken from a legal opinion given regarding ownership of the Prospect in the 1830s, prior to the building of the Royal Hotel. It shows the Pound Inn with its garden, the pound and the Prospect with its four gateways. (HRO BA31/173)

The remaining wall of the Pound Inn now part of the outbuildings of the Royal Hotel.
(Courtesy of the Royal Hotel)

holder of the land, and undoubtedly the earlier Nicholas Fisher, who was grandson to John, son of William Fisher the Quaker, and brother to Sarah and William. This implies that this part of the Bishop's Court extended as far as the High Street corner of St. Mary's Street, and that the three Fisher houses on the west side of the street were encroachments in to what was originally a wide market space or piece of wasteland.

A rent roll for 1687 suggests that Nicholas Fisher (1) was the landlord for the corner house, no.50 High Street, while an abstract of title, shows this house, or part of it, being leased by William Fisher, inn-keeper (son to William senior) to Edward Powell in 1730.[51]

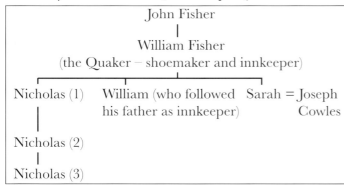

Fisher Family Tree

All the indications are that William Fisher, rather than his son, built the first of these houses in St. Mary's Street and lived in it himself, for part of the land already described 'did lye convenient to the said dwelling house of the said William Fisher' and his garden was separated from the Bishop's Court bank by four 'mere' or boundary stones. Nicholas (1) probably had an adjacent house.[52]

46

William Fisher's house at 7/8 St. Mary's Street — now known as Palace Pound

The Pound Inn was pulled down when the Royal Hotel was built. The front wall partially survives, built into the courtyard wall of the stables. William Fisher's house also survives. Now divided into two, 7 and 8, St. Mary's Street, it is a fine example of a late seventeenth century house. It consists of three bays with a good staircase within the central gable, surmounted by the remains of ornamental plasterwork. The house next to this is now part of Lloyd's Bank and not accessible.

Some time before he died, William Fisher moved out, in old age, to live with his son-in-law, Joseph Cowles. His own house was let to a Richard Bellamy, but he left the two cider mills and the other items in his mill-house to Nicholas (1), a fair indication that they had been living next door to one another. He also left 'the pig pens or stalls that are placed or being in or about my said dwelling', which implies that the area was still, despite the petition mentioned earlier, being used as a pig-market.[53]

In fact, all three houses became the property of Nicholas when William senior died. In his will he left to Nicholas:

> all that piece or parcell or parcells of Land formerly called Bishopps Court now called the prospect adjoining the Churchyard of the parish Church of Rosse aforesaid and all the Lands and tenements thereto belonging which I now hold as undertenant to John Kyrle Esq., who holds the same by virtue of a demise to him made by the right Honourable Thomas Lord Viscount Weymouth.

Pencil drawing of St. Mary's Street in 1821.
(Fred Druce Collection)

All the land on the east side of St. Mary's Street had belonged to John Cowles in the early part of the seventeenth century and was then one property, probably the ancient house seen on the drawing. This property was described as the Reindeer in 1645 and the Old Falcon in 1675. In 1668 the 'causeway leading from the Old Falken to the Church Stallions' (stile, posts?) was ordered to be repaired. The building later became the Duke of Marlborough's Head.[54]

On the corner of the church-yard stood the Church House. This, it is claimed, originally belonged 'to a Suppressed Charity and was appropriated to the teaching of children in the reign of Edward VI.'[55] Other evidence implies that it was the dwelling house for the chantry priest who served the chantry of John de Ros. When chantry property was being disposed of by the Crown after the Reformation, this building was included among the holdings of St. Mary's chantry at Ross, and listed in the Patent Rolls as, 'a messuage in Ross in the tenure of the late chantry priest or incumbent of the said chantry'.[56] It was said to have had an oratory and a private altar, where clergy and other devout persons were probably buried.[57] A piece of land next to the churchyard, 'in the tenure of William Haggar', is also listed as part of St. Mary's property, as is a messuage in the street called Churche Lane. The chantry of St. George also had a house for the priest somewhere in the town.[58]

About 1640 the church house was granted by the then lord of the manor, the Earl of Essex, to Charles Hughes, late father of Blanche Hughes, but it seems to have been used both as a school and as a church hall.[59] When the Quaker preachers came to Ross, their teaching in the church was adjourned to the Church House. Later the building was re-established as a grammar school and it finally fell down in the last years of the eighteenth century and was rebuilt by subscription, but that is part of another story.

6   The Markets and the Market House

The mediaeval market place in the centre of the town was much larger than the present market place. Evidence from title deeds and early rent rolls suggests that it stretched along High Street as far as St. Mary's Street and along Broad Street as far as New Street.[1] By the middle of the fourteenth century the market stalls, recorded in the thirteenth century bishops' rent roll, had become a row of shops and houses and it seems likely that some, at least, of these were included in the 11 messuages and 12 shops, which, by 1377, belonged to the Brotherhood of St. Thomas, which ran a hospice in the town.[2] The buildings were so close to the east side of the Market Place that a mere lane, known as Underhill, separated the two lots of houses.

By the sixteenth century the ancient Market Place contained a High Cross and a Booth-hall where the market tolls were collected, attached to the houses in Underhill and jutting out into the street. The whole area was paved with stone in 1625, when it is recorded in the court rolls that:

> the supervisors of the high waies shall cause to be brought to the high crosse of Rosse aforesaid twoe or three loades of Stones and sand for the pavinge of the markett place and it is ordered that Thomas Jones Bellman shall pitch and pave the said markett place before midsomer next.[3]

The Booth-hall stood partly on the apron immediately in front of the Market Hall. It was joined to the buildings in Underhill by a group of houses, projecting into the Market Place, like the stem of a capital T.[4] By the seventeenth century this building was regarded as unsatisfactory, but although Thomas Webbe, of Ross, left money to replace it in his will of 1612, nothing was done.[5]

It has always been claimed that the present Market House was built by Frances, wife of the 2nd Duke of Somerset and the date usually given is about 1670. This date and attribution comes from a note in Bonner's *Perspective Itinerary*, in which he refers to a lease of 26th November 1672.

> The right noble the Lady Frances Duchess of Somerset, at the request of her tenants, inhabitants of the borough or town of Ross, grants for 21 years, a certain portion of the rents arising from the tolls, and 10 feet of soil round the market-house *then lately erected* etc etc. for keeping it in repair.[6]

The Market House and Underhill from A.F. Pearce
Churches and Houses in South Herefordshire.
(Courtesy of Hereford City Library)

The same view in 2009

The italics are Bonner's and he, somewhat understandably, equated 'lately' with 'the last few years'. Further research has pushed the date back nearly 20 years. Sometime in 1650 the old Booth-hall and the seven houses adjacent to it were pulled down and the present Market House was built. The date can be pin-pointed from several sources, the first a complaint to the bishop by the Ross church-wardens, dated 1661.[7] In this they claimed that they were being sued by the Crown for non-payment of dues on a house near the Booth-hall. The rent of this, they said, was administered by the church for the poor, (actually the endowments of Perrock's almshouses) but, since the house had been pulled down to build the Market Hall, they had received no rents, and had therefore been unable to pay the Crown for the last nine years.

The kings messenger Came and [di]Strained on the said John Hill his Goods for And [*sic*] yerly Rent of Too shillings to the King out of A house du to the Church … The house is now down The Church Receveth no benefite from It And the market house Is Bulded on It And the Town Receveth the Benefite by Receiving the Toule to pay to the pore. And wee the Churchwarddens as our Offis so called the messengger strained of us And enforceth us to pay the said rent with great forfeture Being nine years neglegt …

This record implies that the Booth-hall and adjacent houses came down in the early 1650s. In fact, an entry on the rent roll for 1658 refers to 'the howses which wear puld down to buld the market hows on which wear 7 in number at 6d the piece.'[8]

According to a lease made on the 29th July, 1690 and referring back to this period, the Booth-hall was in the possession of Tobias Feckenham when it was demolished.[9]

There is also evidence that the Market was actually in use by January 1651/2, when the court appointed that 'the Neeps, Cabbages and all other garden stuffe shall stond for sale under the Markett house

Engraving of the Market Place, based on a painting by J.A. Saunders of Bath c.1810 and issued as the illustration for an almanac by the Ross Gazette in 1871

stayers and not elsewhere.'[10] It looks, therefore, as though construction took place in 1650 and 1651 and that the instructions for the vegetable market were issued when space in the new market was being allocated.

Although the new Market House was built on part of the Booth-hall site, it was free-standing, and not attached to the houses in Underhill, as was its predecessor. A description of the ground is given in a later lease, dated 29th July, 1690:

> the said peece or parcel of land whereon the said tenement called the Boothall stood or part thereof being reedifyed and is parte of the land whereon parte of the market house … is now built at the west end thereof.[11]

Since the new building occupied more of the Market Place than the old Booth-hall, the High Cross seems to have fallen victim to the need for more space. It came down at the same time as the Booth-hall, apparently to make more room for stalls, as another order required that 'mipps' (parsnips) should only be sold 'neare unto the Markett place wheere the Crosse in the Markett place did formerly stand.'[12]

The Market House, as might be expected of a public building in use for more than 300 years, has undergone a number of changes. Perhaps the most striking alteration is the substitution of the present staircase for the original outside stairway. A bond, made four days after the lease quoted above, between Tobias Feckenham, son of the first Tobias Feckenham, and Joseph Hawkins, nailer, describes this staircase:

Whereas parte of the stairs ascending in to the Chambers or over floors of the Markett house in the said Town of Ross are now built & erected upon & are – the sd Boothall land att ye Costs and Charges of the Inhabitants of the sd Town of Rosse now if the above bounden Joseph Hawkins his heirs executors admss & assignees doe & shall at all tymes hereafter permitt suffer and allow the Occupier or occupiers Tenant or Tenants of the sd Chambers or over floors of the Markett house, the officers of the mannor of Rosse aforesaid, the Inhabitants, workmen, and all persons attending the Courtes there or otherwise hereto coming to have free ingresse egresse regresse way and passage up & down the sd stairs & from the Chambers or over floors of the sd Markett house without any disturbance or interruption, And alsoe doe & shall at all tymes hereafter continue and keep the said building & structure parte of the sd Markett house now erected & being over the sd Boothall land as also the shopp thereupon built to stand remain & be as now erected.[13]

This document makes it clear that the stairs in question were outside the main structure of the Market House and must have led to a door at first floor level. It provides an explanation for the rather puzzling opening from the upper chamber which faces down Broad Street. Now guarded by balusters of a late seventeenth century style, this doorway was later used as a balcony for civic proclamations, and has always been assumed to have been built for that purpose. If this was a functional entrance, giving access from the street, rather than the ceremonial platform that it later became, the building would make far more sense. Even the asymmetrical position of the doorway, not completely central to the building or the arches below, might be explained if it was balanced in some way by the staircase or a porch. There is no evidence for the fabric of the staircase, whether it was built of timber or stone, or for its form, except that there was space under it for the selling of 'neeps'.

The doorway, now the balcony at the Market Hall.
(D. Skipworth)

The heavy oak internal staircase must therefore have been added after 1690, and there is structural evidence for its secondary construction in the mortises for the original ceiling joists cut into the wall-plate above the stair well. The mention of the need to allow access for 'workmen' suggests that some structural alteration was contemplated at this time and the style of the staircase is reminiscent of that at both nos. 7 and 8 St. Mary's Street, known to have been built in the early 1690s, and Alton Court, where the staircase was added in the late seventeenth century. It is reasonable to suppose that the balusters to the upper door, now redundant as an entrance,

were added at the same time, but the latticework enclosing the stairway may be later, as the handrail of the staircase is moulded on both sides.

The bond also makes it clear that the upper room was used as a courtroom by the manor officials. Structural evidence that the upper floor was designed as a courtroom can be seen at the east end where windows and ceiling are higher than in the rest of the building to accommodate a raised platform. There is also documentary evidence that the courts were held here as early as 1655, when numbers of the townspeople were summoned to appear at the Market House 'for the next Law Day to be holden for the borough of Ross.'[14]

The window sills which conform to the level of the dais in the Market Hall. The photograph was taken during the 1997 restoration. The matchboard dado probably dates from the nineteenth century. (D. Skipworth)

Recent work on the building has shown that the spine beams, supporting the ceiling, are tenoned into the tie-beams at one end only. The other end of each beam was manoeuvred into position by means of a long groove gouged out of the tie beam. This may merely have been the structural solution to the problem of ceiling such a large area, but there is also evidence of nail holes for laths on the underside of the rafters, implying that at some period the trusses were exposed. The combination of these two elements has led to the suggestion that the ceiling in the upper room is a secondary feature. It may therefore be part of the refurbishment that Nicholas Moore has deduced took place at the end of the seventeenth century and which included the insertion of the staircase.[15]

The new Market House and the adjacent space seems to have been a source of pride to the town and efforts were made to keep the area tidy. Problems were caused by the presence of roaming pigs. William Mann was regularly presented for the 'Annoyance of his piggs' and in 1653 it was ordered that: 'William Mann shall not keepe nor feede his piggs at his doore nor his pigs to lye in the Markett howse in Ross.'[16] The pigs presumably found the covered floor shady and cool!

But William Mann was not the only offender. All the inhabitants of Ross were presented 'that doe not ringe and yoke theire piggs and that they keep theire piggs out of the Markett place in payne of 1/8 a peece.'[17]

It appears that it was common practice to leave rubbish heaps in the Market Place and adjacent streets. A court roll entry for 1653 stated:

> we present all the inhabitants of Rosse that bring any Mucke sile or dunnge to the Markett house or Markett place of the said town and that they carrie it away or cause to be Carried away weekly in pyne of 7/8 a peece.

Some of the offenders were influential folk like Mrs. Kyrle, mother of John Kyrle; she was required to remove 'the soyle and rubidg under her stone wall att harterslane end'. Her son, some years later, was presented at court for not removing a dung-heap in front of his dwelling house.[18]

The manor court at which these cases were heard was held on the upper floor of the market hall and here, three times a year, the steward to the lord of the manor would meet with the town's officials to listen to the complaints brought by the parish constables and settle disputes between neighbours. Many of the offences concerned public order and the cleansing of the town, as in the orders already mentioned concerning pigs and dung heaps. The matters dealt with in the manor court covered all aspects of the town's life. There were safety regulations — the dangerous pool in the Horse Fair was to be railed, cellar doors were to be fenced; street-cleaning orders — 'the inhabitants to sweep before their doors every Saturday'; and food laws. Francis Chinn was prosecuted for selling 'stinking oysters'.[19] Road maintenance was an issue. In 1669, the highway from the wooden bridge to the end of 'the Arch leading to Ledbury Road near the Brooke' was ordered to be repaired, an entry that suggests that, in that low-lying area of the town, the bridge over the Rudhall Brook was not the only bridge in use.[20]

Most offences were punishable by a fine, but the town had its stocks and its whipping post for persistent offenders. There is no evidence available for their position in the seventeenth century, but by the early nineteenth century both stood in the Market Place, in front of the Market House facing Broad Street. A nineteenth century report in the *Ross Gazette* tells how 'an old inhabitant … well remembers being held up by his mother, about the year 1829, to see a man flogged at the stocks, and heard the Beadle crying between each stroke, "Honest and true, then!" at every stroke of the whip.'[21] The town also had a ducking or 'cuckynge stool', used, for example, to discipline the wife of Edward Flore, who, in 1624, was presented as a 'Common Scold'.[22] This must have been by the brook or mill-pond. In 1677 the inhabitants of Ross were presented at the manor court for not keeping a ducking stool.[23]

The market tolls and the rents for the stalls were not administered directly by the lord of the manor or his steward, but were rented out to a middle man. Thus William Fisher was in partnership with William Sparry in the 1680s, William Sparry and Ruth Grindall had the agency in the early 1700s and in 1723 John Jones petitioned for a lease of the Market House and requested to fell a poplar tree to make boards fit for standings and stalls.[24] These traders were all Quakers and, as was the custom, they took the 'farm' of the Market House and stalls at a fixed rate and made their money out of the rents they could obtain from the stall holders. From these rents they had to supply the stalls and keep the Market House in repair. In fact, it may be no accident that the staircase at no. 7 St. Mary's Street and that at the Market House are alike. William Fisher, who built the St. Mary's Street house was responsible for the Market House in the late seventeenth century and may have used the same craftsmen for both.

John Jones petitioned to lease the Market House and tolls for 21 years for £60 and, as part of the contract, he agreed that, when the Market House was put in order, he would be obliged to keep it dry.[25] This statement certainly implies that the roof was leaking and that

Left: Staircase at the Market House taken before the installation of the lift in 1997
Right: Staircase at Palace Pound, Wilton Fisher's house

56

Above and lower left: Market scenes in the 1950s

urgent repairs were about to be carried out before a lease could be made to a new tenant. It is more than possible that the cupola was part of this restructuring, although it is now thought that an earlier cupola may have pre-dated the present early eighteenth century structure.[26] The hatch to the roof space with its balustrade has been moved; originally it was several yards to the west of the existing hatch.

Although the Market Place was the focus for trade, other markets existed elsewhere in the town. John Jones' petition for the Market House included the desire that 'his Lordship will let him have the wasteground where part of the market is kept as was granted in the old lease to William Fisher.' This 'wasteground' was probably the area at St. Mary's Street, where William Fisher had had pig-pens and where the 'beast-market' was kept.[27] 'The 'fishboards' were in the High Street, 'nigh the Market Place' and outside nos. 2-6 Broad Street.[28] Part of the Market Place seems to have been used as the cornmarket and, in 1629, it was decreed that the dish market, where crockery was sold, was no longer to be kept on this part but was to move down the hill.

> Noe Crate or Carryer of dishes or glasse or any other woodden ware shall heereafter pitche or put downe their wares neare the cornemarkett, But shall pitche their wares belowe the bellforge.[29]

Later in the seventeenth century sheep were sold in Brookend, where the sheep pens were not to be left standing in the street.[30] By the 1680s the pig market in St. Mary Street was regarded as a nuisance, and the inhabitants of Ross petitioned the court to be allowed to move it to Brookend below the sheep market. Their request does not seem to have been granted, since William Fisher kept pig pens and stalls there until 1709.[31] The 'beast-market' for cattle was also in or near St. Mary's Street. The site of the Horsefair, with its dangerous pool, is unknown.[32]

From this it can be assumed that, when there was a market day, all Ross was in an uproar, that the lowing, bleating and squealing of animals, the cries of the street traders and the rumble of carts, must have resounded through the streets in a manner that would make even the noise of modern traffic seem like a lullaby!

7   The People and the Town

The fortunate survival of the rent roll of the thirteenth century bishops of Hereford has allowed a glimpse of the people of Ross of that time, but for the next three centuries little survives from which to piece together the lives of the ordinary inhabitants of Ross. The little knowledge that does survive comes from official documents and the first entries concern pardons issued by the Crown for various offences.

One of the earliest mentions is of a John Pete of Ross, who, in the 1340s, when acting in some sort of financial capacity for Thomas Blanket of Bristol, neglected to hand in his accounts. The likelihood is that Pete was an agent for Thomas Blanket and responsible to him for goods shipped down the river. He was pardoned for not appearing before the Court of the King's Bench when ordered to do so.[1]

In 1386 Richard Baker of Ross was imprisoned for not preparing to go to Ireland in the king's service when retained by David Russell.[2] Other men found themselves in prison for various reasons. John Gamell, in 1370, and William Goodman, in 1408, were both pardoned for manslaughter, but Philip Singer was not so fortunate. His fate at the hands of his enemies has been noted on p.42.[3] Whether the Bishop's prison was used for all prisoners at this time is not clear.[4]

More pardons were issued in 1394, to Roger Sceymore of Aure and Jevan Jurkyn for not appearing to answer Robert Cok of Ross touching debts of 50s and 70s, while in 1418, the vicar, Thomas Young, as executor of the will of Thomas Hansum, was in trouble because he owed William Erle, one of the legatees, a debt of 100s. The following year he still owed 115s to Robert Burford of London. This was one of the hazards of executorship, and, since few, other than the clergy, could read, the parish priest wrote the wills and acted as executors for many of his parishioners. They were thus more prone to charges of misappropriation.[5] Another vicar of Ross, Richard Lye, was in difficulties in 1444, with a debt of 100s owed to John Greenclere. This time, however, he seems to have 'skipped bail' and the four gentlemen who had stood surety for him were unable to produce him! Each of them was fined 100s. The case dragged on in Chancery for some years, with each gentleman suing him for the bail money.[6]

It is not until the sixteenth century that the documentary sources allow a fuller picture of the town to emerge, and not until the seventeenth that it begins to fill out with any sort of detail. At this point court rolls become available and a number of fascinating details about the

An early Ross lease. (Rectory Box)

lives and circumstances of the townsfolk begin to surface. Rent rolls detail the property and leases have survived which catalogue the changes that have taken place within the town.

The town centre street layout has remained almost unchanged since mediaeval times and the town would still be easily recognised by those who lived there in the late seventeenth century. Their fathers and grandfathers might have had greater difficulty. At the beginning of the century the side roads were hardly built up and were largely service roads between gardens and orchards. New Street — Back Lane — remained in this state until the end of the seventeenth century, so that there was room for the Quakers to site their burial ground there in 1662. Kyrle Street was also gardens. Here, the Congregationalists had space to build their chapel in the late seventeenth or early eighteenth century.[7]

Edde Cross Street was also sparsely built and Copse Cross Street was only built up round the end of Hatters Lane, the Old Gloucester Road. Wilton Gate, comprising the west end of High Street, seems only to have been developed as far as the top of Wye Street. The name Dock Pitch has not been found before the second half of the eighteenth century and it seems that the land immediately outside Wilton Gate was waste or common land belonging to the Lord of the Manor and not available for building. In 1659, William Bennet was fined for not pulling down a cottage he had erected on part of the Lord's waste outside Wilton Gate. Paradoxically, this may have been the start of building in the area, as such fines were sometimes used as a way of collecting rent, allowing the squatters' cottages to became an established part of the landscape.[8]

Until 1625, it seems, neither the Market Place nor the other streets of the town were paved, but in that year there were a number of paving orders, including one made to Thomas

*View from the Market House down Broad Street
towards Brookend*

Jones for paving the Market Place, when stones were to be brought to the High Cross.

In addition to the work on the Market Place, Thomas Jones was to pave the street at Wilton Gate, all upon pain of 7s if he failed to do as required.[9] Another order was issued for the side street just up from the Market Place, and in 1624, John Hill was presented for not paving the street called Church Lane.[10]

The life of the town centred round the Market Place with its Booth-hall and High Cross and to provide for the thirsty tradesmen there were a number of inns. On the corner of Hatters or Harters Lane was the George Inn, the oldest of the known market place taverns, which had been part of the endowment of St. Mary's Chantry, and which, in 1549, was in the tenure of William Tomes.[11] Another inn, the Great Inn, stood at the corner of Church Street, and was kept by Gabriel Hill, perhaps the son of the John Hill mentioned earlier, in the mid-seventeenth century.[12] The Reindeer stood in the present St. Mary's Street, while nearby in 1652, in the present High Street, then Wilton Gate, was 'an ancient inn now known as the White Horse.'[13] There was also an inn called the Griffin.[14] The Crown and Sceptre can be traced back to the late seventeenth century, when the innkeeper was another John Hill.[15] There must have been others, but these are not known by name. These inns, like the other buildings in the centre of Ross, would have been timber-framed and close studded, with jetties to each storey. Timber was not only cheaper and more easily transported than brick or stone, but was the fashionable building material.

Many of the houses in the town were rebuilt in the seventeenth century. The 'John Kyrle house', opposite the Market House, was one of these and was probably built in the first decades of the seventeenth century, and after 1605. In that year Thomas Perrock gave a gift of 10s to Ross charities out of the rent of no. 34, identified at the time as John Chest's house.[16] This suggests that at that date the site was not occupied by a single building but was still in multiple ownership. Originally it was a single, large six bay affair, topped with a row of

Left: John Kyrle's House.   Right: The Saracen's Head

gables. The casement windows were replaced by sashes in the eighteenth or early nineteenth centuries, but there is still evidence of the original row of windows, with their flanking side lights, that graced the façade.

The house that used to be the Saracen's Head, no. 12/13, High Street, on the opposite side of the Market Place, dates from a similar period or perhaps a little earlier. The top storey, added later, has now lost the row of gables that once ornamented the roof line. The inside has been much altered, although the façade was restored by the Alton Court brewery when they bought it in the 1890s. A contemporary account states:

> Recently the open timberwork was divested of the plaster by which it had been barba-
> rously covered up and now (owing to the enterprise of the Alton Court Brewery company,
> the owners of the premises) it is one of the picturesque objects of the town.[17]

It has been claimed that the building was the home of John Farne, vintner and innholder, whose monument is in the church, but no documentary evidence for this has come to light. In 1954, Mrs. Leeds produced the historical section for the book on Ross-on-Wye produced by the Women's Institute. In the text she wrote:

> The 'Saracen's Head' inn is the oldest hostelry now left in the town and dates from early
> Tudor times … Tradition has it that this building has always been an inn and that 'mine

62

host' in the middle of the seventeenth century was a certain vintner, John Farne, who succoured his aged vicar, Mr Price, when the later was evicted, penniless from the living during the Commonwealth and the Anabaptist (Tombes) took his place. John Farne died in 1658 and his monument is to be found in the north aisle of the church near the pulpit.[18]

It must be said that information of this sort, based entirely on oral tradition, is often misleading and has to be regarded with suspicion. This story is the exception, for there is at least some evidence for most of the statements made.

Although the Saracen's Head was hardly an 'early Tudor' building, John Farne was certainly an innkeeper in the first half of the seventeenth century. His will, correctly dated to 1658, but wrongly ascribed to John Tarne, survives in the Public Record Office, but contains little biographical material.[19] His memorial, giving his trade as 'vintner', is in the church. The story of his 'succouring' Philip Price is made more believable when it is found that Mr. Price was living in a house nearby.[20]

A family of Furneys held property in the near vicinity later in the seventeenth century, but, despite the coincidence of the name, do not seem to have been related to John Farne. They appear in Rent Rolls and tax lists until the middle of the eighteenth century in the appropriate position for the Saracen's Head. Moreover they are expressly stated to be connected with the Saracen's Head; in 1675 Richard Furney, paid 4s to the Rector and Churchwardens for a garden.[21] In 1701 the same garden was leased to Alice Furney with a note to the effect that the house, originally on the plot, had been 'consumed with fire'. This garden is identified in later documents as behind the Saracen's Head and was leased together with a 'church way', which passed under the inn to the High Street. In 1812 the site was described as having a public church way 'long discontinued and legally closed' with 'ingress, egress and regress at all times in the daytime through and along the Saracen's Head Yard'.[22]

Richard Furney was taxed for 3 hearths in 1664 and 8 in 1665.[23] It has not been discovered whether he was paying for an extra house in 1665 or whether the inn was being upgraded. This Richard died sometime before 1680 and his wife Alice inherited the business, with her son John.

According to Duncomb, Alton Court, in Alton Street, just outside Ross Borough, was sold by William Vaughan to the Markye family

John Farne's monument

63

Alton Court

in 1602 and the family retained the house until the late eighteenth century.[24] It is possible that it was the site rather than the building that John Markye wanted, for early in the seventeenth century he rebuilt at least one wing of the house, with some flamboyance, with close studding on the walls and herring-bone timbering in the gables. Two large windows, now replaced, in the front façade, lighted the hall and the great chamber over the hall. A probate inventory for John Markye, grandson of the man who built the house, has been transcribed and can be found, together with discussion of the building, in the Appendix.

No. 23 Brookend is another impressive house built by a man of some substance. The rear staircase, housed in a projecting stair-turret, and visible on the upper floors, may be a later addition. There are interesting examples of painted patterns on the ceilings on the first floor.

Not all the houses in Ross were of the quality of those cited above. Some must have been little more than hovels, with neither chimney nor smoke bay. The officials of the manor court saw these as a fire hazard and acted accordingly. As late as 1651 they ordered Margery Endell 'not to make fyer in her house where is no chimney' and this was no isolated example, for in 1655 Elizabeth Bethell was also fined for making a fire against a wall without a chimney.

The painted ceiling at no. 23 Brookend

Blanch Wall, next to the church house, had a chimney but was ordered to 'amend it', so presumably it was considered unsafe.[25]

The rather grand buildings of the town centre were at variance with the state of the streets, where piles of refuse abounded and pigs roamed at will, scavenging for food and acting to some extent as street cleaners. Because of the filth and the rats plague was endemic in these seventeenth century towns and flared up year after year. In common with other areas of the Midlands, the worst outbreak in Ross occurred in 1637 and was an enduring memory to the townspeople, who handed the story from father to son.

This account of the plague was published in 1896, and was taken from a paper, written by Mr. Thomas Jenkins of Ross, a noted antiquary, who died in 1830. He wrote:

> Among the various communications of local interest made to me by ancient people of Ross, this awful visitation, the plague, was never so fully described to me as by my old uncle Roberts, the hatter, that intelligent man, endowed with an admirable memory, was born and spent his days in Ross, where his ancestors, of the same name, had resided for ages. His occasional winter evening's talk with me was to the purport that his father's grandfather witnessed the effects of the plague, the incidents of which were transmitted from father to son, and were to the following effect. That the regular service at Ross Church was suspended; that the market was also dropped; that the buying and sellings of marketings were conducted in the angles and arches of Wilton Bridge; that the money was first thrown into a vessel of water before it was taken by one from another. The dead were buried at night in their wearing apparel in deep graves or pits, numbers at a time, near the cross in the churchyard, and from the cross westward. The bodies were brought in carts and slipped out of the carts into the grave. Good old Vicar Price used to stand on the cross solemnising the funerals by torchlight. The parish records of the period show the number of burials as follows: To the end of the month of July, 1637, 34; in

*Left: The Plague Cross in the churchyard before restoration in 1896. (*Photographic View Album of Ross and District, *Laurence and Fowler). Right: The cross in 1991*

August, 107, September, 99; October 46; thence to the end of the year, 29. Allowing for deaths from ordinary causes more than 250 must have died from the terrible pestilence. During the prevalence of the plague, many of the inhabitants fled to Bridstow, Peterstow, Brampton and other places. Unfortunately some of the refugees carried the plague with them, to the terror of the country. In Brampton, a whole family quickly fell under it.[26]

The parish registers mentioned in this account are no longer extant, but the inscription on the plague cross in the churchyard states that 315 died of plague. Another story, retold by Martin Morris, says that Philip Price continued to minister to the dying throughout the months of plague, and, at 5 o'clock one morning, led the townspeople through the streets chanting a litany with supplications for deliverance. The plague is said to have abated from that time.[27]

No sooner had the country begun to recover from the ravages of plague than it was plunged into an almost greater disaster, that of civil war. Although the town never actually saw fighting, the countryside around was of strategic importance. Goodrich Castle, five miles downriver, was held first, in 1642, by the Parliamentary army under the Earl of Stamford, who had occupied Hereford, and then by Henry Lingen for the king, between 1644 and 1646.

Wilton Bridge with Castle. (W. Callow, 1842)

Both these armies lived off the land, exacting money and goods from the neighbouring towns and villages. A chilling tale is told of how the Parliamentary captain holding Goodrich Castle plundered the vicar of Goodrich and his wife of all they had, taking even the children's food and clothing.[28]

Between 1642 and April 1644, apart from a brief period in 1643 when Parliamentary troops occupied Hereford, the area round Ross remained quiet and in Royalist hands. But in the spring of 1644, the borderlands between Gloucester and Wales once again became of strategic importance. The king's forces had tried and failed to gain control of Gloucester. Colonel Massey, Parliamentary governor of the city, became bolder, and, at the beginning of 1644, threatened Newent. One of the king's commanders, Colonel Mynne, duly fortified Ross churchyard. Webb says:

> His entrenchments, taking in the church appear to have formed nearly a square. The sunken road on the east was probably one, the southern was on the edge of the present upper burial ground and adjoining garden, and ran between them and the former vicarage (pulled down many years ago) to the face of a precipice bounding the work on the west: the northern trench passed through the middle of the lower churchyard, opening out upon the same precipice, and crossed the area of the palace.[29]

Colonel Mynne's stay at Ross was cut short when Colonel Massey began to advance on Hereford. Mynne moved to intercept him, sending some of his troops to Monmouth and some to Hereford, leaving Ross open to occupation by Parliament. Massey promptly took advantage of this manoeuvre and moved up to Ross with two pieces of ordnance, making for the bridge over the Wye at Wilton.

The westernmost arch of the bridge had been broken down, and had been spanned by a drawbridge. Massey found the crossing guarded by troops, including 30 musketeers from the Royalist garrison at Goodrich Castle under the command of Captain Cassie. Despite this precaution, the Parliamentary troops forded the river below the bridge and drove the guards back to the castle, taking a number of prisoners.

Part of Massey's force then occupied Ross and remained for about a week, during which time he mounted an attack on Monmouth which was repulsed, with some casualties on both sides. During that week he summoned the local gentry to pay their contributions and, we are told, a number of the yeomanry then declared themselves for Parliament, no doubt feeling the wisdom of so doing. After a week, however Massey evacuated Ross and hurried his force away to cut the road between Oxford and Bristol.[30]

Once again the town was part of Royalist held territory. Massey had levied taxes to support the Parliament cause; now the king's commissioners exacted their dues. A list of tax-payers in the Royalist assessment of 1644 for Ross Foreign, survives among the parish papers. It is headed:

An assessment made for the Forren of Rosse the 28th day of August 1644 by vertue of A warrant from his Maties Commissions for this county of hereford for the some of 15li 12s 00d for his Maties contribucon for the Moneth of July last past 1644.[31]

These 'official' extortions were, of course, in addition to the plunderings of greedy and hungry garrisons.

The worst depredations seem to have taken place in 1645, when the Scots army under the Earl of Leven and Sir David Leslie besieged Hereford, on behalf of Parliament. The pay of Leven's troops was

(6)

The severall losses and dammage sustained by the severall Inhabitants in the severall Parishes within the Hundred of Graytree.

	l.	s.	d.
Taken and plundered from the Brough and and Forren of Rose to the value of	1189	18	00
Taken and plundered from the Inhabitants of Much Martle to the value of	1104	11	04
Taken and plundered from the Inhabitants of Eaton Tregos to the value of	0238	16	00
Taken and plundered from the Parishioners of Ashton Iguram to the valew of	0178	04	10
Taken and plundered from the Parishioners of the Lea to the value of	0134	19	68
Taken and plundered from the parishioners of Linton to the value of	0487	16	11
Taken and plundered from the Parishioners of Woollhoye to the value of	0650	00	00
Taken and plundered from the Parishioners of Sollershop to the value of	0094	09	00
Taken and plundered from the Parishioners of Upton Bishop to the valew of	0074	12	08
Taken and plundered from the Parishioners of Westton under to the value of	0742	05	08
Taken and plundered from the Inhabitants of Waford to the value of	0091	05	10
Taken and plundered from the Inhabitants of Brampton to the value of	0439	15	06
Taken and plundered from the Parishioners of Putney to the value of	0073	13	00
Taken and plundered from the Parishioners of Mancels Hope to the value of	0063	00	00
Taken and plundered from the parishioners of Dorrington to the value of	0328	08	02
Taken and plundered from the parishioners of Mordeford to the value of	0490	00	00
Summe	6979	08	08

Page from Miles Hill, A true and Impartial Account of the Plunderings, Leases and Sufferings of the County of Hereford *(1645)*

greatly in arrears, and the soldiers scoured the country, carrying off not only provisions and crops, but anything that might be valuable.[32]

The Herefordshire solicitor, Miles Hill, who was appointed by Parliament to provide for the Scots army, was horrified by the plunder and sent in a report to his masters, listing the damage in the county. Of all the parishes Ross seems to have fared worst.

> Taken and plundered from the Brough and Forren of Ross to the value of £1189. 18. 00

Much Marcle lost £1,104 11s 4d.[33]

The siege of Hereford was lifted on 1st September 1645, when news of an army, advancing from Worcester, with King Charles I at its head, reached the attackers. We are told that they withdrew 'like a Scottish mist' and King Charles entered the city three days later. After a stay of a few days he set out for Raglan and it is asserted that he passed through Ross, spending the night at the Great Inn, then belonging to Gabriel Hill. Webb, quoting the local historian, Mr. Thomas Jenkins, says that the apartment he used was called the King's Room until the early 1800s, but adds that other evidence conflicts with the claim that he stayed in Ross overnight.[34]

With the lifting of the siege, the Royalist garrison of Hereford under their commander Sir Barnabas Scudamore, were free to attack local Parliamentary strongholds. Nicknamed the 'roysterers from Hereford', they captured Abergavenny, burnt Eardisley Castle and are reputed to have plundered the market at Ross. Scudamore also seized the opportunity to pay off old scores. Sir John Bridges, of Wilton Castle, had held himself aloof from the fighting and, although not in arms for Parliament, had refused to allow his house to be garrisoned for the king. This enraged Scudamore, who together with Henry Lingen, ordered the burning of the place. Tradition says that the burning occurred while the family were in church, and left the place in ruins.[35] The present house, amid the towers of the ancient castle, is mainly a nineteenth century building.

The continual financial drain occasioned by the up-keep of the opposing forces put considerable strain on the resources of the area. When, with the surrender of Goodrich Castle, the conflict finally came to an end in this part of Herefordshire, there must have been many who cared little which side won. Nevertheless, there is little evidence of the reaction in Ross to the cessation of fighting and the town had to settle down under the more repressive regime imposed by the new masters.

In particular, they had to adjust to a new vicar. It has been described on p.39 how the 'good' Philip Price was ejected from the living, in 1646, when he refused to give up the Prayer Book liturgy and how Jonathan Smith was set in his place. He, like many of the intruded ministers, had no academic training and was stigmatised in later years as:

> the Thrum Vicar, sometime an apprentice in Canterbury to a tailor, and afterwards a broken draper or stocking seller in Sandwich, [who] upon the day of his Majesty's unhappy loss and danger at Worcester did celebrate the memory of it with cake and ale.[36]

This 'unhappy loss' was the defeat of the future Charles II in 1651, at the Battle of Worcester, which Cromwell had hailed as a 'crowning mercy'. It set the seal on a new regime, decreed by a presbyterian Parliament and put into practice by the new church leaders acting through the manor officials. Feasts became fasts, Christmas ceased to be celebrated, personal behaviour became the concern of the courts.

In 1655, they not only presented 'William Ball in the Brookend for making a bludshed upon William Taylor', but also 'Anthony Alder and Henry Walker for suffering theire serv-antes to prophane the Lordes day'.[37] The inn-keeper at the George, Stephen Endall was presented for keeping a shuffle-board table. He seems to have been a somewhat notorious character as he, together with his mother and his wife Jane, was involved in the fight in the Brookend with William Taylor.[38]

Although there were supporters in Ross of Jonathan Smith and his teaching, there were also those who resented the discipline imposed by the church and, in particular, the Solemn League and Covenant that had been enacted by Parliament to abolish bishops and establish a church on the presbyterian model. When Charles II finally gained his throne in the summer of 1660, it was ordered by the new Royalist Parliament that the Covenant should be burned. On June 1st 1660, the king's birthday, the celebrations took place in the Market Place. The occasion was described thus:

> Upon Wednesday, being the happy day of His Majestie's birth, as well as his and the Common Prayer Book's restoration, the most and most considerable persons in Ross thought it not enough to celebrate the day with praise and prayer, as well as sermon, but to express this inward joy of heart the better they caused a face of wood to be cut, which being dressed with a long mantle and a cape, with a solemn league and covenant upon his breast, was carried on a pole by a chimney sweep (instead of a hangman) dressed in his holyday apparel, that is, as black as he could be; two of the same quality carried up his train, and in this triumphant manner after evening prayer he was solemnly carried quite through the town, the drummer and guard of musqueteers beside the pikemen attending him, till at last he was brought to the market-place, fixed in the ground, the covenant having the inscription –
>
> 'Who set three kingdoms in a flame,
> Tis just, should perish by the same'
> And so burned to ashes with acclamations of great joy not easily to be paralleled, ...[39]

The construction of John Kyrle's house, Alton Court and the Saracen's Head, each with hall and great chamber above, is typical of large houses built in the west midlands at the end of the sixteenth and beginning of the seventeenth centuries. As the seventeenth century progressed, so the pattern of building changed still further. The houses of the early 1600s were timber built throughout, but the façade, rear and side walls of no. 53/54 High Street were built of stone, with a space left in the rear wall to accommodate a timber-framed wing. It has been suggested that this wing is earlier in date than the main house, but the same type of carpenters' mark appears in both parts of the building. The house, probably built

The frontage of 53/54 High Street

in the 1650s, still contains original fireplaces and panelling and the front room is separated from the passage by an original wainscot screen surmounted with balusters. Aquila Smith, a physician, who occupied the house in 1665, had seven hearths, which fits well with those which, even now, can be identified.[40] There is evidence that the section of the rear wing beyond the kitchen was always a separate building and was certainly used as such in the eighteenth century.[41]

As the century wore on timber-framed houses became less and less fashionable. Stone and the new-fangled brick became the chosen materials. The rubble stone, available in Ross, would have been plastered and then lined out to represent dressed stone blocks. Ross had little local brick, but at the beginning of the eighteenth century a Ross resident wrote:

> The house that Mrs P – lived in, was built of Wood, and plaister'd over, then painted in Imitation of Bricks; and as she but seldom went from Home, was very fond of gazing at Strangers, who commonly walked in the Church-yard … I very often brought Strangers opposite to her Door, by telling them, I would show them a House, that none could guess what the Front was built with; and everyone thought t'was Bricks 'till I had convinced them to the contrary.[42]

The end of the seventeenth century saw improvements not just in the houses in Ross, but in the town generally. The new development in the area of the church has already been touched on, but attention was also paid to pitching and paving the streets, to providing a water-supply and above all to the laying out of the Prospect. These changes in the town have been attributed to the Man of Ross, John Kyrle and no doubt he was the instigator of many of these innovations.

Ever since Alexander Pope celebrated the benefactions of John Kyrle in verse, he has been Ross's most lauded son. Everything from pubs to river steamers has been named after him and much of the adulation is deserved. He was born at Dymock in 1637, to Walter and Alice Kyrle. Walter, the second son of Sir James Kyrle of Walford Court, was a lawyer and acted as steward of the manor for the Countess of Somerset. He and his wife lived in the impressive timber-framed house by the Market House in Ross, and this John Kyrle inherited after the death of his father in 1650. Alice continued to live in the house until her death in 1661 and her probate inventory gives a good understanding of the modest but comfortable lifestyle of the family.[43]

The inventory, in which much of the furniture is described as 'old', is typical of the home of a well-to-do tradesman or farmer, but in no way equates with the elegant furnishings that might be expected in a gentleman's home. This preference for frugality and modesty, inherited from his parents, epitomises John Kyrle. It appears in the stories of his simplicity of dress, of his refusal to have his portrait taken and his insistence on drinking only beer and cider.[44]

John Kyrle owned property in Gloucestershire as well as in and around Ross, including the manor of Cleeve to the south of the town. In part of the Cleeve estate he laid out his famous 'Walk'. Heath described it a 100 years after Kyrle's death as:

> A neat gravel path, which … runs parallel with the course of the Wye. Towards the middle it is carried near to the edge of a rocky eminence, partially clothed with underwood, and shaded with beech and other timber in a thriving state. The trees planted by Mr. Kyrle, which had grown to a very fine and large size, have, since his death been cut down. At the extremity of this Walk is placed a
> ### SUMMER HOUSE
> Which affords an agreeable retreat, as well as a pleasing view of the river and country.[45]

The income from John Kyrle's estate cannot have been large, as it is claimed that he made his many benefactions from an income

Excerpt from Alice Kyrle's probate inventory, 1661

'The Man of Ross' — John Kyrle distributing bread to the poor, by J. van Aken, c.1730.
(Courtesy of Hereford Museum and Art Gallery)

of £500 a year. Pope listed the laying out of the Prospect with its fountain and water supply, the causeway to Wilton Bridge, the re-building of the church spire and the endowing of almshouses as the results of his charity.

Bonner, quoting from Dr. Johnson's *Life of Pope*, has this to say:

> The truth is, that KYRL was a man of known integrity and active benevolence, by whose solicitation the wealthy were persuaded to pay contributions to his charitable schemes: this influence he obtained by an example of liberality exerted to the utmost extent of his power, and was thus enabled to give more than he had.[46]

Top: Drawing of the entrance from the Prospect to the churchyard from The Wye Tour, *1896.*
Bottom: The Prospect Gate in 1999

Johnson's summing up of Kyrle's liberality seems to have been remarkably accurate. Although it is not known what methods Kyrle employed to fund the building of the causeway to the bridge, or to subsidise the repair of the church tower, sources indicate that the waterworks was set up by a partnership, and that the Quaker, William Fisher had shares in the project. In 1705, he, with three other Ross men, took over a lease of the One Mill and Rix Meadows skirting the river, which had been made out to John Kyrle eight years before. The millpond was to supply the power for the waterworks which pumped water from the river up to the town, and the leat to the engine ran through the meadows. By the following year the waterworks was an accomplished fact.[47]

The laying out of the pleasure ground called the Prospect was certainly Kyrle's brainchild, but after leasing the land by the church from Lord Weymouth, part of the same package that included One Mill and the meadows, and setting out the design, he sublet the land to William Fisher, with the proviso that Fisher should maintain the grounds and keep the walks in repair.[48] It is worth noting that the site was known as the Prospect from its inception and is so called in 1709 in William Fisher's will.[49]

The church spire was repaired in 1721 and the entry in the parish register says nothing of Kyrle's involvement, though the booklet, The Life of John Kyrle, asserts that he convened the parish meeting which took the decision to rebuild.[50] It seems that John Kyrle may have initiated these useful schemes, but was not necessarily the sole patron.

John Kyrle's Prospect fell into decay, and the fountain he set up there for the convenience of local people became choked with rubbish, but his principles lived on. In the nineteenth century his Prospect was reinstated, and his water supply, reorganised several times, and provided with new pumping equipment, continued to supply soft water to the town until the 1950s.

8   The Impact of Nonconformity

The middle of the seventeenth century saw the rise of a ferment of new political and religious ideas, released and stimulated by the lifting of censorship that accompanied the ousting of the Anglican bishops in the early 1640s, at the start of the Civil War. The result was a great increase in the number of 'free-thinking' Christians, who read their Bibles, listened to the new preachers and produced ideas of their own. Some of them felt able to remain within the Church of England; indeed the Church changed to accommodate them, with the old clergy who supported the bishops and the king turned out of their livings to make way for ministers with Baptist, Congregationalist and Presbyterian views. John Tombes, a clergyman in the Church of England with marked Baptist views, was actually parson of Ross for a short time in the 1640s.[1]

With the Restoration of the king in 1660, these freedoms came to an end. The supporters of king and episcopacy returned and the nonconforming ministers had to make way in their turn. One such minister was John Skinner the 'Baptist' minister of Weston-under-Penyard. Ejected from his parish church, he founded a 'conventicle' in the village and it has been suggested that a handful of Baptists from Ross travelled to this house in the hamlet of Ryeford to worship.[2]

Another minister with Independent leanings, the Rev. Anthony Collier, moved to Ross when he was turned out of his living first at Moreton-on-Lugg and then at Moreton Valance in Gloucestershire. He, too, began to lead a conventicle in the upper room of his house in Copse Cross Street, as did the Rev. Jonathan Smith at Walford.[3] The authorities, now once again in favour of episcopacy and traditional church doctrine, were not prepared to countenance these deviations. The adherents of these groups were regularly presented by the rector at the Bishop's Consistory Court and fined for their obduracy.[4]

From the lists compiled by these courts we can get some idea of who were the more affluent members of Collier's congregation. Only Jonathan Smith and his wife Ann, Nathaniel Wood and his wife Mary, Walter Hall and his wife Grace, John Bennett and Jane Garway, widow, appear regularly with Anthony Collier. Of these Nathaniel Wood, and John Bennett both had substantial houses with three hearths.[5] Jonathan Smith seems, by this time, to have been an assistant to Anthony Collier and he also attempted to take over the grammar school at Ross. In this he was prevented by the rector, Dr. Newton.[6] By the 1670s the rector seems to have had an enlightened policy towards his erring parishioners. He only presented those he thought could pay the fines![7]

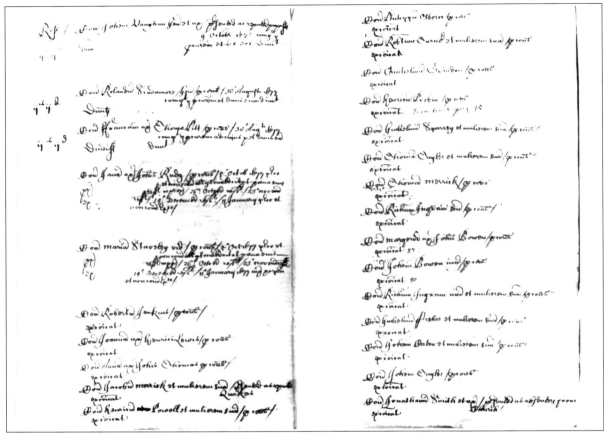

The Act Book of the Consistory Court of the Bishop of Hereford giving lists of the names of those dissenters presented at the court. (Courtesy of the Bishop of Hereford)

The Independents — later known as Congregationalists and now part of the United Reformed Church — established themselves in Ross and, sometime at the end of the seventeenth or the beginning of the eighteenth century, built themselves a meeting house on the south side of Kyrle Street, just round the corner from what is now Broad Street.[8] The church building survives, although it has been drastically altered, but was replaced in 1867 by a new church in Gloucester Road. The early Independents seem to have made little impact on the town and even the 'church book' can offer little for the first hundred years of the church's history.[9]

This cannot be said of the Society of Friends, the other nonconformist group which grew up in the town. The Quakers, like the Baptists and the Independents, grew out of the nonconformity of the Commonwealth era. The established church of the Restoration could see little difference between the various groups. Although Anthony Collier and his followers were often described as 'absenters from church' or 'non comers to church', they were also called 'Anabaptists', and were regularly confused with the Quakers. The Quakers of Ross, however, were prominent, organised and vocal. Their impact on the town was considerable.

When the Yorkshireman, Thomas Goodyear, and his colleague George Scaife, followers of the Quaker, George Fox, came to Ross, in December 1655, they found a community open and ready to listen to their radical brand of Christian teaching.[10] Led by James Merrick, a tanner, to whose house the preachers first came, a group of townspeople assembled in the 'steeple house'. There their discourse was interrupted by the Baptist preacher, John Skinner, of Weston-under-Penyard, who tried to break up the meeting — the Quakers were as feared by their fellow nonconformists as they would later be by the established church after the Restoration. The presence of the four parish constables, of whom Merrick was one, all eager to hear the new teaching, prevented any real disruption and the audience

> did withdraw into A house Called ye Church house, Joyning to ye Steeplehouse yard; and there both Tho: Goodeyar and Geo: Scaff declared the Lords Everlasting Truth Boldly without Interruption.

Many were convinced, including all four constables — John Cowles, Guy Lane, Thomas Nickells and James Merrick.

James Merrick was to be prominent in the new Society of Friends and he and his family figure repeatedly in the early history of the group. Indeed, the first meeting was established at his home. There both Goodyear and Scaife were entertained and also George Fox when he visited Ross in 1663.[11] James Merrick was probably already living on a site in the Brookend, Brampton Street area where his family held property.[12]

The account from which the founding of Ross meeting was taken was written in 1707, by eyewitnesses William Fisher and Richard Ingram. They attributed the success of the new teaching to a group already in existence

> who were desierouse And in Expecktation to here truth declared, who had for some time before seperated ymselves from ye Publicke worship of the world, who did see ye End of ye Priests Teachings, & would many times sitt in silence & noe perticular person Appointed to speak or Preach Amongst ym.[13]

The names and the dwellings of many of these early Friends are known and, even without the testimony of Fisher and Ingram, it could be deduced from their places of residence that some were already dissenters. Dissenters in the seventeenth century tended to band together for mutual protection, and dissenting landlords let to tenants of like mind. It is therefore significant to find in a rent roll of 1648, that Thomas Taylor, Thomas Brown, Margaret Chapman and John Cowles lived in the High Street, on the north side backing on to Back Lane — now New Street. There were also a number of families associated with the area north of the town called Over Ross, north of the mill; out of 15 families owning land in Brampton and Ledbury Streets, five are known to have become pillars of the Quaker community.[14] It might be thought that this last concentration of Friends resulted from the presence of the Meeting House in Brampton Street, but this was not the case. The Osbornes, the Prichards, the Preeses, the Merricks and the Grindens were already in Over Ross area in 1648, seven years before the Quaker preachers visited the town, and 18 years before the construction of the meeting house next to James Merrick's own house.

The seventeenth century Quakers held strong beliefs. Their conviction that all men are equal in the sight of God led them to spurn the conventions of the day. They refused to raise their hats to their betters, and gave offence by addressing all men with the familiar 'thee' and 'thou'. They took seriously Christ's instruction to 'swear not … but let your yea be yea and your nay be nay', and refused on this ground to take the oath of allegiance. Totally repudiating established religion and its structures, they would not attend the parish church, an offence in itself, nor would they bury their dead in the churchyard or pay tithes. To the government of the day, national and local, beset by strange sects and the apocalyptic extremes of the Fifth Monarchy Men, this behaviour was tantamount to anarchy. It must be said that the Society of Friends took early action to deny any such intention, and declared in their 'Peace Testimony' sent to Charles II in 1660: 'Our principle is, and our practices have always been to seek peace and ensue it … All bloody principles and practices we do utterly deny.'[15]

This declaration had little practical effect and even under the Commonwealth, when other dissenters flourished, some of the Quakers were sorely persecuted.

Little more than a year after the preachers' visit, the Quakers in Ross were in trouble. In May 1657, a number of the Ross Friends were arrested by two constables on their way to a meeting organised at Kings Caple at the house of the 'aged' Joan Merrick, mother of James. One of the Friends was put in the stocks and the meeting itself was disrupted by a 'rude Rabble, with Dogs and Staves … whooping, halloeing, pushing their Staves in at Windows, and throwing in Sticks and Dirt.'

The mob continued to interrupt the preaching and then followed the Friends back to Ross, 'striking one of them, Giles Milton, so violently that he became lame in one of his arms.' The following year it was John Merrick in trouble. He, though, like his relative, a tanner of some wealth, fell foul of certain gentry for refusing to doff his hat. In one incident he was 'beaten and sorely abused' by the servant of the famous John Kyrle.[16]

The villagers of Kings Caple displayed considerable antagonism to the Quakers and seized their opportunity when Joan Merrick, in keeping with Quaker practice, was buried by her sons, James, Walter and Thomas, in her own garden, rather than in the churchyard. They claimed that Thomas and Walter had murdered their mother, and this despite sworn statements from other witnesses at the inquest that she had died a natural death. Since the brothers, in accordance with their principles, refused to take the oath, the coroner fined them and bound them over to the Quarter Sessions. However, no further action appears to have been taken by the authorities.[17]

The garden at Kings Caple, at this time in the hands of Walter Merrick, seems to have been used as the burial ground for the Ross meeting until 1663, and Giles Milton and his son were probably buried there in 1661. However, by 1663, the Ross Friends had a need for a burial ground of their own and so they bought for £5, from Thomas Brown, one of their number, a parcel of land which was set out, bounded and used as a buryeing place situate and beeing within the Towne and Burrough of Rosse aforesaid in a street there called Back Lane, lyeing betweene a messuage of Thomas Taylor apothecary in the possession or occupation of one Moses Hungerford, and another Messuage or tenement of Margarett Chapman widow in the possession or occupation of one John Hungerford and abutting on the garden of one John Cowles on the south side thereof.[18]

According to the rent roll for 1648, Margaret Chapman, Thomas Brown, Thomas Taylor and John Hungerford all had houses in the High Street and as the plot lay at the back of these houses it was protected from malicious intrusion. Two of the parties cited in the deed, Thomas Taylor and John Cowles, were prominent Friends and their names feature in the early minute books of the Society, along with the Merricks and William Fisher.[19]

As time went on, the authorities in Ross seem to have softened their attitude to the Friends, while still considering that their views were misguided. In a letter to a diocesan official, the rector, John Newton wrote in 1674:

> the case is very hard with John Cowles who is wrongfully presented, and more there is to be said on his behalfe than I am willing to set downe in a letter.

He went on:

Copy of the presentment made in 1674.
(Courtesy of the Bishop of Hereford)

If you make any further proceeding against any let Phillip Osborne be one who is lately drawne in to be a Quaker by James Merrick & it is believ'd yt if his purse did once smart for it it would be a means to bring him into his witts again and he is able to bear the charge.'[20]

This enlightened policy did not last and during the late 1670s and 80s, when the political climate was very unsettled, a number of the Ross Friends were heavily fined and authorities 'lockt up the [meeting] House, and took away the Key, so that they were obliged afterwards to meet in the Street.' Even so it was only the better off who suffered.[21]

Apart from their role as prominent Quakers, the Merricks helped shape the area at the junction of Brookend and Brampton Street. The family had owned a house in

Brampton Street since the beginning of the century and in 1670 James Merrick decided to extend his holding. He negotiated for and bought another old house 'called or known by the name of the Porch house', from William Hill, Glover, and his wife Sybil, next door to his house in Brampton Street. In a separate transaction he also bought the two rooms — a lower room and a chamber over — which formed the dwelling house of the Hills and their daughter, Joan.[22]

In buying this land Merrick had two objects in mind: his first intention was to build himself a new house and his second, to provide a purpose built meeting house for Friends in Ross. His own house was put in hand almost straight away for when he made his will five years later he left the new house to his wife Elizabeth:

> My house I lately built standing upon the ground I lately bought of William Hill and the Tenement belonging to the said house with the Outhouses, Garden, Courte and appurtenances belonging to the same (except the part before bequeathed) now in the possession of me the said James Merrick, and alsoe an Entry, Backside, Stable and Barne lying and being in Brampton Street.[23]

Brook House built by James Merrick in the early 1670s

Now known as Brook House, James Merrick's house has been divided into flats. The front, with its dormers, modillioned eaves cornice and hooded doorway, must be much as James Merrick built it. It is also said to have a staircase with heavy, turned balusters. A wing has been added to the rear of the building, which may have contained the malthouse mentioned in a document of 1703.[24]

Pevsner has dated this house to the early eighteenth century and commented on its similarity to the house next to the mill, until recently the Railway Hotel. Though the building date is somewhat earlier than Pevsner suggests, the similarity is not in doubt.[25] The two houses were built by cousins, both Merricks, both tanners, both Quakers, and apparently at much the same time. Perhaps the same builder was employed. The mason may have been Henry Powell who was a Friend and a trustee for the burial ground. He was also employed by the meeting to do repairs to the meeting house and burial ground.[26]

John Merrick's house was probably built slightly before James' dwelling, and was in existence by 1670, when John settled the property on his son John on the occasion of his

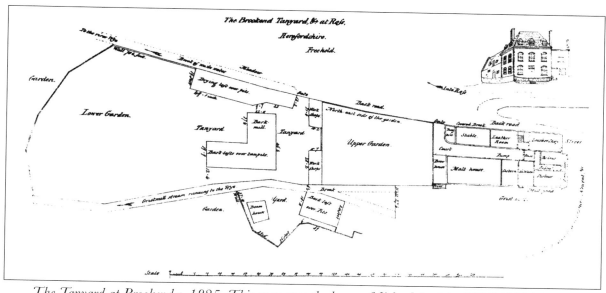

The Tanyard at Brookend c.1825. This was once the home of John Merrick. (HRO BA31/188)

marriage.[27] A drawing of the house made in the early nineteenth century shows that by this date the windows and the door had been altered to conform to later fashion.[28] The inside has a charming staircase and panelling but is all much later than John Merrick's day.

The Friends' Meeting House

The part of the property described in James Merrick's will as already bequeathed, was the plot that Merrick had intended for the meeting house next to the dwelling house. He had already made it over to the trustees of the meeting house, together with access through his entry and court. It also included

> all that part of Oake Timber I bought this last Summer and allsoe the sume of Forty Pounds to erect and build a house upon the said piece of ground.[29]

In 1677, a year before he died, James and his wife formally granted the meeting house to trustees.[30]

Like so many of the early nonconformist places of worship, the building was tucked down a narrow alley between two dwelling houses. The structure was, we are told in a questionnaire dated 1824, 'altered in 1803 and enlarged', but the shell remains essentially that built by Merrick's executors.[31] The house on the south of the entrance, much altered and now made into two flats, still survives and the seventeenth century roof trusses and some of the framing can be seen inside the building. The other, to the north, was pulled down sometime before 1825 and the land used to build a 'Women's Meeting Room'. The houses were let out to Friends, and in the Monthly Meeting Book for 1700 there is a note asking

> Elizabeth Bennett in the house adjoining next the meeting house that shee doe not lett filth comeing from ye piggs Cots to come through Thomas Osbornes butery.[32]

Elizabeth Bennett was probably one of Anthony Collier's congregation.

Behind the meeting house was a piece of land which James Merrick used as a garden. In 1702/3 it was agreed that:

> Whereas Tho Merricke doe lay something of claime to part of ye garden Addionyng to ye meeting house it is unanimously Agreed by ye said Thomas Merricke & friends yt wch ever friend of Ross have occashion for a Burying place yt yt peec. of ground shall be made use of for a Burying ground.[33]

In 1729 Edward Prichard was instructed to divide the burying ground from the garden, the rear part of the plot which contained the stable and barn referred to in Merrick's will. This was 'parted from the Garden with Pales'.[34] Recently this part of the garden has been sold and the flats called Southall House built on it.

The Merricks were not the only Quakers to invest in bricks and mortar. In the Brookend area they were joined by a number of well-to-do Quaker tanners, like the Prichards and the Osbornes. The Prichards built Millbrook House, while Thomas Griffiths, who certainly had

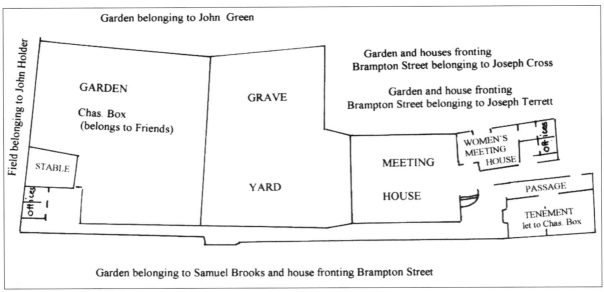

Sketch plan of the Friends' Meeting House in 1823, taken from a plan in the Friends' House Library, London

The Will of William Fisher, 1709, with the entries for the pigpens and the waterworks

Quaker connections, built no. 35, which was described as 'all that newly erected Capital messuage in Brookend' in 1730.[35]

While they were revitalising the neighbourhood at the foot of the town, William Fisher, as has already been shown, transformed the area known as Palace Pound. Although John Kyrle laid out the Prospect, William Fisher was responsible for maintaining it. He also had shares in the newly developed water-works and rented the Market House and the market tolls, the first of a series of Friends to administer the property.[36]

It has been suggested that 'Quakerism' was 'most influential among the hard-pressed middle classes', but this is hardly borne out by circumstances in Ross.[37] The Merrick cousins both owned tanyards and had sufficient capital to build themselves substantial houses. Thomas Taylor was an apothecary of some status — perhaps the only one in Ross, whilst William Fisher inherited from his father one of the best sites in the town, in addition to his lease of the market.[38] His partner in this market enterprise was William Sparry but they fell out over 'ye Pitching pens and Setting up of Standings etc'.[39] Two Friends, one of whom was William Grindall, were appointed to reason with them and urge them to end their differences. William Sparry and William Grindall were both salesmen or (probably) auctioneers and both families

83

had interests in the Market House after William Fisher's death.[40] Once again William Sparry proved a difficult man to do business with and again two Friends tried to mediate:

> there is some diferance between Wm. Sparry and Ruth Grindall About ye (sic) theyr consernes being Partners in ye marketthouse.[41]

Ruth Grindall was prepared to abide by the agreement drawn up, but William Sparry had to be persuaded to 'have his hand on the sd paper' and the end result is in some doubt.[42] His quarrel with Thomas Merrick over the mortgage he held on Merrick's house and the settlement when Elizabeth Merrick married William's son, was never resolved and remained an issue until Sparry's death.[43]

By the end of the second decade of the eighteenth century the founders of the Quaker meeting had all died and a new generation had taken their place. A new family name appears in Ross with the advent of Edward Prichard from Almeley, in north-west Herefordshire. Prichards would, from this time, play a prominent part the affairs of the meeting. It is true that there had been Prichards in Ross at an earlier period and that a David Prichard appears in the records but he was hardly an asset, being rebuked for leading 'a disorderly life'![44] The Players, Joseph and his son John, the Cowles, John and his son and grandson, Joseph and John, Samuel Lodge and his sons, and the James Morgans, father, son and grandson, were all leaders in the Society of Friends in the eighteenth century.

These men were solid businessmen and owners of property, but they do not seem to have had the drive of their forebears. Not until the nineteenth century would the Friends again make their mark on the life of the town.

9   Charities and Care

The parish church and those less fortunate living in the small town of Ross have benefited over the centuries from the generosity of the townspeople. In the past the better-off inhabitants have bestowed gifts, endowed charities, founded hospitals, established almshouses and started schools. A number of these were suppressed at the Reformation, others have been lost, but many have continued to the present day together with a genuine care for the community.

Towards the end of the thirteenth century bequests were made to the church in the form of chantries from the wealthy parishioners. However, most of the Ross charitable institutions date from the seventeenth century, though an early deed exists relating to a house in Hatters Lane which Richard Worcester endowed as a hospital in his will of 1511. During the reign of Henry VIII 'this same Hospital (for four poor persons) was endowed by Charles Perrock, and Thomas Perrock the younger' in the early 1600s. Now known as Perrock's Almshouses in Old Gloucester Road, it was rebuilt in 1771 and has since been altered and restored. Charles Perrock's endowment of 30s was, by tradition, used for lamp-money for the church altar. This amount was added to by Thomas Perrock with his annuity of 26s, both endowments being originally charged on property then situated at the Booth-hall in the market place. In 1809, the hospital and its endowment was conveyed to Thomas Jenkins in trust for the Rev. Thomas Underwood and others. In 1810 it was reported by the churchwardens that 3¼d was paid weekly to each inhabitant which totalled 4d per annum more than the endowment.[1]

Another early almshouse foundation understood to date from the fourteenth century was 'the ancient gift of Mr. Birt, and held in trust by ye family of Rudhall, by which later name it is usually distinguished.'[2] This attractive row of almshouses in Church Street was repaired by William Rudhall in 1575, then generously endowed by Thomas Perrock, mercer, in 1605; Alice Spencer, a servant at Rudhall, in 1677; and Herbert Westfaling Esq. in 1741 who left a yearly sum of £5 to be paid 'to five poor persons, inhabitants of the parish of Ross — three of them to be men, and two women.' When restored in 1960 by the Ross Charity Trustees the five original houses were converted into three almshouses 'without altering their Tudor front.'[3]

Thomas Webbe was another great benefactor to the town. He was a carpenter from Monkton in Llanwarne who died in 1612 and in his will left 'the sum of one hundred pounds, for building a Hospital in Ross for seven poor parishioners of Ross and also seven hundred pounds for the endowment thereof.'[4] Apart from these almshouses, which stand in Copse

Rudhall's Almshouses in 1892

Cross Street, he also left £200 to free Wilton bridge of its toll, and money to replace the old Booth-hall in the Market Place, a request that was not carried out — see page 49.

A contemporary of Thomas Webbe was the Rev. William Pye, vicar of Foy, who in 1615 left 'an ancient Messuage (sometime a school house) unendowed, for four poor parishioners.' In 1648 this 'school house' in Edde Cross Street was leased by 'the Widow Scott'.[5] The building was rebuilt in 1679 as almshouses and moved to its present site in 1792 due to the buildings being in a ruinous condition and in an inconvenient position for Mr. Walter Hill, whose properties overlooking the Wye surrounded the charitable institution. In 1854 these almshouses in Edde Cross Street benefited from an endowment from Thomas Roberts, the son of John Roberts, a bookseller and former clerk of the Bank of England.[6]

In the mid-seventeenth century Philip Markye, presumably from Alton Court, gave 'an Almshouse, Burgage and Garden in Edde Cross Street — for the use of the poor of Ross.' All the almshouses were described as being in a dilapidated condition in 1844, and although Markye's Almshouses were unfit for habitation in 1866, they remained standing until they were demolished in 1961. The proceeds from the endowment and sale of the site was paid into the Ross Almshouse Charity and forms a permanent endowment.[7]

With the presence of so many almshouses in Ross, it is not surprising that in 1667 a poor, worn out schoolmaster from Llanwarne applied for 'an Almsman place in the Almshouse in Rosse.' After 43 years of teaching, Thomas Hooper described himself as having 'an extraordinary paine in my head caused by long and frequent bawlings of boyes: My sight is dimme my hearing bad and my body Crazie weake and full of Infirmities.' He considered that 'though the weekly allowance be but 1s 9d yet then I shall have a hole to put my head in and not be driven to perish in the highway.'[8]

ROSS.—NOTICE IS HEREBY GIVEN

That a VESTRY MEETING will be held on Friday, the 16th of August instant, at the hour of Three in the Afternoon, for the purpose of taking into consideration the present DILAPIDATED CONDITION of the ALMS HOUSES, of the Parish, with a view to form a plan for putting them into a state of Repair, and to provide a permanent Fund for their preservation in future.

Dated this second day of August, 1844.

WILLIAM PRICE, WILLIAM BONNOR, Churchwardens.

CHARLES HENRY HUGHES, JAMES GRIFFITHS, STEPHEN BUTT, RICHARD WEAVER, Overseers.

(Courtesy of Hereford Record Office)

Surviving charity records reveal some interesting details about the people and places of Ross. In 1614 Thomas Addis from Netherton Farm in Brampton Abbotts left 2s 6d 'towards the reparashons of the church of Ross', and bequests to his wife included 'my best featherbed with the furniture thereto, and the third parte of all my household stuffe, and foure oxen, viz: Lion, Brownie, and the Two Blacke.'[9] Many other interesting 'Benefactions to the Church and Parish' are displayed on two boards in the church tower. Now almost illegible, the text was published by J.A. Stratford in The Wye Tour over 100 years ago. It includes such items as:

1607. – John Baker, sometime of London, Gent., gave fo the Sunday Evening Lecture £20 per annum for ever.

1635. – The Youth of this Parish gave the Second Bell in peal.

1783. – The Associates of Dr. Bray, deceased, presented the Parochial Library.

1846. – Mrs. Elizabeth Mills, Relict of the Rev. James Mills, formerly Curate of this Parish, bequeathed £100 sterling for bread, to be purchased with the Interest, and to be distributed on Good Friday of every year, at the discretion of the Curate for the time being, among 50 poor widows or single women above 60 years of age, residing in the parish of Ross.

In a list of 'Certain gifts and bequests given by several persons to the use of the Church and poore of Rosse', are names of properties recorded in 1645, now almost forgotten. 'The Rein Deer, later by the name or sign of Marlborough's Head', was an inn which stood near the corner of St. Mary's Street and High Street nearest the Market Place. In 1705 William Mann, a glover, left a 'sum of forty shillings yearly to the poor of the Town and Forren of Ross', paid out of 'my Messuage Burgage or tenement called the Bell Forge' (see also pp.20-1).[10]

Amongst the 80 plus recorded gifts, bequests and endowments to Ross church and the poor, is one person who received special mention, Jane Furney. This pious gentlewoman was born into the Merrick family in 1660 and married John Furney around 1681. Apart from mothering her ten children she was 'cherisher of the young, the comforter of the aged, and a Pillar in the House of our God' and was described as a 'venerable matron', 'Munificent – devout – and unassuming'. After the death of her husband in 1705, Jane gave to the parish church 'a Paten of Silver for the Holy Sacrement, and also a Pulpit Cloth and Cushions of crimson velvet, tasselled and fringed with gold.' Then in 1728, two years before her death, 'That excellent Benefactress Mrs. Jane Furney of this parish, widow, of pious Memory – amongst other worthy acts – gave in her life time, the now Workhouse of this parish with the now Garden thereto adjoining and belonging to the use of the poor of the parish [Ross] forever.'[11]

The workhouse continued to be used after her death, administered by the church-wardens, overseers of the poor and the governors. The vestry minutes of 1750 record their concern about its state. In 1751 two boys and two girls were allowed shirts and shifts, and in

1764 when Mr. Jones was appointed by the overseers of the poor as Master of the Workhouse, it was proposed to furnish it with 'Clothing and bedding'. When old enough the children were placed out as shown in a list dated 1786:

Josiah Jackson to Mr. Wm. Llewellin
George Hoare to Mr. Joseph Smart
Wm. Collins to Mr. Joseph Hardwick
John Nicholls to Mr. James Powles
Sarah Dunn to Mr. Charles Prosser
Frances George to Mr. Roberts Staymaker
Eliz. Scott to Mr. Rich. Panter
Richard Scott to Mr. John Jarvis.[12]

ROSS DISPENSARY.

APPEAL.

The Committee of the Ross Dispensary earnestly appeal to the Inhabitants of Ross, and the Neighbouring Parishes, for subscriptions towards raising a sufficient sum to enable them to purchase the Premises in which the Institution is now held.

The Committee are informed that the Premises are likely to be sold. Considering the thorough suitability of them for the purposes of the Institution, both with reference to general internal fitness, and excellency of situation—The great difficulty and heavy expense already experienced, in which the Committee would be again involved, if driven to substitute other Premises—The very moderate amount of ascertained purchase money—Considering, these and other equally cogent reasons, the Committee EARNESTLY recommend the purchase of the Property, and throw themselves on the liberality of their neighbours and friends, to enable them to raise the requisite amount.

The Committee feel it unnecessary to allude to the great amount of benefit which the Institution has conferred, and is still conferring, on the Poor of Ross, and the surrounding Parishes; or to the desirability of placing it on a sounder and more permanent footing.

Subscriptions will be thankfully received by any Member of the Committee, the Treasurer and Honorary Secretary, and at either of the Banks in Ross.

COMMITTEE.

WILLIAM BRIDGMAN, Esq.,	THOS. HILL, Esq.,
REV. T. P. SYMONDS,	REV. W. HULME,
CHARLES BURMESTER, Esq.,	K. M. POWER, Esq.,
REV. T. WEST,	WM. STUBBS, Esq.

TREASURER AND HONORARY SECRETARY.

J. W. R. HALL, Esq.

This workhouse was situated near Copse Cross Street, but it is not possible to locate its exact site. In its last days it housed 18 adults and five children before being replaced by the Ross Union Workhouse. This opened in 1838 and was run by an elected Board of Governors under the Poor Law Amendment Act. After additions and alterations the Workhouse ceased in 1914, becoming the Poor Law Institution.[13]

Between 1819 and 1837 information was gathered for a report made by the Charity Commissioners for the 'Borough and Parish of Ross'. The charity schools, almshouses and bread charities were described in detail, together with the later Baker's Charity which dates from 1835. James Baker was a nailer from Ross who moved to London and became a successful ironmonger and marine store dealer, and in his will left a large sum 'for the benefit of the Poor of the parish of Ross.'[14] The 1837 report was followed by a Supplementary List in 1891, which added four important institutions founded by prominent citizens of Ross — the Prospect Gardens laid out by John Kyrle in 1696; The Dispensary started by James Wallace Richard Hall in 1825; the British and Foreign School, which opened in 1836 due to the exertions of Captain George Adams and James Wallace Richard Hall; and Thomas Blake's Free Library and Reading-room of 1873. All of these foundations are described in other parts of this book. Another worthy of the town, Nathaniel Morgan, contributed to the 'Charities of the Society of Friends' recorded by Mr. Good in 1868.

From the reports and 'Inquiries Concerning Charities' published during the nineteenth century, the Charity Commissioners recorded the loss of charities in the names of Alice Spencer 1677, Christopher Mutlowe 1717, Eleanor Dubberley 1749 and James Maddocks 1759, although the latter two re-appeared on the Charity Commissioners scheme of 1957.[15] Others were never recorded by the Commissioners including the Ross Maternal Charity founded in 1800 and the Organ Benefaction of 1827. It does appear that some charities originated from an earlier date as recorded in a list of the 'Committee of Charitable Uses' dated 1675. Others of interest, not officially recorded, appear on the Benefaction Board.[16]

During the twentieth century other charities were founded, known as Brookfield Villas Alms-houses, Cawdor Gardens Trust, and the Minnett and Skyrme Trust. It is understood that the latter Trust was named after H. Minnett and J.H. Skyrme who conveyed the land where the Board School in Cantilupe Road was built in 1873. This Trust was only registered in 1990 after the sale of part of the land for the building of the new library, and its funds are used to provide financial assistance towards the education of people aged under 25 who live in Ross.[17] In 1957 a

Thomas Matthews, J.P.
late nineteenth century chemist

'Scheme of the Charity Commissioners' was adopted, which amalgamated most of the 'Charities in the Ancient Parish of Ross under the Ross Charity Trustees.'[18]

The sick, injured and dying of Ross were attended by surgeons, apothecaries, physicians, midwives as well as those with no qualifications. Apothecaries were chemists who were licensed to prescribe, prepare and sell drugs, whilst surgeons specialised in surgery, and physicians were legally qualified as doctors of medicine. In 1784 John Bond, Walter Pearse and Thomas Paytherus served as the surgeons and apothecaries in the town. By 1822 there were two physicians and five surgeons and apothecaries including Samuel Philpot Brookes and George Rootes, both situated in the Market Place. Brookes practised from the Man of Ross House until his death in 1829, when the property passed to William Cary Cocks, an apothecary in 1830. He remained there until 1868 and was succeeded by Thomas Roper, then by Thomas Matthews, a chemist and druggist, in 1876.[19]

A subsequently internationally known doctor of nervous diseases was born in 1786 at Millbrook House in Brookend. He was Dr. James Cowles Prichard, a descendant of the prominent Quaker family, who qualified as a doctor in 1810, and specialised in diseases of the nervous system. He became one of the world's leading authorities in anthropology and master of a dozen languages. In 1809 he joined the Church of England, and was buried at Sellack in 1848 where his son-in-law was vicar.[20] A physician in practice from the start of the nineteenth century was Richard Evans in the High Street. By 1835 he had moved to his home in Edde Cross Street, where he died in 1843 aged 77.[21] A few years later another physician, George Strong, was residing at the Chase, which had been rebuilt by his father-in-law John Cooke. Strong was obviously interested in the surrounding area with a 'desire to catch the faint and dying echoes of the Past' which led him to produce his Handbook to Ross and Archenfield in 1863. The Chase in 1877 was listed as 'void' as Strong had moved to Merrivale Villas and was offered for sale a year later.[22]

After 1788 the sick or disabled who had contributed to the Ross Friendly Society were entitled to an annual payment, but only after belonging to the Society for over 12 years.[23]

The less fortunate of Ross who suffered from ill-health relied upon the charity of the Parish Overseers. But the treatment given was basic, as evidenced in 1766, when 3d each was paid for the 'Bleeding of Mary Holloway' and John Underwood.[24] In 1822 the vestry appointed Mr. Edward Wilmott 'Surgeon and Apothecary' to the poor at a salary of £20 a year, for which he was expected to find 'all necessary Medicines' and 'all Midwifery where a woman Midwife can't officiate.' Assistance from the Ross vestry was often requested by the poor parishioners to pay for the doctor who attended the sick and ailing.

The problem of how to treat 'lunatics' also needed addressing. In 1844 the case of 'James Reed a Lunatic from Peterstow', came before the vestry but the case was 'considered too doubtful to give their decided opinion,' although it was agreed the pauper should be removed to another parish. For 'lunatics' from wealthy families, a Lunatic Asylum had been established at Whitchurch near Ross in 1834. Here for a fee patients were 'treated as much as possible like rational beings' by the 'Resident Medical Man', Mr. Millard, and his family.[25]

Both Cary Cocks and Strong served at the Ross Dispensary in Brookend Street. This venture, providing a much needed service for the less wealthy, was opened in 1825 mainly through the efforts of James Wallace Richard Hall, a solicitor, banker and benefactor to the town.[26] From its site in Brookend the Dispensary moved to New Street and by 1876 had become the Ross Dispensary and Cottage Hospital. In 1879 a new Cottage Hospital, in Gloucester Road, was opened with great celebration. It had cost £1,500 to purchase the land and build the hospital, and was paid for by fundraising, together with bequests and

Ross Cottage Hospital, 1905

91

legacies from the rich and wealthy. The Cottage Hospital was to benefit the 'working classes' who, when accidents occurred, could be treated locally instead of suffering an uncomfortable journey by cart or train to the infirmary at Hereford. From that time a caring staff and dedicated supporters raised further funds to enlarge and extend the hospital, adding an operating theatre in 1897 and an X-ray ward in 1919. The much loved Cottage Hospital was eventually replaced by the Ross Community Hospital in 1997.[27] It is apparent that a real effort was made by a caring community to look after the poor, sick and homeless of Ross; the church and individual benefactors all played their part, now mainly taken over by the state.

10   Schools and Education

Over the centuries there have been many attempts to establish schools in Ross. A record of 1675 which says that 'another house hath beene used as a schoolhouse' may be referring to Pye's Almshouses which were described by the Charity Commissioners as 'an ancient Messuage (sometimes a schoolhouse).'[1] This was the house in Edde Cross Street described as the 'school house' in 1648. Another existed in the early eighteenth century when William Dobbs' mother kept a very large school in a house adjoining the churchyard in Ross, which Mr. Kyrle often visited 'for the purpose of enquiring what children were objects of encouragement, and what of reproof.' William Dobbs served as Sexton of the parish for many years before he died in 1798 aged 86.[2]

However, the earliest school in Ross probably dates from mediaeval times when one of the chantry priests taught in a 'free school' as one of his duties. This was either held in the church aisle, in a chamber over the porch or in the chantry chapel. The subjects taught would have been based on the scriptures, with an emphasis on reading and writing with some instruction in arithmetic.[3] The school was 'called or known by the name of the Church-house otherwise Saint Maries School', and after the Dissolution it was allowed to continue as a place for 'the teaching of schools.'[4]

In 1537 John Scudamore as a Receiver at the Suppression reported to Thomas Cromwell that two lads 'singularly well learned' had arrived in Ross. Both appeared to have been schoolmasters in Exeter, and one intended to keep a school in Ross, an event which may have led to the re-establishment of the Churchyard School as a Latin Grammar School.[5] In the 1660s it appears that the Latin Grammar School was in disarray when Jonathan Smith, the ejected minister, attempted to take over but was prevented by the vicar, Dr. John Newton. He became the rector of Ross in 1675, and was an advocate of educational reform, 'protesting against the narrowness of a system which taught Latin and nothing else to boys ignorant of their mother tongue.'[6]

Dr. Newton, a mathematician and astronomer, wrote many learned works including *The Scale of Interest* and *The Compleat Arithmetician*, which were both written for the use of an English Grammar School to be set up in Ross. The doctor obviously intended to replace the existing school, then in a bad state of repair, and appealed to John, Viscount Scudamore, at Holme Lacy, and other landowners to support and endow an English School in Ross, where 'children may be the easier taught what religion is, as well as instructed in those arts and sciences which will conduce to their more comfortable substinence and present being.'[7]

Eighteenth century schoolmaster holding a children's class, by J. Van Aken.
(Courtesy of Hereford City Art Gallery and Museum)

It is doubtful whether this school was established during Newton's lifetime, because of a dispute over ownership and the building 'went gradually into decay' during the late seventeenth century until John Kyrle decided to settle the ownership question. His investigations concluded that the churchwardens could show no legal title and that their management of the site began in error. The rector could show evidence of a claim of the chief rent, though even this had not been regularly paid. Hence it was adjudged that the lord of the manor of the borough, in whom the estate was vested, was the rightful owner.

In 1704 the then lord of the manor, Thomas Lord Viscount Weymouth, gave and 'delivered to Charles Whiting D.D., Rector of Ross, and John Kyrle esq., the possession of the premises to the intent that the same should be and remain to the use of the said Dr. Whiting as the master of the grammar school there, and the future masters of such school for ever' and for the instruction and education of youth therein, according to the doctrines and usages of the Church of England as established by law. This was followed in 1709 by Lord Weymouth charging his 'Manors of Weobley and Ross with £400 per annum for several stipends to augment Livings and to Schoolmasters,' which included a 'Sum of Ten pounds' to be paid to the Ross schoolmaster. The school was to teach the tenets of the established church.

In 1759 the Rev. Mr. Jenkins was 'Master of the Grammar School' and was given free seats in the gallery over the south door of the church 'for the use of his Scholars to sit kneel and hear Divine Service.' Towards the end of the eighteenth century the greater part of the 'Church house' had 'fallen in' and its remains were in such bad condition that it was 'hazardous and dangerous to go near' and the Churchwardens were instructed to take it down.[8] As the master's salary continued to be paid until 1793 the children were obviously taught somewhere else in Ross.[9]

In 1801 the Rev. Thomas Underwood, Rector of Ross, proposed reviving the Grammar School 'which for several years has been discontinued to the great detriment of the town and neighbourhood,' and a subscription list was started the following year to fund the rebuilding. The rector was supported by the bishop of Hereford, the marquis of Bath, local gentry, landowners and some tradesmen. Unfortunately the amount of £529 13s 11d collected by 1808 was not enough to complete the building.[10]

While the school was being rebuilt the Grammar School children were taught by the Rev. James Mills at his house in the High Street, and the writing or primary school was held at Mr. Delahey's house in the churchyard. This writing school was taught by a temporary master in such undesirable surroundings that the Rev. Underwood and others had removed their children from it. By 1810 only the walls and roof of the new school were built and the builders were demanding payment. This led to further discussions over funding, which were not straightforward due to the tension between the Anglicans and the nonconformists, both subscribers of the project.[11] It appears that the Grammar School remained at Rev. Mills' house while the nonconformists were seeking to hold their school, which opened the following year at the Market House. By 1821 a Sunday School opened in the lower room at the new school building, and in 1822 the upper floor was let out as a Commercial or English Grammar School called St. Maries, on the understanding that the master instruct two boys free of charge. The proceeds of Lord Weymouth's endowment paid towards the expenses of

A book bill for St. Maries School in 1826. (Rectory Box)

the Sunday School and to settle the outstanding debt owed to the builders. Other rooms were let out occasionally to the Ross Fruit and Flower Society, the Ross Savings Bank, and the Ross Society of Fine Arts.[12]

The Churchyard School, now St. Mary's Hall

In 1811 a society was formed to promote National Schools for the 'Education of the Poor in the Principles of the Established Church' and took over many existing schools such as the churchyard one in Ross which by 1830 appeared to have re-established itself as a writing school affiliated to the national society. Although Directories from 1830 record a National School in Arthur's Lane (Old Gloucester Road) which became the Infant School. In 1834 the Writing School at Church House was reorganised to form a National School.[13] By this date the English Grammar School had become extinct, but the Congregational minister, Rev. William Byrne, was offering a classical education in Kyrle Street. The school continued and at a later date, with Henry Jowling as master and Agnes Sloane as mistress from 1868 the school moved its pupils to the new Board School in Cantilupe Road which opened in 1873.

Board Schools were established under the 1870 Education Act, which aimed for the education of the entire population by setting up district schools that were secular and undenominational. The 'Ross School Board' was founded in 1872, and the following year a new school was erected on two pieces of land in Cantilupe Road acquired from H. Minnett and J.H. Skyrme. The 'handsome pile of buildings' accommodated 420 children and were erected by Mr. William Bowers, of Hereford, from the design of Mr. George Pearson, of Ross. The total cost of building was £6,137. The foundation stone was laid by Thomas Blake, chairman of the Board, on 24th May 1873 and the school was opened by him on 1st June 1874.[14]

Maybe it was the foundation of the Society for the Propagation of Christian Knowledge in 1698 that had prompted interest in education in Ross at the start of the eighteenth century, for the parish certainly saw an increase in educational activity. Apart from seeing the revival of the old Grammar School in the churchyard, a new school known as the Blue Coat School was founded in 1709 by public subscription. This was a charity school for poor children which aimed to educate, clothe and apprentice them to a trade. Due to lack of funds in 1728 'The number of Children taught was reduced from 50 to 35' which made an immediate saving on clothing, materials and salaries.[15]

The site of the original Blue Coat Charity School is unknown, and the only surviving record is an account book dating from 1709 to 1788. This shows that a Thomas Hardwick taught the boys for 40 years and illustrates the quantity of blue woollen cloth, blue and

Blue Coat Charity School Accounts. (Rectory Box)

white linen, shoes and stockings that were purchased for the girls' and boys' uniforms. In 1779, at the end of Thomas Hardwick's long teaching career, the school was 'running down', and attempts were made to revive the establishment. However, by 1786 it appears that the 'South Isle of the Parish Church' was made available for the children on certain days as a replacement for the school building.[16] Four teachers were appointed including the young William Hill, who continued to teach the children of Ross for over 50 years.

When the school became 'almost derelict' it was visited by a former pupil, Walter Scott, who as a boy had received 'the little learning I have' from John Blount at the Blue Coat School. Walter was a native of Ross, the 'son of John Scott and Elizabeth his wife' and was baptised in January 1716. After his short education and the death of his parents, he left Ross for London, where he worked for his uncle as a plasterer. At a later date he inherited the business, and before his death decided to use his wealth to re-establish his old school in Ross.[17]

Walter Scott died in 1786 and the proceeds of his will paid 'for the ground and building the school-house' on a parcel of ground at the lower end of Hatter's Lane (Old Gloucester Road). It was duly opened on 5th January 1799 as Walter Scott's Charity School' and was subject to a long list of rules and regulations including a 'Schedule' of clothing. During 1823, 60 children were educated and clothed by the Master and Mistress, William and Theodosia Hill, who were paid a total of £50 a year.[18]

The following year the minute book reveals the 'sale of more of the school funds' in order to 'increase the number of scholars from 60 to 70 for a year, and the salaries of the Head

Master and his wife to be raised by 6 guineas for their extra trouble.' The faithful treasurer and governor of the school, Thomas Jenkins, died in 1829. He was recorded as 'a gentleman of extraordinary talent and ability, whose general knowledge and powerful research were sought after by all.' Perhaps his loss was keenly felt for the secretary soon reported that 'the National Society has received this school into Union at the request of the Governors.' In 1833 William Hill was at an 'advanced age' so his son, the master of the Free School, assisted his father, teaching the boys from both schools together. Six years later a complaint, over harsh punishment by an ageing and infirm Mrs. Hill, led to her resignation and replacement in 1840 by her daughter-in-law.[19]

The school curriculum at the Walter Scott School was simple. The children, all aged between six and 14, were taught reading, writing and arithmetic. Boys were also taught wood-work and the girls plain needlework. In addition all pupils were instructed in the Christian faith continuing the tradition established by the original Blue Coat School.[20] After restoration in 1887, and renovation in 1900, the 'Scott School' continued to teach until 30th March 1928, when 'all working materials, books. etc.,' together with 'twelve scholars' were moved to the Ross Urban Council Senior Mixed School, formerly the Board School.[21] Proceeds from the endowment and the sale of the property in 1948 continues to be paid out in grants by Ross Educational Foundation.

Walter Scott's Charity School in 1820. (Courtesy Hereford Library)

In 1808 the followers of Joseph Lancaster, a Quaker, had founded the Royal Lancastrian Society which carried out his educational ideas, though it changed its name to the British and Foreign School Society two years later. The schooling was based on the monitorial system, so allowing a great number of children to be taught by older and better educated pupils, and keeping paid staff to a minimum. Its aim, to educate children from different backgrounds and religious denominations attracted support from nonconformists.

By 1811 the nonconformists in Ross led by Thomas Prichard were seeking a site to hold a school run on the monitorial system. At a meeting of the newly established Grammar School, the rector, Thomas Underwood, left 'under a full conviction that the Town Hall was the place' instead of the Church House for such a school due to 'incapatibility with the principles of the Grammar School.' He also added that Mr. Prichard was 'employing a person to survey the necessary repairs' at the Town Hall.[22]

The same year the 'Free School' opened in the Town Hall (Market House), and called 'free' as it was 'supported solely by voluntary contributions'. At first this school was for boys only, but in 1812 the two upper rooms at the Walter Scott School were altered to accommodate girls. This was reluctantly accepted by the Scott School Governors at a rent of £8 a

The British & Foreign School, 1837. (Courtesy Hereford Record Office)

99

year, 'although the teaching of the said new School in this House is manifestly inconvenient,' but extra income was always required to maintain the school and keep the large building in repair.[23]

In 1823 the monitoring scheme was still under discussion by the Vestry, who requested 'the Committee to enquire and investigate the several cases which the Parents of poor children receive parish pay in consequence of their children being in the Lancaster or other Schools.' Although there is mention in 1835 of a Lancastrian School in the churchyard, it seems that this was an error and that it refers to that held in the Market House. This was the school attended by Thomas Blake in 1828 where he 'learnt his letters by tracing them with the forefinger of his right hand in sand.'[24]

In 1834 the Government made grants to elementary schools, including those run by the British and Foreign School Society. This encouraged Captain George Adams, James Wallace, Richard Hall and Mr. Kedgwin Hoskins to establish a separate building to house the British and Foreign School in Ross. A public meeting was held in 1835 at the Swan Inn, and a committee was formed under the able chairmanship of Nathaniel Morgan, a respected Quaker and businessman. A subscription list was duly started 'for the purpose of raising sufficient funds in aid of the Government Grant to erect a school house.' George Adams married Mary, a daughter of Joseph Lloyd, a papermaker at Bill Mills in Weston-under-Penyard. They lived at Vaga Lodge in Dockhill Pitch (Wye Street) and they both contributed to the British and Foreign School Building Fund.

As this project was an 'important step forward in the provision of additional educational facilities for the town', the committee decided the school should receive Royal patronage. Captain Adams therefore approached the Duchess of Kent 'with a view to securing the name of Princess Victoria, Britain's future Queen as patroness of the new school.'[25] This approval was forthcoming and the school was duly named The Ross and Archenfield Royal Victoria British School.

On 29th April 1836 the foundation stone of the new building was laid by Nathaniel Morgan, and on 19th September 1837 the boys' school was opened. A further grant and contributions enabled the girls' school to be completed and this opened on 14th July 1840. The school was built of stone in the Mock Gothic style on a piece of ground between Wye Street and the newly constructed Wilton Road. It cost a total of £1,859, and could accommodate 400 children and house the teachers under the same roof. By 1842 the school attracted pupils from outside Ross mainly from the 'agricultural population who found it to their advantage to place children with a friend or in lodgings in Ross and send provisions with them.'[26]

Captain Adams kept a meticulous record of the school, and his private journal relates the day to day happenings, numbers of pupils, list of subjects, reports of examinations, clothing sales, and an important event on 25th January 1842, the 'Christening of His Royal Highness the Prince of Wales', also reported in the *Hereford Times*:

> On Tuesday last, the day appointed for the christening of his Royal Highness the Prince of Wales, the children of the [Royal Victoria British] School, to the amount of nearly two hundred, assembled in the boys' school-room, to celebrate the event, by partaking

of what the liberality of the Committee and friends of the Institution had provided for them. The room was tastefully decorated with banners and appropriate motoes, and at the northern end an orchestra was erected, and covered with green and gold paper, forming a very chaste and pleasing appearance, for the accommodation of the members of the Ross Band, who had guaranteed their services for the occasion.

Despite the rector's refusal to aid and support the British and Foreign School, donations, subscriptions and modest fees kept the establishment going throughout the mid-nineteenth century when William Parker and Ann Sayres were Master and Mistress. They were replaced by Mr. Cook and Miss Caddick before the school closed, although the building briefly housed the Board School before the new school building was opened in 1874. The British and Foreign School was sold and the proceeds from the sale were 'applied in scholarships or exhibitions to children attending a public elementary school by schemes established by Order of Board, 1876.'[27]

By 1885 the Board School had replaced the National School in the churchyard, the British and Foreign School in Wye Street and the Infants School in Old Gloucester Road, which all ceased to exist. In 1889 the school was enlarged at a further cost of £800, and in 1902 a further Education Act enabled the newly established County Councils to set up and supersede school boards and make provisions for secondary education. It does not appear that any dramatic changes were made at the Cantilupe Road School, except that it became known as the Ross Council or Elementary School. This school continued into the twentieth century.

Ross Board School in 1920. (Leeds Collection)

Private schools had existed in the Ross area from the eighteenth century.[28] Their numbers increased during the mid-nineteenth century, when a total of nine were recorded in the town. These day and boarding schools offered an alternative education for 'young ladies and gentlemen' than that provided by the church and charity schools. The earlier private establishments included the Rev. Byrne's Classical School in Kyrle Street, and Clairville House in Copse Cross Street, where girls were later taught by Madame Du Beau and Miss Wolstenholm.

Another mid-nineteenth century school was run by Mr. Charles Smith, also a photographer, in New Street which became the 'Ross Academy' at Vaga House in Dock Pitch (Wye Street). Here boys were 'carefully instructed in all the various branches of a sound education, including – without extra charge – Drawing, Land and Timbering Measuring and Mapping.' There was also Mr. Thomas Evans' boys' school at Palmerston House in Ashfield, which apparently originated at the Bank House in Broad Street.[29]

Other private schools near Ross included the Misses Halls' establishment at Rose Cottage, Weston-under-Penyard, and the Blenheim House Academy at Lea. At the latter, 'conducted by' Mr. Irving, the boys were prepared for 'the learned professions, Military, Naval and Civil Service, the Oxford and Cambridge Middle Class

"Clairville"
Ross-on-Wye
Ed J Burrow del 1896

Clairville School

ROSS-ON-WYE,
HEREFORDSHIRE.

- - - - - - - - - - - - - - - -

Boys' Boarding & Day School.

- - - - - - - - - - - - - - - -

Head Master - T. E. MADDOX, F.R.G.S.
Assisted by Resident and Visiting Masters.

TERMS ON APPLICATION.

Grammar School staff and pupils, 1912

Examinations and Commercial pursuits.' Pupils aged over 12 years of age were charged 25 guineas a year for board and tuition, plus 2 guineas for 'washing' and another 4 guineas each for 'Latin, Greek, German, Drawing, Dancing and Fencing.'[30]

Despite changes, at least two of these establishments survived into the 1900s. Palmerston House became a 'school for girls' and Clairville a 'Boarding School for Boys'. The aim of this last school was to 'impart a good sound moral training, combined with a thoroughly practical education: to train the pupils in habits of diligence and accuracy: to install right principles and gentlemanly habits' all provided in the 'comforts of a home'.[31] Both of these were listed in 1941 with Mrs. Parsons at Palmerston and Miss Morling at Clairville as principal of the Ross High School.

The Grammar School, originally called the Ross Secondary School, was founded as a direct result of the 1902 Education Act. After political delays, enough money was raised by 1911 to erect the school at Ryefield Road. The opening took place on the 20th January 1912, and two days later the headmaster, Mr. A.E. Barker, and his staff met the new pupils. In 1916 it was considered that its name 'did not seem to meet with the approval of the general public, who had the idea that it was a second class school', so the name was changed to the Ross Grammar School.

The curriculum included geography, algebra, arithmetic, English language, English literature, geography, history, music, woodwork, art, metalwork, French, domestic science and chemistry.[32] An index to the Grammar School Admission Register reveals examination results, entrance to universities and training colleges, transfer to Private Schools and employment after leaving.

The Grammar School continued into the 1920s under the headship of Mr. Frank Leeds, whose wife Winifred made an important contribution to recording the history of Ross. The school had always taken a few scholarship children from the Council School, but the majority of pupils were fee paying. The Education Act of 1944 abolished the fees, introduced the eleven-plus examination, raised the school-leaving age and enabled a Secondary Modern School to be built.

11   Travel and Tourism

As Ross grew and developed into a prosperous market town its communications by river and road were improving. From the late eighteenth century those seeking the picturesque were attracted by the town, with its scenic situation above the winding Wye and below the wooded hills of Chase and Penyard. By 1855 Ross was connected to the railway network, which added to its accessibility, prosperity and popularity as a tourist town.

When Ross became a manor of the bishops of Hereford and a market town, roads developed from an existing network of ancient routes. The road and causeway leading to the river crossing at Wilton needed constant attention as recorded in the Bishop's Registers of 1418, 1474, and 1518. In the latter date the route was described as a 'great stone public road bridge leading from Ross' to the river crossing where there was an established 'free passage of the bishop's servants' using a ferry from Shipmede pasture.[1] The right of a ferry, in some cases, allowed the erection of a temporary bridge made of wooden planks, as was observed by Leland in the early 1500s.

From 1555 the responsibility for the maintenance of roads was transferred from manors to parishes under the terms of the Highway Act. At this time Ross was 'an ancient and great market town' and 'a very great thoroughfare, passage or portway' leading from Hereford, Monmouth, Brecon and South Wales to London and other parts of England. The town's only disadvantage was the unpredictable crossing over the Wye at Wilton, where the 'furious and dangerous river' caused the drowning of people and livestock packed into overladen boats. This was resolved in 1597 by the passing of the Wilton Bridge Act.[2]

The fine six arched stone bridge at Wilton was completed by 1600. It opened as a toll bridge until this payment was freed by the proceeds of Thomas Webbe's will of 1612. Towards the end of the seventeenth century John Kyrle raised sufficient funds by public subscription to restore the fourteenth century causeway leading from Ross to the bridge.[3] The completion of the causeway was commemorated by a pillar, which has since disappeared, but the inscription is remembered and recorded:

> At this spot was cheerfully begun what is now happily completed, the labour of this causeway, winding in the parishes of Ross and Bridstow, hence to the Black Pool Bridge, and thence in a connected line to Lady Pool arch.

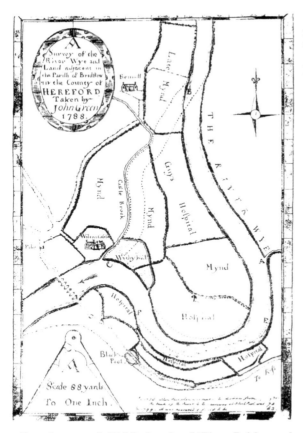

Green's map of 1788 showing Wilton Bridge and Causeway. (Courtesy Hereford Record Office)

Isaac Taylor's map of 1786 showing part of Ross. (Courtesy Hereford Library)

During the seventeenth century the roads in Herefordshire were in a 'wretched state'. Travellers 'journeyed in ditches, in narrow forest lanes, or antiquated hollow ways, deeper than the head of a horse and rider; a troop of horses might pass between the steep banks of the trackways almost from one side of the county to the other – so little were the roads above ground: and these were the remains of original British ways, the wear of centuries, in which an opening rarely occurred where two carriages could pass.'[4]

In 1675 when John Ogilby published his Britannia depicting the 'Principal Roads', the routes around Ross were already established. His survey was followed by Isaac Taylor's detailed county maps of Herefordshire produced in 1754 and 1786. Taylor, the map maker, not to be confused with other engraver of the same name and period, was from Brentford, Essex. He married Eleanor, and in 1765 was recorded at Ross when his daughter Mary Newman was born. He lived with his family at 53/54 High Street and travelled the country to make surveys for his numerous county maps. In 1788 the 'geographer' died and was buried at Ross.[5]

With the increase in trade, travel and transport in the early eighteenth century, it became important and necessary to improve the neglected roads of Herefordshire, so the turnpike system was adopted. This had already been tested on the New Great North Road in 1663 and was introduced into Herefordshire in 1721 and spread rapidly throughout the county. The main Hereford to Gloucester route through Ross was turnpiked in

Anno vicefimo fecundo

Georgii II. Regis.

An Act for repairing and widening the feveral Roads leading into the Town of *Rofs* in the County of *Hereford*.

Whereas the feveral Roads here- Prean
in after-mentioned and defcrib-
ed, that is to fay, the Road
leading from the Town of Rofs
in the County of Hereford, to
Harwood's Inn, being Five
Miles, or thereabouts; and alfo the feveral Parts of the
Road leading from the faid
Town of Rofs towards the City of Gloucefter (which lie in
the faid County of Hereford)
being Five Miles, or thereabouts; and alfo the Road leading from the Town of Rofs aforefaid, to Hoarwithy, being Four Miles, or thereabouts; and alfo the Road leading from a Place called the Town Brook, in the Town of
Rofs aforefaid, to a Place called the Perry Tump in
the Parifh of How Caple in the faid County of Hereford,
being Four Miles, or thereabouts; and alfo the Road
leading from the Town Brook aforefaid, to a Place called
the Smith's Shop, in the Parifh of Much Marcle, in the
faid County of Hereford, being Five Miles, or there-
 6 U 2   abouts;

RICHARD WHEELER'S
REGULAR STAGE WAGGON,
FROM HIS
WAREHOUSE, BROAD STREET,
Adjoining the Half Moon, and opposite the Mitre Inn,
HEREFORD,
To and from the undermentioned places, viz.
LONDON, per Dawe's Waggon,
To the Bell Inn, Warwick Lane; Moore and Griffin,
Green Man and Still, Oxford Street, and Gloucester
Warehouse, Mondays, Thursdays, and Saturdays.
OXFORD,
Tredwell's Warehouse.
CHELTENHAM,
Dawe's Van Waggon and Office, Winchcomb Street.
GLOUCESTER,
J. R. Heane, Walker's Warehouse, and Lower George
Inn, Mondays and Thursdays.
ROSS,
Mr. Thomas Gurney's, Brookend, Tuesdays and Fridays.
GOODS REGULARLY FORWARDED TO
HAY, KINGTON, LEOMINSTER & BROMYARD,
AND ALL ADJACENT PLACES.

R. W. respectfully begs leave to acquaint the Public that
he has commenced carrying Goods to and from the above
places, and hopes, by regularity, care, and moderate charges,
to receive a share of their support.

The Proprietor will not be accountable for any parcel
above Five Pounds value, nor for breakage or loss of any
parcel containing money, plate, jewellery, watches, writings,
paintings, glass, or any brittle article, unless entered as such
and paid for accordingly, loss by breakage of casks will not
be accounted for.

N.B. Please be particular in ordering per Dawe's Waggon,
from London to Gloucester, and from thence per Wheeler.

HEREFORD, BRISTOL, & LONDON.
TIGER COACH.
MESSRS. WARD, PEAKE, & CO. beg to re-
turn their sincere thanks to their numerous
Friends and the Public in general for the favours already
conferred on them, and soliciting a continuance of the
same, beg to say the above Coach will, on Monday,
Aug: 20th, leave the MITRE INN, HEREFORD, at
5 A.M., on MONDAYS, WEDNESDAYS, and FRI-
DAYS, and arrive at the RUMMER HOTEL, BRIS-
TOL, at 1 o'clock P.M., and at the GERRARD'S
HALL, Basing-Lane, LONDON, at 6 A.M.
FARES from HEREFORD to LONDON, Inside
46s. Out, **24s.**; or Parcels and Luggage, 2d. per
lb. No Fees to Coachmen and Guards from Bristol to
London. Any Passengers travelling by the above
Coach, can remain a Day in Bristol, if required, and by
4s. Out, or 10s. Inside, shall be forwarded by a Day
Coach, performing the journey in 12 hours, and no Fees.
These Coaches start from the GERRARD'S HALL,
LONDON, every Morning at ½-past 6, and After-
noon at 2; and BRISTOL, at 10 o'clock. TUES-
DAYS, THURSDAYS, and SATURDAYS, and
arrive at HEREFORD at 6 in the Evening.
ROUTE—ROSS, COLEFORD, CHEPSTOW,
BRISTOL, BATH, MARLBOROUGH, AND
READING.

Above: Ross Road Act of 1749
Above right: Advertisement for a stage wagon service, 1837
Right: Advertisement for a coach service, 1838
Both advertisements are from the Hereford Times

1726, and Ross established its own Trust in 1749. The first meeting of the Ross Trustees was held at the King's Head, though it was probably attended by only a handful of the hundred named trustees.

The Ross Road Act of 1749 turnpiked eleven routes leading from Ross covering a total of 43 miles. Further Acts of 1773, 1791, 1815 and 1862 allowed these routes to be shortened, extended, diverted, widened, altered, realigned and replaced. The tolls collected from the road users were spent on these improvements, and on appointing surveyors, employing toll keepers, repairing the roads and erecting milestones. Between 1749 and 1873 the Ross Trust made many significant changes, which included replacing the 'inconvenient' routes to Linton and Deep Dean, realigning the Hereford road at Bridstow and improving the road to Gloucester after Thomas Telford's proposals of 1824.

Communications from Ross were further improved during the early nineteenth century when the turnpike road to the 'Quern' was extended to William Partridge's iron works at Bishopswood. It prompted the surveyors to plan alternative routes avoiding Ross and using the ancient river crossing at Goodrich. These proposals were not carried out, although a bridge was constructed at Kerne Bridge in 1828. During the next decade a major new 'Turnpike Road between the Town of Ross and Ledbury' was constructed as a typical twisting turnpike road built to ease the gradient for horse-drawn vehicles.[6]

Within the town 'the several Streets or Highways leading through the said Town of Ross called The Brookend, The Bell Forge, Behind the Hill, The Hill, The Bull Ring, The Market Place, Corps Cross Street, Hatter's Lane, The High Street, and The Townsend'

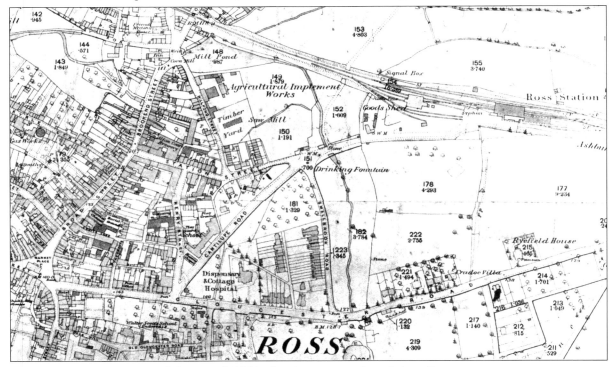

OS map of 1887 showing new roads and the railway

were also repaired and improved by the Turnpike Trustees after the 1815 Act. A few years later the streets of Ross were transformed with the addition of the present Gloucester Road around 1825, the Wilton Road in 1833 and Station Street after the opening of the Hereford, Ross and Gloucester Railway in 1855. By 1889 Henry Street and Cantilupe Road had been constructed together with 'New Chase Lane' replacing 'The Old Chase Lane'.[7]

From its source on Plynlimon in mid-Wales, the River Wye flows through a varied and dramatic landscape, and meanders around Ross in a great horseshoe bend. The Wye has probably always been used by man for navigational purposes, but it was not until 1662 that a serious effort was made to establish the river as a commercial waterway. Further Acts and schemes attempted to improve its navigation, but the river's numerous weirs, shallow fords and variable water levels were a constant hindrance.[8]

In the 1720s Defoe observed that Ross 'was a good old town, famous for good cyder, a great manufacture of iron ware and a good trade on the River Wye.' Docks were established either side of Wilton Bridge where Luke Hughes, John Mason Vaughan, William Porter and Edward Tamplin constructed quays, wharves and warehouses to serve the river trade of the eighteenth century.[9] The barges were hauled by a team of men, and horses were used after the opening of the 'Horse Towing-path' following an Act of 1809. A note of 'Wages to Bargemen' from Bishopswood in 1828, reads 'Horses from Lydbrook to Hereford from £2 to £2 10 0 for two that will haul a Barge each from 15 to 24 Tons this depends on the state of the River and I say the quantity of water in the River.'[10]

During the 1820s many tradesmen and residents of Ross were listed in the Terrier Valuation for the use of the 'Dock'. The names included Richard Collins, a boot and shoe maker; John Hardwick, an ironmonger; Joseph Evans, a basket maker; John Morgan, a cabinet maker; John Evans, a maltster from Wilton; and Mr. Tovey from the Waterworks. Most of the Ross riverside was then in Bridstow parish including 'Dock Meadow', except

Barges on the Wye at Ross in 1838. (Courtesy Ross Old Books)

WYE STEAM BOAT COMPANY.

THE Company's STEAM TOW-BOAT the PAUL PRY, being now equipped and fit for Work, they are ready to receive TENDERS from any one willing to Contract for the Transport of Goods or Merchandise to or from Chepstow to any part of the Rivers Wye and Severn.

For further particulars and information apply (if by letter, post-paid,) to the Agent of the said Company, at Mr. Lucy's, Dry-bridge House, Hereford.

Advertisement for the Paul Pry *steam tow-boat on the Wye, 1827, from the* Hereford Journal

the 'Wharf' on the south side of Wilton Bridge. This was the property of the Guy's Hospital Estate, also the owners of Wilton Castle and the quays, wharves and warehouses on the opposite side of the river.[11]

Barges up to 65 tons carried 'Great quantities of cider, hops, oak-bark, wool, wheat, and timber' down to the tidal limit at Brockweir, where the goods were shipped to London, Bristol and Ireland.

Coal from the Forest of Dean, slates, deals and other heavy goods were conveyed upstream from the lower Wye. Other commodities carried on barges were cases of wine, hat boxes, iron pots, chests of soap, bags of nails, barrels of pitch, bales of leather and many other items.[12]

In 1828 the 'Wye Steam Boat Company' had equipped and fitted a 'Steam Tow-Boat the Paul Pry' to transport goods on the Wye. On her first trip 'She left Chepstow on Wednesday, and reached Monmouth the same day towing a barge after her. On Friday she proceeded from Monmouth to Lydbrook, which she left the next day, towing a barge as far as the Kerne Bridge and arrived at Wilton' but she did not reach Hereford until Monday evening.[13]

After serving as a vital route, the river trade began to decline due to improved roads, the construction of the horsedrawn tramway from the Monmouth Canal to Hereford in 1829, the completion of the Hereford to Gloucester Canal in 1845 and, more dramatically, the opening of the Hereford, Ross, Gloucester Railway in 1855.

Apart from hindering the navigation of the Wye and making the fords and ferries impassable, the river's numerous floods caused damage, tragedy and inconvenience over the centuries. Only the great floods of 1735, 1795 and 1947 are inscribed on the Ross side of Wilton Bridge. Others recorded include 'the greatest flood ever known' in 1768 when 'the causeway between Ross and Wilton was so much under water, that several people in returning from Ross Market missed the causeway, and must have been drowned if some boats had not fortunately come to their assistance.'[14] In 1831 the Wye overflowed its banks 'to a considerable extent', although 'the flood was not so high as in November 1824', but still caused distress and damage as reported in the *Hereford Journal*:

> At Ross the Wye continued rapidly rising till the middle of Wednesday night; and the communication between the town and Wilton became hourly more difficult and dangerous. The heavy set of water over the causeway leading from Ross soon broke down a considerable portion of the parapet at the west-end of the bridge; and the road

began to blow up. In consequence of this circumstance several persons on horseback, and an individual in a cart, were precipitated into the hollow formed by the water, but they were extricated by the prompt assistance of boats and boatmen; and every person, after the accident of the cart, was warned of the danger. The scene was animating in the highest degree, from the numbers passing and repassing, it being Ross market, and several sailing boats were manoeuvring about upon the large sheets of water near the town. The mail and other coaches from Ross landed their passengers at Wilton, whence they were ferried over. The damage done to the road must be considerable.

From around the mid-eighteenth century the untamed and virtually unknown beauty of the River Wye attracted the attention of poets, writers, artists and 'gentlemen of taste' seeking the 'Picturesque'. The romantic scenery of hanging woods, lofty rocks and rapid water provided natural artistic views that were best admired from the river. A boat trip was taken from Ross which became known as the Wye Tour with its origins attributed to the Rev. John Egerton.[15]

Rev. John Egerton, Rector of Ross 1754-1771.
(Courtesy St. Mary's Church)

John Egerton served as rector of Ross from 1745 until 1771 when he became the Bishop of Durham. He was the eldest son of the bishop of Hereford and was well connected through birth and marriage. From 1750 he often entertained his wealthy friends and relatives at Ross, and would treat them to a boat trip down the Wye. He was a diligent and conscientious man, a liberal supporter of many religious and educational institutions, yet in his private life was amiable and hospitable.[16]

Egerton's notable guests were so impressed by the discovery of the Wye's hidden beauty that it created a fashion. By 1760 'boats were first let to hire', but it was William Gilpin's *Observations on the River Wye* and Thomas Grey's tribute of praise, both describing their Summer Tours of 1770, which increased the popularity of the Wye Tour. Grey wrote 'The principal light and capital feature of my journey was the River Wye, which I descended in a boat for near forty miles, from Ross to Chepstow. Its banks are a succession of nameless beauties.' Gilpin, obsessed with the Wye's 'Picturesque

Beauty', also sketched some dramatic scenes. Despite bad weather at the start of his voyage, he remarked 'the picturesque eye also, in quest of beauty, finds it almost in every incident, and under every appearance of nature.'[17]

Accounts were written by Shaw, Ireland, Farrington, Heath, Bloomfield, and Fosbroke amongst others, and as a result the Wye Tour became commercialised by boat proprietors and innkeepers. Craft were hired from Ross for a leisurely journey, with time to write, sketch, picnic and explore on foot the delightful scenery of the Wye Valley. Permanent visible reminders of this period are the water colour views sketched by James Wathen between 1788 and 1802. By 1827 a single boat was insufficient to cope with the demand — 'since the pleasure of the excursion has been known, they have increased to eight, and more are sometimes wanted to accommodate the company. The price of the boat from Ross to Monmouth is £1 11s 6d. From Ross to Chepstow, £3 3s. besides provisions for the boatman.'[18] In 1836 a steam boat called *The Man of Ross* offered a 'Tour of the River Wye' between Ross and Chepstow in one day for the cost of 10s.

The opening of the Hereford, Ross, Gloucester Railway in 1855 increased the number of visitors and tourists seeking 'Pleasure Boats' to hire for a 'Tour of the Wye'. Boats were available from two places, Joseph Evans basket maker and postmaster, claimed '40 years experience, in succession to his father, and has during that time made the Trip 1200 times.' William Newton at the Hope and Anchor Inn, offered both large and small pleasure boats 'fitted up with every suitable convenience' with boatmen 'well skilled in the navigation'. A tourist of the time wrote 'Having provided ourselves with a few substantial comforts, so that we lose no time in attending to any physical want, we take our seat punctually at the hour appointed and our gallant little bark, manned by stout oars and

TOUR OF THE
RIVER WYE,

From Ross to Goodrich Court and Castle, Symond's Yat, Whitchurch, New Weir, Monmouth, Tintern Abbey, and Chepstow.

THE admirers of the beautiful and romantic Scenery of the River Wye will now have an opportunity of making the deservedly celebrated Tour of the River from ROSS to CHEPSTOW, in ONE DAY; and at the same time be afforded AMPLE TIME for an attentive survey of the numerous attractions its Banks present; by the Establishment of a Safe, Commodious, and Elegantly Fitted up

STEAM BOAT,
CALLED
"THE MAN OF ROSS,"

which made her first Trip on Monday last, the 27th of June, 1836, and will continue to Ply to and from ROSS and CHEPSTOW, TWICE A WEEK, during the Summer Season.

The times of Starting during the present and ensuing Months, are as follow :—

ROSS TO MONMOUTH.			MONMOUTH TO CHEPSTOW.		
Monday July	4	10 morn.	Monday July	4	4 after.
Thursday ..	7	5 morn.	Thursday ..	7	11 morn
Monday ..	11	8 morn.	Monday ..	11	2 after.
Thursday ..	14	10 morn.	Thursday ..	14	4 after.
Monday ..	18	10 morn.	Monday ..	18	4 after.
Thursday ..	21	10 morn.	Thurs. 21 not sail from Mon.		
Monday ..	25	7 morn.	Monday ..	25	2 after.
Thursday ..	28	10 morn.	Thursday ..	28	4 after.

CHEPSTOW TO MONMOUTH.			MONMOUTH TO ROSS.		
Tuesday ..	5	8 morn.	Wednesday ..	6	8 morn.
Friday ..	8	10 morn.	Saturday ..	9	8 morn.
Tuesday ..	12	1 after.	Wednesday ..	13	8 morn.
Friday ..	15	5 morn.	Friday ..	15	12 noon.
Tuesday ..	19	6 morn.	Wednesday ..	20	7 morn.
Friday 22 not sail from Chep.			Friday ..	22	8 morn.
Tuesday ..	26	2 after.	Wednesday ..	27	8 morn.
Friday ..	29	5 morn.	Friday ..	29	11½ morn.

FARES :
Ross to Chepstow 10s. Ross to Monmouth 5s. Monmouth to Chepstow 5s. Chepstow to Ross 10s. Chepstow to Monmouth 5s. Monmouth to Ross 5s. Children under twelve years of age half-price. Dogs 1s. each.

A considerable allowance will be made in the Fares to Families and large Parties. Persons returning within a week to either place will then be charged half-price.

Refreshments may be had on board, on moderate terms, and every attention will be paid to the comfort and convenience of the Passengers.

Any further information may be obtained by applying at the King's Head Hotel, Ross; Packet Office, Dock Pitch, Ross; Ship and Castle on the Quay, Monmouth; and Steam Packet Office, Chepstow.

Advertisement from the Hereford Times, *1836*

Boats for hire, 1905

an obliging and experienced Captain, glides rapidly down the stream.'[19]

Towards the end of the nineteenth century Ross became known as 'The Gate of the Wye'. The additional railway route from Ross to Monmouth was completed in 1873 which closely followed the scenic Wye, but it was considered that 'nothing should tempt the tourist to give up the water for the shorter trip, because the charm of the river scenery cannot be fully witnessed from the land, or sufficiently realised during the speedy transit of a railway journey'.[20] By 1914 it appears that the term 'Wye Tour' was replaced with 'Boating on the Wye' with the hiring of boats gradually declining throughout the century.

As for the railways themselves, in 1844 Mr. Collins, a town solicitor and turnpike trustee, was discussing the 'possibility of a railway communication being extended into the neighbourhood.' Various routes were suggested in 1846, but it was not until 1851 that the Hereford, Ross and Gloucester Railway Company served a notice to the Ross Turnpike Trustees of their intention of opening.[21] By 1851 James Wallace Richard Hall, a turnpike trustee from Ross, was acting as solicitor and Hon. Secretary for the railway company negotiating purchase of land and financial compensation. He later became a director of the company and organised its opening at Ross on 1st June 1855.[22] Of the latter, the *Hereford Journal* for 6th June reported:

The Hereford, Ross and Gloucester Railway at Ross, from The Illustrated London News, *1855*

Among the first to arrive at the station was J.W.R. Hall and Charles Richardson, Esqrs., the former one of the indefatigable Directors (to whose unceasing exertions the event of the day may in great measure be contributed), the latter the resident engineer of the line. The trains having deposited and received their passengers, proceeded on their way. The decorations of the interior of the station were the striking feature of the place. Flags of every description were suspended from the iron girders of the roof, the most conspicuous being the Union Jack and French tricolor, and long may they float side by side. Over the doors of the various offices were hung the crests of the Directors and gentlemen who were mainly instrumental in getting the bill passed through Parliament.

Ross Station in the 1900s. (Courtesy Mary Powell)

The company had been financially assisted by the Great Western Railway and by 1860 the latter 'thereupon agreed to purchase absolutely the undertaking of the Hereford, Ross and Gloucester Railway' which took place in 1862.[23] This was followed in 1873 by a further extension of railway communication with the opening of the Ross and Monmouth line. This closely followed the banks of the River Wye along a most picturesque route which attracted a number of excursion trains during the holiday season.

Both railway lines were served by the station at Ross which was rebuilt in 1892 by the Great Western in a typical railway station style. The twin-turreted building housed a booking office, waiting rooms, a refreshment room and staff quarters. Two platforms were linked by a footbridge, and surrounding the station were the goods sheds, engine shed, signal box and sidings.[24] Despite the mammoth effort put into constructing the railway, excavating the tunnels and erecting bridges, this important form of transport only served the town for a little over one hundred years. There are remains of the railway including a railway arch, an engine shed, weighbridges and disused railway track to be seen in the town together with an interesting display at Five Ways, at the bottom of Brookend. This features the history of 'Rails to Ross' on pictorial panels together with a small stationary display of railway memorabilia.

Inns existed in Ross from early times, but only brief recollections remain of the Griffin, the Rose and Crown and Gabriel Hill's Great Inn. Gabriel Hill did live in Ross and was named in a deed dated 1664 and a Tax Assessment of 1661. Another inn 'known by the

The George Hotel. (Courtesy Martin Morris)

Barrett's Royal Hotel in 1838. (Courtesy The Royal Hotel)

name or sign of the Rein Deer and later by the name or sign of Marlborough's Head' was documented in 1606.[25] After that date improved communications attracted more traders, travellers and tourists who sought places to rest, refresh and hire horses after their travels, a service that was provided by the numerous inns, many of which blossomed into coaching inns and post-houses.

The George was an old inn described in 1549 as 'the messuage called Le George and a garden in Harters Lane in the tenure of William Tomes.' By 1771 this inn had become 'a good convenient and well accustomed house, having a soft and hard Water Pump, Five Stables, and a good cellarage.'[26] When the present Gloucester Road was constructed around 1825 the George probably altered its position and certainly its address. By 1851 it had become the 'George Inn and Commercial Hotel' in Gloucester Road run by Thomas Roper, but the inn failed to survive into present times, although its sign is housed at the Market House Heritage Centre.

During the eighteenth century the principal coaching inns were established. In 1722 the London and Oxford Flying Coach ran a service every Wednesday from the King's Head. This was followed by Thomas Pruen's New Coach and John Phillpott's New and Elegant Mail Coaches from the King's Head, King's Arms, George and Swan and Falcon. After being advertised for sale in 1779 the King's Arms, the former house of John Kyrle, was closed as an inn in 1805, and the Swan and Falcon was eventually replaced by the Swan Inn.

The Castle Hotel in 1943. (Leeds Collection)

During the 'Golden Age of Coaching' in the 1830s it was possible to travel from Ross to London and Milford on the Royal Mail, to Brecon on the Paul Pry, to Carmarthen on the Nimrod, and to the local towns of Monmouth on the Rapid, to Ledbury on the Man of Ross, to Gloucester on the Rising Sun and to Hereford on the Champion.[27] All this activity combined with the improved roads and the popularity of the Wye Tour led James Barrett to construct his grand hotel in 1837.

James Barrett, the former innkeeper of the Swan and Falcon, purchased the Pounds Inn, the Beast Market and the Prospect where he erected his purpose-built hotel in the picturesque style for a cost 'upwards of £15,000'. The hotel commanded extensive views and became a successful coaching inn, posting house and 'a favourite starting point of summer parties who make the celebrated tour of the river Wye.' The 1851 Census recorded James Barrett as a hotel keeper with a staff consisting of a milliner, bar maid, waiter, chambermaid, under waiter, kitchen maid, boots, a hostler and two house keepers.[28]

Ross had now become a popular tourist centre with inns and hotels offering 'well aired beds', 'superior post horses', 'Pleasure Boats', 'homebrewed beers', 'excellent stabling' and an 'Omnibus to meet every train'.[29] By 1876 24 hotels, inns and taverns were listed in the town including the Castle Inn, the Pheasant, and the Nag's Head which were later taken over by the Stroud Brewery Company. The Crown and Sceptre, The Plough and the King's Head are the only inns that have survived from the seventeenth and eighteenth centuries without altering their names.[30]

Over the centuries Ross had a share of famous visitors sampling the hospitality of its inns. There is a tradition that 'In a house formerly an inn opposite to the king's head, is a chamber called the King's chamber, where Henry IV lay when he went to see his Queen then ready to lie in at Monmouth'. This was called the Griffin which stood at the corner of Church Street opposite Gabriel Hill's Great Inn, where Charles I supposedly stayed in 1645.[31] Ross was taken by surprise in 1821 when an unexpected George IV passed through the town 'almost unobserved'. His journey was delayed by a road obstructed by waggons, so he waited at an ale-house later known as King George's Rest. Mr. T.W. Purchas of Ross made the following record of the visit:

The visit of King George the Fourth to Ross ... was caused by the ship in which he crossed from Ireland having been driven out of her course by bad weather, landing him in South Wales, instead of at Holyhead or Liverpool. He entered the town by the old Wilton-road and Dock Pitch (then the only way), and after a change of horses, and taking a glass of wine that was handed to him by Mrs. Mary Howells, the landlady of the King's Head, much to the disappointment of the inhabitants, he drew down the blinds of the coach, intending to hurry on as quickly as possible. Greatly to his disgust, however, on arriving at the Nag's Head, an unexpected obstacle barred his progress for a time. The carrier's waggon had arrived, and, before unloading, the horses had been taken out. The place was so narrow that the King was obliged to wait while the horses were brought out again, and the waggon moved out of his way. This incident led to a great improvement of the town, as, shortly afterwards, notice was sent from London that, unless a better way was made through the town, the mail would be taken off the road, in consequence of which the present Gloucester-road was constructed.[32]

The pony presented by Dickens to Dolly's children.
(Courtesy Hereford Library)

Literary notables associated with the inns of Ross include the Hon. John Byng who stayed at the Swan and Falcon while touring South Wales in 1787. The poet Samuel Coleridge penned his lines about the 'Man of Ross' in 1794 at the King's Arms, and another, Robert Bloomfield, stayed at the Swan and Falcon in 1807 when 'touring with friends along the Wye'. In 1867 when the Royal Hotel had become a 'Family, Commercial and Posting Establishment', its doors were entered by Charles Dickens. He had travelled by train to Ross to visit his friend and manager, George Dolby, at Wilton House and to discuss his American tour with Mr. Forster. Dickens's visit to the Royal is commemorated by a plaque erected in 1915.[33]

On 25th July 1802 Lord Nelson with his guests arrived at Ross while touring South Wales. They breakfasted at the Swan and Falcon before walking through the beautiful grounds of Walter Hill's garden at Merton House. Followed by a party of inquisitive townsfolk they descended to the river and embarked on a pleasure boat to Monmouth.[34] Further famous visitors to the town's hostelries include the Duke and Duchess of Teck in 1891, who stayed at the Royal Hotel with their daughter, the future Queen Mary.

12   Improvement and Change

The nineteenth century was a period of major development in Ross. Dilapidated buildings were demolished, the streets were cleaned, lowered and widened, roads were constructed, gas lighting installed, the water supply was improved, the railway arrived and the town adopted a mock gothic style. A population of 2,347 in 1801 had more than doubled to 4,897 by the end of the century. This transformation of Ross was mainly due to the two Improvement Acts of 1830 and 1865.

Even before 1830 the streets of Ross had been 'greatly improved', sewers had been laid to 'carry off the filth' and a nightly watch had been 'lately established'. The only government the town had was 'a Sargeant, who is dignified with the title of Mayor, four Constables, two Searchers and Sealers of Leather, a Fish and Flesh Taster, two Market Keepers, a Hayward, and two Scavengers, together with the Town Crier.'[1] The appointments are mainly self-explanatory, but the hayward's job was to repair fences and hedges and impound stray live-stock, whilst the scavenger cleared the rubbish and refuse off the streets. With reform of government becoming a national issue it was understandable that certain Ross citizens chose to enhance their market town.

With the passing of the 1830 Act for 'paving, cleansing, draining, lighting, regulating, and improving the Town of Ross', Town Commissioners were appointed. These were the lord of the manor, the rector, the mayor, two lawyers named John Cooke and John Stratford Collins, as well as Nathaniel Morgan, Thomas Prichard and Edward Prichard who were bankers and Quakers, together with Dr. Richard Evans. At their meetings during the 1830s various improvements were discussed, and the sale of certain 'Lands and Commons' was agreed to produce capital for paving, removing obstructions from the streets, establish a gas works to light the town, provide a lock-up for prisoners, sink wells with pumps and form a police force.[2]

Neither the Gas Works nor the Water Works were undertaken or managed by the Commissioners, but were let out to private individuals. They paid a fixed rent, administered the enterprise and took the profits. The Gas Works was erected in Kyrle Street before 1835 under the proprietorship of 'Wall and Lewis'. In December 1849 the gas works was in a profitable and efficient state so the Commissioners made plans to purchase the works, but by January 1862 it was 'inadequate for increased demand'.[3] It was then decided to sell the Gas Works, and an offer from James Harris from Middlesex was accepted. With gas lamps lighting the streets, the commissioners decided it was 'desirable to secure the sites of the houses of the middle row' in the Market Place which were 'to be pulled down for the purposes of widening and improving the thoroughfare.'[4] This dilapidated but quaint row of tenements known variously as Behind Hill, Underhill or Middle Row housed a variety of trades before its removal in 1862, including two eating houses and the Boar's Head Inn.[5]

Ever since the time of John Kyrle the supply of water had been an important issue. In 1713 the Water Works instigated by John Kyrle and his partners at the Dock had changed hands, but still pumped to the reservoir in the Prospect.[6] During the eighteenth century 'iron was substituted for wood, both for pumping machinery and mains, and the Prospect fountain was filled in. A reservoir, to hold 10,000 gallons, was constructed under the wide pathway in the churchyard, near the entrance from St. Mary's Street, and the cast iron hatchover for this reservoir is still to be found in the churchyard wall.'[7]

In the 1820s John Tovey was in charge of the Water Works when there were very few pumps for the town which 'supplied water from an engine, which, by means of pipes, furnished every house with an abundant quality, at a reasonable rate.'[8] This 'Engine' was described in 1844 as '25 Horse Power, with Overshot Wheel' and 'Pipes and Works used for supplying the Town of Ross with Water.' The engine was powered by a 'Stream of Water' running from the One Mill on the Rudhall Brook along the Rope Walk to the Ross Water Works near the Hope and Anchor Inn.[9]

In the mid-nineteenth century Samuel Bennett Wall, coal merchant, was also the proprietor of the Water Works, Weighing Machine and Wye Baths.[10] He served as an Improvement Commissioner when various schemes were discussed, but financial difficulties made it impossible to improve the water supply, so a second Improvement Act was passed in 1865. This

ANNO UNDECIMO

GEORGII IV. REGIS.

****

Cap. xliii.

An Act for paving, cleansing, draining, lighting, watching, regulating, and improving the Town of *Ross*, and for disposing of certain Common and Waste Lands and Rights of Common within the Parish of *Ross*, in the County of *Hereford*.
[29th *May* 1830.]

WHEREAS the Town of *Ross* in the County of *Hereford* is extensive and populous, and it would greatly tend to the Benefit, Convenience, and Safety of the Inhabitants thereof, and of Persons resorting thereto and passing through the same, if the several Streets, Lanes, Thoroughfares, and Places within the said Town were more properly paved and repaired, and the same Streets, Lanes, Thoroughfares, and Places well and sufficiently cleansed, drained, lighted, watched, regulated, and otherwise improved, and made more commodious and safe, and all Obstructions, Nuisances, Annoyances, and Encroachments removed, and for the future prevented within and throughout the said Town : And whereas there is within the Parish of *Ross* aforesaid a certain Open Common or Waste, called *Ross Marsh*, of little Value in its present State, containing Six Acres One Rood and Ten Perches, or thereabouts : And whereas there are also within the Parish of *Ross* aforesaid certain Common Meadows, called by the several Names of *Broadmeadow, The Ricks,* and *Maud's Meadow,* containing together Sixty-seven Acres, or thereabouts : And whereas there are also within the said Parish of *Ross* certain Common Arable Fields, called by the several Names of
[*Local.*] 9 *I* *Cawdor,*

The Ross Improvement Act of 1830

Left: Underhill in 1848. (Courtesy Hereford Museum and Art Gallery). Right: Before 1860

had powers to 'construct Waterworks' and to 'purchase Waterworks from Samuel Bennett Wall', as the town had grown in size and population and the existing water supply of poor quality was now inadequate. This project was keenly followed and supported by another Commissioner, Thomas Blake.

The Ross Town Commissioners in 1867 were Thomas Blake, accountant; Thomas Roper, chemist; Richard Brendon, grocer; J.E. Perris, another chemist; Henry Perkins, ironmonger; Samuel Bennett Wall, surveyor; and Benjamin Brunsdon, another grocer. The chairman was Henry Southall, a draper and Quaker, with the solicitor William Hooper as Clerk. They were later joined by Alfred J. Purchas, a wine merchant, and Joseph Turnock, a brewer and founder of the Alton Court Brewery. When Purchas became chairman in 1882 he appealed to the town to support The Ross District Water Act which attracted some opposition.[11]

Various attempts were made to secure an improved water supply including a scheme proposed by Mr. J.L. Piddocke, a solicitor. At his own expense he obtained an Act of Parliament empowering him to construct water works for the town and parish of Ross. Water of good quality was found at or near Rudhall and surveys were made, levels taken, and plans matured for the purpose of obtaining this water supply. Three years were allowed under the Act in

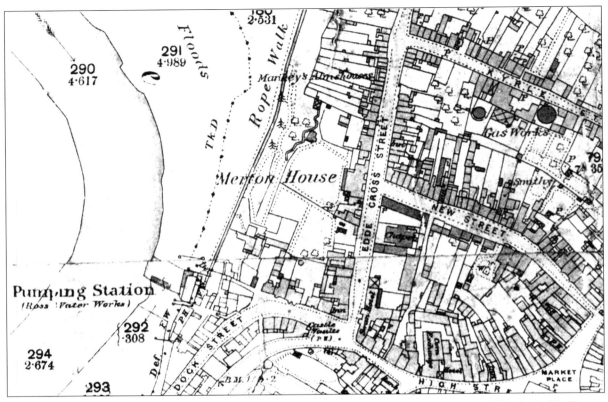

OS map of 1887 showing the water pumping station and the gas works. (Courtesy Elizabeth Okell)

which to commence the work, but for some unexplained reason no steps were taken during that time to begin the necessary operations, and consequently all the powers under the Act lapsed.[12]

Joseph Turnock, another citizen keen to solve the water problem, and his sister had moved to Merrivale by 1881 and while there 'he erected a reservoir and pumping station to supply the town with water, but many difficulties prevented the Merrivale Water Works from being the success he anticipated.'[13] Shortly after this Thomas Blake investigated the possibilities of supplying fresh water from artesian wells above the town, which led to the establishment of the Alton Court Water Works in 1887. The works were under the complete control of Blake and enabled the whole of Ross 'to receive the water which arrived, fresh and limpid pure, in every kitchen.'[14]

Blake also purchased the Merrivale Estate and the Rope Walk Water Works, and in 1891 he made an agreement with the rector, 'to lay Water Pipes along the Churchyard path from the existing Reservoir near the Entrance Gate, St. Mary's Street, to the Reservoir I am now constructing in the Prospect.' This held a capacity of 50,000 gallons and in 1945 'an oil driven pump (with alternative electric motor drive as stand-by) raised water to an underground reservoir at The Prospect from which it is distributed to the industrial water consumers, the chief of which are the Railway Company and the Brewery.'[15]

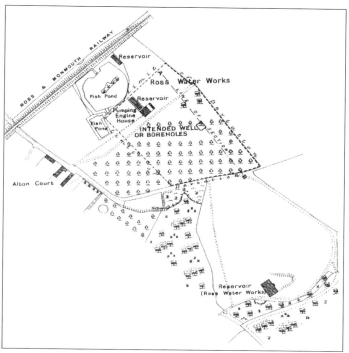

Plan of the water works in 1928. (Courtesy Ross Old Books)

Another main concern of the Town Commissioners was sanitation and the prevention of disease. Stink traps were installed, drains and ditches were cleaned, and houses were inspected 'to compel inhabitants to drain either into sewers or proper middens.'[16] In 1870 a letter from the 'justices' outlined their concern of 'the large amount of epidemic diseases which have for some time past prevailed in the town', which they considered was due to the 'defective state of the sewerage'.[17] Improvements had obviously been made by 1896 when Ross was described as being 'famous for the longevity of its inhabitants who are healthy as well as long-lived.'[18]

In November 1821 William Cobbett in his *Rural Rides* wrote 'The market at Ross was very dull, no wheat in demand, no buyers', then he listed the poultry prices 'Fowls 2s a couple; a goose from 2s. 6d. to 3s.; and a turkey from 3s. to 3s 6d.' The livestock market held around the Market House would have been cramped and crowded — vegetables and garden produce continued to be sold below the upper chamber of the Market House, and dairy products were sold in the streets. In Upper Church Street (St. Mary's Street) was the site of the 'beast-market' and Parish Pound beside the Pounds Inn.[19]

By 1851 the Market House was in 'a very decayed state', and its range of chambers were mostly used as a warehouse for deposits of grain. A few years later in 1860 the 'Ross Corn Exchange and

The Market House in 1853. (Courtesy Ross Old Books)

Public Building Company' was established to provide and maintain a suitable building for a 'Corn Exchange, the sale of Butter, Cheese, and Poultry, and for Public Rooms with or without a Library.' The premises were designed by Thomas Nicholson from Hereford and erected in 1862 at a cost of £4,000. The imposing building, recently restored, boasted a 'capacious hall' which was used for lectures, concerts and meetings. One Reading Room was 'handsomely furnished' for gentlemen and tradesmen, and the other with a Public Library, was for the use of 'mechanics and others'.[20]

Under the terms of the Improvement Act of 1865 the Town Commissioners were able to purchase the Town Hall (Market House), the rights to take Market Tolls and the Parish Pound. As the market place and streets of Ross were inconvenient and unsuitable for the 'Sale of Cattle and other Animals', it was agreed a proper livestock market would be provided. This was erected in 1871, away from the town centre at the bottom of Edde Cross Street. Here, within a short distance of the railway station, the Cattle Market remained until its removal at a later date to a site adjacent to the motorway network.

28° VICTORIÆ, Cap. cviii.

Ross Improvement Act, 1865.

The SCHEDULES referred to in the foregoing Act.

SCHEDULE (A.)

Tolls in respect of Articles and Things sold in or brought for Sale to and in respect of Rents and Stallage in the Markets.

CORN AND SEEDS.

	s.	d.
For every Bushel of Wheat, Peas, Beans, Vetches, Flour, Meal, or Malt	0	3
For every Bushel of Barley, Oats, or Rye Grass	0	2
For every Fourteen Pounds Weight of Clover, Trefoil, Turnip, or other Seeds	0	2

And so in proportion for a greater or less Quantity.

CHEESE.

	s.	d.
For every single Cheese weighing above Two Pounds and not more than Twenty-eight Pounds	0	1
For every Half Dozen or less Number of Cheeses, each weighing not more than Two Pounds	0	2
For every additional Half Dozen or less Number	0	2
For every Quantity of other Cheese, not exceeding One Quarter of a Hundredweight	0	1½
Exceeding One Quarter and not exceeding Half a Hundredweight	0	3
Exceeding Half and not exceeding Three Quarters of a Hundredweight	0	4½
Exceeding Three Quarters of and not exceeding One Hundredweight	0	6

And so in proportion for any greater Weight.

BUTTER AND EGGS.

	s.	d.
For every Tub, Cask, or Jar of Salt Butter, or any less Quantity	0	4
For every single Basket of Fresh Butter or Eggs	0	3
For every double Basket of the same	0	4½

FISH.

	s.	d.
For every Stall for the Sale of Fish :—		
For each Market Day	1	6
For each Fair Day	3	0

Market Tolls as set out in the Ross Improvement Act, 1865

Damage and death by fire always presented a major threat to the inhabitants of Ross. In 1809 a Subscription Fund was started 'for Purchasing a New Fire Engine for the Town of Ross', and 'to determine the best means of constructing a Reservoir, for supplying the

Ross Cattle Market, 1904. (Courtesy Hereford Library)

Engine with Water.'[21] Mr. Delahay was put in charge of the fire engine which consisted of a bucket, leather pipes, two pumps and a 21 foot ladder. Presumably this was used in October 1812 when the churchwardens paid the 'Nags Head for Beer given to the men at Mr. Brown's fire.'[22]

In 1825 the vestry were looking for a 'proper person' to care for the fire engine, and by 1827 there were 'plugs [for water] in the street, in case of fire'. From an account in 1852 it appears that the Ross Fire Engine was inadequate, as engines from Wormelow and Hereford attended a 'Dreadful Fire and Loss of Life', as described in the *Hereford Times*:

> A fire took place in this town ... which was of a most appalling character, striking dismay into the inhabitants from the suddenness of its discovery, the rapidity of its progress, and the extent of destruction, which it threatened, as well as the loss of life which it occasioned. Never did the writer witness before such alarm, and, as may be supposed, the following account is written in a state of great excitement.
>
> About half-past four this morning as some workmen were proceeding down New-street, they discovered that the large premises occupied by Messrs. Hall and Minett, were on fire, the flames were at this time raging violently through the windows fronting the street, an alarm was of course immediately given, and a messenger was disaptched to Llandinabo for the fire engine, from that place which was soon on the spot, as well as the engines belonging to Hereford. The fire raged with great vehemence and notwithstanding every exertion was made not anything could be saved. The messenger meanwhile arrived in Hereford, and the engines were quickly started with four horses to each, and such was the speed at which they went, that only an hour and 45 minutes elapsed from the time the messenger left Ross till the engines arrived. Such however was the terrific character of the fire, that the whole of the premises were destroyed before they arrived.

Ross Fire Brigade and engines dated 1809, 1850 and 1899. (Courtesy Hereford Library)

Ross Lock-up, no date

Shortly after this disaster the Ross Fire Brigade was formed. In 1858 William Blake was appointed as Superintendent, and by 1867 the 'Fire Engine House' was in Kyrle Street with the 'Fire Escape at Brewery Yard in Henry Street'. In 1869, £87 4s was paid by the Improvement Commissioners for 'Building Engine and Fire Escape House etc., Repairs to Fire Escape, and incidental to the Brigade', and £24 10s on 'Reservoir near the Royal Hotel Tap'. This refers to the 'recently erected buildings' in Edde Cross Street, and arranging to collect water from the churchyard tank in case of fire.[23]

A 'New Steam Fire Engine' was purchased in 1899 with a 40 foot fire escape, 900 foot of hose and new clothing including helmets for the men, on a day that was described by the *Ross Gazette* as 'a red-letter day in the archives of Ross'. The engine was called John Kyrle, and was drawn by two horses, although it was light enough to be drawn by hand. The Fire Brigade moved to the site of the old Parish Pound in 1906, and stayed in St. Mary's Street until moving to Woodside in March 1969.[24]

Although at the beginning of the nineteenth century there were 'Offices of Police for the Borough',[25] Ross Vestry held a 'special meeting' in 1824 to discuss 'building the Prison or Lock-Up House' which was to 'be immediately erected in the Garden of the Workhouse'. Due to later objections this proposal was never carried out.[26] The 1830 Improvement Act therefore empowered the Town Commissioners to appoint 'Watchmen' and 'provide a proper Watch-house or Lock-Up House containing two or more Cells.' A site was found 'on old stables in New Street', where the Lock-Up was built in 1838.[27]

In the 'Rules for the direction of the Ross Police' drawn up in 1838, the policeman was to 'reside in the Lock-Up House and devote his whole time to the Service of the Town as Policeman.' While on duty he was to 'wear his uniform or some mark or Badge that he maybe known to be a Police officer' and was 'held responsible for the safe Custody of all prisoners', to 'regularly Patrol every part of the Town' and 'pay particular attention to all Public Houses, Beer Shops and Cider-Houses.' In case of fire he was ordered to 'give immediate alarm by springing his rattle'.[28]

During 1842 a policeman was not employed due to 'the distressed state of the town'. But after the passing of the Constabulary Act, the commissioners were instructed by the county to seek a new Station House. They in turn suggested that the beadle and constable, appointed by the Vestry for various duties including those of Town Crier, Mace Bearer and for generally keeping law and order, were to live rent free in the lock-up after mending the windows and airing the building 'before entry'.[29] Plans were eventually confirmed in 1844 for a new lock-up and constable's house to be erected in Brampton Street. Based here the constable was paid 10s a week in 1853, and in 1863, when Mr. Edwin Colville Moore was Superintendent of the Ross police, his four constables were paid 2s 7d a day.[30] Before the end of the century the force expanded and in 1958 was moved to a new establishment in Old Maid's Walk on the site of the former rectory.[31]

In step with the rest of the nation, the nineteenth century saw a surge in religious activity and many changes made to church and chapel. At St. Mary's 'an organ chamber was built on the south side of the chancel' in 1874, and 'upwards of £4,000 were laid out on its restoration in 1877-78' under the rectorship of the Rev. R.H. Cobbold. During his 20 years of ministry, the 'Mission-Room

Congregational Church, 1896

127

Mock Gothic walls and tower in 1906. (Leeds Collection)

and Sunday School' at Overross was built in 1880 at an estimated cost of £1,000, this was 'free to all' and was extended in 1897 to commemorate Queen Victoria's Diamond Jubilee.[32]

By the late nineteenth century 'various denominations of dissenters' were provided with 'commodious chapels' in Ross. The 1860s was a particularly busy period — the old Independent Chapel in Kyrle Street was replaced by a 'handsome building' in Gloucester Road, and the Wesleyan Chapel in Edde Cross Street was erected at a cost of £1,000 to replace the 1834 chapel in Overross Street. The Plymouth Brethren built a 'neat Chapel' in Henry Street, but the Catholics only 'contemplated' a replacement of St. Mary's Cottage in the Crofts.[33]

The Quakers remodelled their Meeting House in Brampton Street in the early nineteenth century and added a new burial ground. This was later funded by a trust set up by Nathaniel Morgan in 1852. The Baptists had already erected a chapel in 1819, but by 1881 the Broad Street chapel 'was so much out of repair' that another generous benefactor, Thomas Blake 'came to the front, with offers to replace the old building with a new one of a larger size, and the present well built handsome and commodious chapel is the result.'[34] The 'Particular Baptists' were in Wilton Road, and another 'Baptist Chapel' was marked on the Ordnance Survey of 1887 in Cantilupe Road.

Ross became 'thoroughly and expensively medievalised' during the 1830s, continuing John Kyrle's 'public-mindedness' in beautifying the town and landscape. Apart from his legacies, only a polygonal tower of the late eighteenth century in Edde Cross Street, and a former summerhouse in the grounds of Merton House appear to have been built in a similar style. Other follies in the tradition of towers were built, including a 'Castellated Summer House approached by a Battlemented Terrace' at Lincoln Hill, and a tower summer-house built by Mr. Vandervort Kyrle at the end of the John Kyrle Walk. At Merrivale Joseph Turnock concealed his water pump and farm buildings with a castellated wall and a towering chimney.[35]

Gazebo and hotel tower, c.1840. (Courtesy Hereford Record Office)

The mock-gothic Summerhouse in 1905

While the Ross Turnpike Trustees and the Town Commissioners were busy carving out the new Wilton Road during the 1830s, James Barrett was developing the Palace Pound site with his grand hotel. Presumably the surplus of red sandstone cut away from the cliffs was used to construct the stone walls with arrow-slits and oriels, and the Gazebo tower all built above the new road.[36] There is evidence of a lower tower, but in 1870 stones were removed from its summit because they were loose.[37] It has since been dismantled.

This mock-gothic theme was continued with the building of the British and Foreign School in 1837, the Lock-Up in 1838 and a summerhouse in John Kyrle's garden described as 'a small gothic building of red sandstone'. Although known as John Kyrle's Summerhouse it was built much later. The deeds indicate that it was constructed in 1834 by William Cary Cocks, apothecary, possibly 'on the site of a room formerly occupied by the bankers Jones and Love'. The garden and summerhouse were visited by the Duke of Cambridge in 1835 and were 'ornamented at an immense expense'.[38]

Other features of this architectural style may be identified on buildings in the town, especially in Palace Pound and Wye Street including the gable ends of the former Castle Inn added in 1838.[39] This active and dramatic period of development during the 1830s significantly altered the western approach into Ross. 'Although pseudo-medieval buildings were popular at that time, maybe this style was used to balance and harmonise with the genuine fourteenth century ruins of Wilton Castle standing on the opposite bank of the Wye.' Or was the 'palpable reason for going so medieval in this place: the existence of a house of the

Bishops of Hereford.' Alternatively, was there a connection with the three towers which stood on 'Bishop's Court' in 1696? They were sufficiently important as summerhouses or follies to have keys and be kept in repair.[40]

The improvements and developments in Ross during the nineteenth century were mainly carried out by the businessmen, tradesmen and professionals living in Ross. Names of Improvement Commissioners that stand out from 1830 include John Stratford Collins, William Cary Cocks, Samuel Bennett Wall, Nathaniel Morgan, James Wallace Richard Hall, James Barrett, William Powell Hooper, Henry Minnett, Alfred Purchas, Samuel Llewelyn, Joseph Turnock, Henry Southall and Thomas Blake who all had vested interests, and undoubtedly made a personal gain. One unpleasant issue that many of them were involved with was the controversy over access onto the Prospect.

This happened after James Barrett had established his Royal Hotel and laid out ornamental plots and well kept walks in the Prospect, but enclosed a portion adjoining the hotel. The public, who understood they had free access since the time of John Kyrle onto the whole of the Prospect, decided to protest in 1848. This was reported in the *Hereford Journal* of 19th July 1848:

> It is known to all the world that Mr. Barrett, many years ago, purchased the property at the Prospect and erected there as elegant and accommodative an hotel as is to be found in any part of the kingdom. Conceiving, therefore, that he had the right to the whole charming promenade at the Prospect, the public were shut out from a part which has been enclosed by a laurel fence, and called the Lower Garden, but not without great dissatisfaction, for they conceived that the benevolent individual referred to had secured in perpetuity this beautiful and healthy walk to the inhabitants of Ross. During last week the belligerent spirit was at its height, crowds assembling, and on Wednesday night there was a furious contest for possession, or the right of walking in the Lower Garden, Mr. Barrett and his servants being arrayed on the one side, and numbers of the inhabitants, headed by respectable individuals on the other.

Another protest occurred in 1863 followed in 1869 by 'Serious Rioting and Destruction of Property at Ross' reported by the *Ross Gazette* of 15th July 1869:

> Soon after 6 o'clock, a signal was given for the work of destruction to commence, and very soon the peas, beans, potatoes, and cabbage plants were strewed and trampled about the ground, amidst the cheers of the hundreds of spectators who were present by that time. Many of the handsome plants in the ornamental portion of the grounds next fell a victim to the fury of the mob. The gates attached to these gardens had all been thrown open during the day by the instructions of the hotel managers, thus giving the public the right of free ingress and egress, and the inhabitants, we need hardly say, made the most liberal use of the privilege. The members of the Barrel Friendly Society (who were celebrating their anniversary that day) took the opportunity thus afforded them of marching round the gardens, headed by the Trafalgar band, after leaving church in the morning.

This last riot led to a Special Meeting held by the Town Commissioners on 16th July to respect the people's rights to the Prospect. By 1870 the Prospect affair had been 'settled' by conveying the outer part to the Commissioners and instructing the hotel company to erect a wall at the bottom end. This account from the Commissioners Minutes varies slightly from a version of 1904 written in the *Life of Thomas Blake* which records:

In order to end the controversy with the townspeople as to their supposed right to the Prospect, Mr. Blake succeeded in purchasing, anonymously (through the medium of the late Mr. John Skyrme, solicitor), the entire freehold of the best and largest portion of the Prospect, with all rights thereunto belonging, and presented it to the town by deed for the use of the town for ever. For over two years no one but Mr. Blake and Mr. Skyrme knew who had at first proposed and carried out the purchase. This happily ended the cause of perpetual strife; and while the hotel company have benefited by having at the same time a decision of a high court of law, declaring the portion of the ground they had enclosed as strictly private (for this was part of the arrangement), the people have now the Prospect secured to them by deed for their enjoyment for ever.

View from the Prospect in 1896

13   Industry, Trade and Commerce

From early times Ross was ideally situated to develop its trades and industries. Water from the Rudhall brook and other streams powered its forges, mills, tanyards and breweries, and raw materials were readily available nearby, or from the Forest of Dean. With two important crossings over the Wye at Wilton and Goodrich communications to the market town were adequate with road and river transport improved and later replaced by the railway.

Camden in 1607 noted that 'Ross maintains its reputation for iron works and drives a considerable trade in cyder and wool.' Although iron-working had been carried out in and around Ross, by the nineteenth century there was 'no manufacturing carried on in an extensive way.'[1] The same Joseph Hawkins associated with the exterior stairs to the Market House was a nailer at Brookend in 1693, and although the industry probably continued it was due to John Partridge, an iron master in the late eighteenth century who apparently imported from 'Harborne, near Birmingham, upwards of a hundred skilled workmen and established them in New Street, in a long row of nail shops.' By 1813 John Hardwick 'ironmonger' and John Rudge were producing nails and the industry continued until the mid-nineteenth century, when the iron foundries of Samuel Kell and Esau Palmer became established.[2] They were followed by William Blake at the corner of Brookend and Station Street with Perkins and Bellamy at the 'Broad Street iron works', in the 1870s.[3]

In Elizabethan times the 'Borough of Rosse' traded in 'all kinde of Cattell, as of Corne'.[4] Also associated with the rich agricultural land of the area were the woollen, milling, tanning and brewing industries. Wool was an important commodity with markets or fairs held in the churchyard before being moved in 1696. In 1784 Panter, Wood and Lloyd were listed as Woolstaplers, a business continued by William Lloyd and Sons in Copse Cross Street. At this time the Market House was 'filled with Sheep's Wool as fine as any in the Kingdom.' The Lloyds were followed by other woolstaplers at Copse Cross Street until the 1860s when Edwin Yates opened his warehouse in the High Street. Next to the One Mill was a 'Tuck Mill' which was associated with the woollen industry. This was recorded in the 1620s and in 1813.[5]

Corn was produced in great quantities on the rich Herefordshire soil. For example in July 1791 '60 bages of whete' were transported by barge from Hereford to Wilton, followed by a further delivery of '40 Bages to Wilton at 4d pur bag' in May 1792.[6] Corn was ground at three different mills in Ross, the Chest or Chace Mill, the Town Mill and the One Mill. James Powles was the miller at the Chace Mill in 1794,[7] but shortly after 1813 'Old Chase'

ROSS.

ESAU PALMER,

GENERAL AND FURNISHING IRONMONGER,

DEALER IN ALL KINDS OF

BRONZED, PLATED & JAPAN GOODS,

CANDLE AND SOLAR LAMPS,

GAS PENDANTS, GLASSES & FITTINGS,

Cutlery, Kitchen Furniture and Tools,

Brush Factor, and Dealer in Iron, Steel, Copper, Brass, Zinc, and Tin ;

MANUFACTURER OF

Entrance and other Gates, Palisading, Verandahs, Invisible Park and
other Fencing, Iron Hurdles,

AGRICULTURAL AND OTHER MACHINES,

WROUGHT CASEMENTS & WINDOW FRAMES,

Stocks and Dies, Press Screws, Axles, Chains and Nails, together with
every Description of Plain and Ornamental Ironwork, as also of

ROPES, TWINES, LINES, & CORDAGE.

SMITH, BRAZIER, COPPERSMITH,

TINMAN, LOCKSMITH,

BELL-HANGER, GUNSMITH, & BRASS FOUNDER.

HOT HOUSES AND CONSERVATORIES,

Heated by Steam or Hot Water, on the most improved plan.

CASTINGS IN IRON, BRASS, LEAD, AND ZINC ;

OILS, COLOURS, PAINTS,

VARNISHES, PITCH, TAR, RESIN, &C.;

PALMER's CANDLES ;

HIP, SLIPPER, SHOWER, SPONGING, AND VAPOUR BATHS ;

KITCHEN RANGES,

STEAM COOKING APPARATUS AND GRATES,

IN EVERY VARIETY ;

Pumps of all kinds, and Smoke and other Jacks ; Fire Bricks and Squares.

Repairs and Work to Order, on the shortest notice.

AGRICULTURAL IMPLEMENTS SUPPLIED AT THE MAKER'S
PRICES.

Examples of industries and trades in Ross.
Above: Iron & Brass Founder, 1851
Above right: Tanning, 1836
Below: Woolstapler, 1836
Below right: Saddler, 1896

EDWIN JAMES YATES,

WOOLSTAPLER.

OFFICE AND WAREHOUSE, HENRY STREET, ROSS.

AGENT FOR THE

WESTERN FIRE AND MARINE INSURANCE COMPANY,
LIMITED,

AND FOR THE

SOVEREIGN LIFE ASSURANCE COMPANY.

TO TANNERS, CURRIERS, FELLMONGERS,

BREWERS, AND OTHERS.

To be Sold by Private Contract,

OR LET FOR A TERM OF YEARS,

AN

EXCELLENT TANYARD,

CONTAINING 82 PITS,

with Bark-mill, Drying Lofts, Store-rooms, Currier's Retail
Shop, &c. in complete repair, to which the Currying Business
is attached and in full work ; and to which that of a Fellmonger
might with convenience be added, as there is a good stream of
water constantly flowing through the yard.

THE DWELLING HOUSE

is large and commodious, with Vaulted Cellars, large Malthouse,
Stables, Gardens, and every convenience for carrying on an
extensive trade.

THE PREMISES ARE FREEHOLD

and advantageously situated in a rich and picturesque country,
having easy communications by land and water with surrounding markets, and an abundance of the finest Bark and Barley
growing in the immediate neighbourhood. There is no Fellmonger within Eight Miles. The Premises might easily admit
the establishment of a capital Brewery, in addition, with every
prospect of success in that line.

Address, (post paid) P. R. at Mr. L. Cook's, No. 1,
Maiden Lane, Covent Garden, London.

W. FOWLER, PRINTER. CIRENCESTER.

For every description of
SADDLERY, HORSE CLOTHING,
STABLE REQUISITES,
Or any Article connected with the Horse,

GO TO

T. W. BAILEY,

Saddler and Harness Manufacturer,

HIGH STREET, ROSS.

was replaced by a mansion house and the mill became disused. By 1830 William Hart was the miller at the Town Mill, which was re-erected as a corn grist mill, and the One Mill was worked by the Morgan family, and subsequently John Prosser in 1867. By 1887 the One Mill was 'dis-used', the Town Mill was still working as a 'Corn Mill', but the Chace or Chest's Mill was long forgotten.[8]

Tanning, converting raw hide into leather, progressed over the centuries into a complicated and lengthy process using oak bark. In the seventeenth century there was a tanyard at Brookend owned by the Merricks. Oak bark was plentiful from local woods and forests and was transported by barges along the Wye. At the tanyard a water-driven bark mill ground the oak bark before it was mixed with water to form a solution. This was poured into a series of tan pits where the hides were immersed, passing from a weaker to a stronger solution over a period of about 18 months. The business passed out of the hands of the Merricks and was sold in 1808 to James Frere, a former currier. It then consisted of pits, drying lofts, bark mill, beam house, leather room and shop together with a Brew House and Malt House. His third son, Charles, took over the business but ran into financial difficulties. The tanyard and contents were sold and the Brookend Tanyard ceased production in the late 1830s.[9]

From the early nineteenth century another tannery was operated by Mrs. Boughton in Over Ross Street. This was probably the same site reused by Elles Lee Sanders for his 'extensive tannery' established in 1837 and later run by Messr. Smyth & Co. Towards the end of the century this Ross Tannery with its tan pits covered a large area along the Rudhall brook approached by a lane now known as Tanyard Lane. Other tanners only worked for short periods in Broad Street and Edde Cross Street, where John Tranter's 'Skinhouse Yard' was situated in the 1820s.[10]

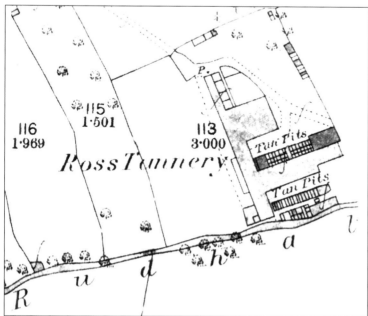

The OS map of 1887 shows the site of Ross Tannery at Overross

The leather produced by the tanyards was used for making gloves, boots, shoes, books and saddlery. Reference has already been made to a pair of 'Rosse boots' given to the Earl of Shrewsbury by his son in 1576. In the eighteenth century there was 'John Scott of London, leather gilder' and William Mann, a glover, at the Bell Forge. Later that century there was a 'Wholesale Boot and Shoe Warehouse' run by Walter Watkins a 'Skinner and Glover'. In 1806 John Meek was making shoes in 'a certain street called Edd-Cross.'[11] From the early nineteenth century there was a rapid growth in boot and shoemaking, saddlery and book-binding, which continued to flourish throughout that century.[12]

Another Ross industry was brewing and malting. A brewery was established at Fownhope by Mr. Purchas in the late eighteenth century, but beer was not generally brewed commercially until the nineteenth century.[13] During the early 1800s barley was malted and beer was brewed mainly on the premises of inns and at the Brookend Tanyard in a small way. It appears to have been John Hill who started the first brewery at Ross, from his 'House, Malthouse, Stable etc.' in Brookend, where several other malthouses were sited in 1824.[14] About two decades later this was taken over by former grocers Joseph and Benjamin Turnock. Known as the 'Ross Brewery', it moved to Station Street and became a limited company called the Alton Court Brewery in 1865.[15]

In 1893 the Alton Court Brewery underwent 'complete renovation', and in 1897 the company was licensed to

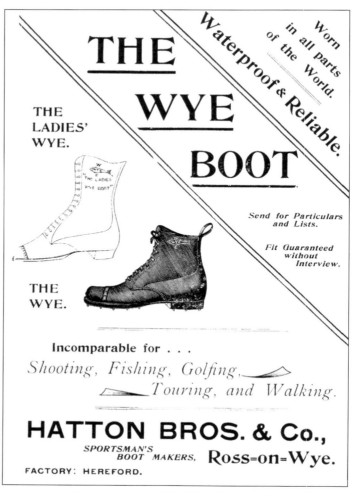

Advertisement for The Wye Boot in 1896

'carry on a wines and spirits business in connection with the brewery.' At this time the premises of the 'Brewers, Maltsters and Aerated Water Manufacturers' extended from Brookend Street along Station Street to Henry Street. Harvest Ale, Mild Ale, and Bitter were brewed on site together with Golden Crown and Golden Hop 'Brewed especially for Private Families'. 'Stout and Porter' were 'carefully brewed on a new and improved principle' and were 'strongly recommended – more especially for invalids.'[16] During the 1950s the Alton Court Brewery ran into financial difficulties. The company was taken over by the Stroud Brewery in 1956 and the premises in Ross were closed down.

It was the Purchas family from the Fownhope Brewery who established themselves in Ross as Wine and Spirit Merchants in 1790. From New Street they moved to Broad Street in a house formerly known as the Black Lion Inn.[17] It was soon followed by other outlets including the Nag's Head offering 'Wines and Spirits, Home-Brewed Beer, Ale, Porter, Cider etc.' and the 'Wine and Spirit Vaults' in St. Mary's Street.[18] The firm of 'Purchas and Sons' continued

Advertisement for The Alton Court Brewery in 1896

into the next century, and the family is commemorated in Ross Church together with a much earlier 'vintner', John Farne, who died in 1658.

Other industries were carried out on a small scale, such as the making of bricks by Charles Prosser, John Bevan and John Viner in 1794. In the 1840s Ephraim Blewett and John Robinson were the 'Brick and Tile Makers' in Broad Street and Arthur's Lane (Old Gloucester Road). The 1840 Tithe Map shows a Brickyard Meadow adjoining the Stock Meadow, and a 'Coal Slate Timber Yard and Sheds' in Millpond Street. This was the site of J.B. Kemp and Sons' steam saw mills and timber, slate and cement yard. Another 'Sawpit Yard' in Brampton Street was worked by William Lewis in 1847.[19]

Timber was an important commodity for building, furniture making and firewood. There was a plentiful supply from the local woods and forests and many sales of 'Timber and Coppice Wood' were advertised in the Hereford Journal, including an auction of 'OAK, ASH, and ELM TIMBER' at the Swan Inn on 18th December 1806. The timber was 'all numbered with white paint' and 'worthy of public attention' at Kings Caple and Much Marcle.

Other industries flourished in the neighbourhood — paper was made at Tressack, Hoarwithy, Guns Mills in the Forest of Dean and at Bill Mills in the parish of Weston-under-Penyard. Here paper was manufactured from the 1680s to 1832 mainly by the Parker and Lloyd families.[20] Coal came from the Forest of Dean, but there were 'cole mines' at Walford owned by Gabriel Hanger in 1747. Lime was equally needed for agriculture, building, tanning and medicinal purposes. Lime kilns were scattered over the hills of Walford, Whitchurch,

Fownhope and the Forest of Dean. From the 'Vention Lime-Kilns near Lidbrook' a 'Barge Load' of lime delivered to Wilton and Ross cost 9s in 1824.[21]

Stone was required for building and road repairs, but in and around Ross there is little evidence of any extensive quarrying except along the Rope Walk below Edde Cross Street. In 1839 the quarry at Bishopswood was inspected 'to view stone to be used by the Turnpike Trust instead of from Coppett Wood.' It was delivered to Kerne Bridge and then conveyed by barge to Ross.[22] A number of stonemasons worked in the town, the best known and longest serving being 'A.W. Ursell Waterloo Monumental Works' at Cantilupe Road, who also advertised 'Landscape and Portrait Photography' in 1896.

Withies, hemp and water were the required materials for basket and rope-making, a trade which developed along the Wye at Ross. From the eighteenth century it was the families of Joseph Evans and John Newton who dominated these trades for nearly 100 years. From nearby withy beds 'the workers cut and harvested the osier branches, then they had to be peeled and boiled so as to obtain a finished component' for the basket-maker who 'by skilfully combing, weaving, knotting and plaiting produced the finished basket.'[23] Rope was manufactured from hemp, and this operation took place in the 'Rope House' and along a length of about 300 yards of roadway known as the Rope Walk.[24] In 1779 the rope-maker John Newton had a 'Workhouse in Wye Meadows' which held his 'Utensils and Stock' valued at £150. The churchwardens' accounts of 1813 record 'To Mr. Newton for Bell Rope and Cord 7s 8½d', and again in 1816 'Paid Mr. Newton for Bell rope repairing 16s 6d.'

Top: Advertisement for T.W. Purchas & Sons showing their premises
Bottom: An 1867 advertisement for coal and lime

Osier stripping in preparation for basket making. (Alfred Watkins; courtesy Hereford Library)

In 1782 Joseph Evans, the basket-maker was paying a fire insurance policy for 'Four Tenements under one Roof situate aforesaid in the Tenure of himself, Edw. Hill Glazier, John Newton Flax Dresser and Stephen Lane Victualer.' Newton's property beside the River Wye was built of brick, plaster and tiles, and valued at £300. Another 'Flax Dresser' was Joseph Hardwick at Dock Pitch. In 1785 his 'Household Goods', 'Utensils and Stock' were valued at £460, whereas his 'dwelling house' with a 'Stable and Workshop' were only valued at £340 for insurance purposes.[25]

For many years John Newton, rope-maker, rented 'The Ricks', 'Rope House' and 'Rope Walk' from various owners and in 1847 Joseph Newton was paying £3 13s 6d a year for the Rope House 'recently put into good repair.'[26] The Newtons were also recorded as flax dressers together with Joseph Hardwick, and during the eighteenth century large amounts of flax were purchased by the Ross Overseers including '3 Stone of Flax £1 2s 6d' in 1767.[27] From 1835 William Newton also sold 'Beer and

SARAH NEWTON,

HOPE & ANCHOR INN,

NEAR THE RIVER, ROSS,

BASKET & SIEVE MAKER.

PLEASURE BOAT PROPRIETOR.

Boats for Excursions on the Wye to Monmouth, Tintern Abbey, and Chepstow.

BOATS OF EVERY DESCRIPTION CONSTANTLY ON HIRE.

Advertisement placed in 1851

Ale' from a premises called the Hope & Anchor which his family continued to run as an inn until George Hobbs took over around 1870 and which is still in existence as a pub today.

Since the eighteenth century boats had been available for hire from the dock at Ross, but there is no evidence of boat-building apart from a John Powell listed as a boat-builder in 1835, and a barge Rival built at Wilton in 1804. It was only at the end of the nineteenth century that Henry Dowell and Sons became boat-builders. They were also the sole proprietors of the steam wheel launch Wilton Castle and their business continued well into the 1920s.[28]

The industries and trades needed lawyers, bankers and accountants to administer their affairs. 'Attornies' of the eighteenth century appeared to have worked outside the town such as Thomas Harvey from Overross and 'his uncle Mr. Mynd'.[29] During the next century the lawyers were more conveniently placed. John Cooke, who replaced 'Old Chase' with a mansion house in 1818,

Coracles on the Wye at Ross in 1860.
(Wight Collection, Hereford Record Office)

had his office in Lower Church Lane (Church Street) with his 'stable and gig house'. William Hooper was at Merton House, which had been recently erected in Edde Cross Street, and John Stratford Collins, from the Walford family, had his offices in Upper Church Street (St. Mary's Street).[30] After the developments in Ross during the 1830s, his house known as Palace Pound featured a 'substantially-built Tower, Castellated Buildings, Parapets, and Walls'.[31] Now called the Gazebo it was called Collins' Tower when newly erected.

With a growing population and expanding trades, there were openings for enterprising solicitors

Merton House in the 1950s

and the established attorneys were joined by others in the 1830s. One was the ambitious James Wallace Richard Hall, already practising in Hereford, who started the partnership of Hall and Humphrys in New Street. After his marriage in 1823 he lived above the town at Springfield off Brampton Street (now demolished) and devoted his life as a 'counsellor, adviser and benefactor' to the town of Ross. His firm passed to Minnett, then Piddocke before becoming Burt, Evans and Shawcross in the 1930s.[32] Succeeding members of the Hooper family continued as solicitors until the death of William Powell Hooper in 1870, whilst the Collins' practice was taken over by George Okell in the early 1900s.

The bankers of Ross were represented in the late eighteenth century by Mr. Jones, 'an intelligent, smart, spirited man', whose 'conversation upon Agriculture, Trade and Politics is sensible and solid, and his behaviour is highly pleasing and agreeable.'[33] Was he the partner of 'Messrs Jones and Love, bankers' situated in the High Street and to whom a former 'Vault' may have belonged which was described in a deed of 1834? In 1822 Josiah Newman and Edward Prichard were at Ross Old Bank and John Jones, Richard Jones and Nathaniel Morgan were running the Ross and Archenfield Bank. Morgan, a Quaker, was a 'vigorous, kindly and astute man' who formed his bank in 1820 and which together with the other Ross bank survived the financial crisis of 1825 caused by the after effects of the Napoleonic Wars and political unrest.[34]

By 1840 the solicitor James Wallace Richard Hall had established his Ross and Forest of Dean Bank in New Street. After the death of Nathaniel Morgan in 1854 and Wallace Hall in 1860 the three remaining independent banks, which in 1858 were listed as the 'Ross and Archenfield Bank' in the Market Place, the 'Old Bank' in the High Street, and 'Ross & Forest of Dean Bank' in Broad Street, were taken over by larger companies — the Gloucester Banking Company, the National Provincial Bank and the West of England and South Wales District Banking Company. These, in turn, have since been absorbed into the banks that exist today.

In 1816 the 'Saving Bank for Ross' was established 'to give persons of the labouring classes and others, the opportunity of investing ... small sums of money.' It was held in the 'upper room of the School-House, in the Churchyard, Ross, every Monday evening.' The patron was Sir Hungerford Hoskyns from Harewood, and the Treasurers were the bankers Messrs. Newman and Prichard. By 1876 it was still held in the church-yard school and open twice a week for 'any sum received from a penny to £20.'[35]

Houses, land, household goods and farming stock were sold by auctioneers, many also acted as surveyors and estate agents. In 1815 John Tristram auctioned two acres of land on the south side of 'Horsemill Lane otherwise Frog Lane other-wise Badges Lane otherwise Bad's Lane.' (Greytree Road). Later, John Morgan and Sons were named in 1833 as auction-

Nathaniel Morgan, 1775-1854. (Courtesy V. Morgan)

141

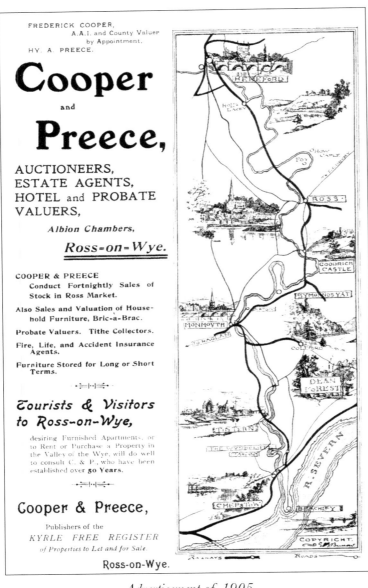

FREDERICK COOPER,
A.A.I. and County Valuer
by Appointment.
HY. A. PREECE.

Cooper

and

Preece,

AUCTIONEERS,
ESTATE AGENTS,
HOTEL and PROBATE
VALUERS,

Albion Chambers,

Ross-on-Wye.

COOPER & PREECE
Conduct Fortnightly Sales of
Stock in Ross Market.

Also Sales and Valuation of Household Furniture, Bric-a-Brac.

Probate Valuers. Tithe Collectors.

Fire, Life, and Accident Insurance
Agents.

Furniture Stored for Long or Short
Terms.

·=∣·∣=·

*Tourists & Visitors
to Ross-on-Wye,*

desiring Furnished Apartments, or
to Rent or Purchase a Property in
the Valley of the Wye, will do well
to consult C. & P., who have been
established over **50 Years.**

·=∣·∣=·

Cooper & Preece,

Publishers of the
*KYRLE FREE REGISTER
of Properties to Let and for Sale.*

Ross-on-Wye.

Advertisement of 1905

eers on the sale particulars of 'The Cleeve formerly the Property of the Man of Ross', on the sale notice dated 1836 of 'Neat and Clean Household Furniture' from Charles Frere's Tanhouse, and on an auction notice of the One Mill and Water Works in 1847.

By the second half of the nineteenth century, the auctioneer, John Innell was serving as an accountant, estate and insurance agent, with Henry Dowle from Vaga House, whilst Rootes and Wintle operated from the Market Place offering the same services.[36] The accountant Thomas Sherwood Smith listed in 1851 at St. Mary's Street was presumably the author of a useful publication, *The Tourist's Guide to the Wye*, first published in 1855. A notable accountant was Thomas Blake, 'The Pious Benefactor of Ross', who rose from being a modest post office clerk to become an influential businessman and Justice of the Peace. In politics Blake was a Liberal and on three occasions was returned as a Member of Parliament, twice for Leominster and once for the Forest of Dean. As a devoted nonconformist he spread the gospel by preaching over a wide area, and laid the foundation stones of several local chapels.[37]

These accountants, bankers and especially the solicitors wielded an enormous amount of influence as business advisers and legal administrators, before later reforms in law, education and voting qualifications distributed power more evenly. However, many shopkeepers and tradesmen owned their own business and other property in the town, which gave them their own status and financial standing. From the mid-nineteenth century Ross shops were selling a variety of products, and skilled tradesmen offered a range of services. It was said that

Thomas Blake, 1825-1901

The inhabitants of Ross were kept informed of news and events by reading local newspapers. The *Hereford Journal* — 'the organ of Conservatism' and 'one of the oldest papers in England' — was established in 1713. It ceased in 1932, and is not to be confused with the existing *Hereford Journal*. The *Hereford Times* was founded over a century later in 1832 offering 'liberal politics'. In 1855 two Ross newspapers were started — the *Ross and Archenfield Gazette* printed by Thomas Farror in the High Street, which only lasted a few weeks, and *The Man of Ross* which was published for over 35 years.[40]

The bookseller, printer, stationer and bookbinder William Hill, founded the *Ross Gazette* in 1867, advertised as 'The Largest, Cheapest, and Best Weekly Newspaper in the District'. Published every Wednesday it boasted 'the best medium for Solicitors, Auctioneers, Tradesmen, Advertising Agents,

the High Street 'positively rang with enterprise', Brookend was 'a hive of industries', Broad Street 'held the monopoly of the town's refreshment rooms', and the Market Place 'had reached a scale hitherto unknown'.[38]

Even with an established postal service by mail coach, dating from around 1784, it was not until the 1820s that the first postmaster, Richard Dee, was appointed in Ross. One of his successors was Joseph Evans in 1850 who was also a basket and sieve manufacturer, pattern and clog maker, dealer in fancy goods and pleasure boat proprietor. He must 'have been an early riser, for the first of the mails arrived with the letters at 4.30 a.m.'[39] By 1876 the Post and Telegraph Office had moved to new premises in Gloucester Road, and a Stamp Office was available at the Man of Ross House.

William Hill, 1833-1891.
(Courtesy Martin Morris)

and others, to make known their announcements to the Public.' Apart from reporting 'full and accurate reports' of the local news it also contained 'a carefully compiled summary of the Home and Foreign intelligence of the Week.'[41] This popular newspaper still serves the community of Ross and district, although in 1998 'it was reported that after 130 years the *Ross Gazette* has ceased to be an independent newspaper and has become part of Tindle Newspapers Ltd.'[42]

14   The Twentieth Century

With Victorian England nearly at its close, and the nation, including volunteers from Ross, involved in the Boer War, the entry into the twentieth century made little impression on the town. The *Ross Gazette* of 4th January 1900 featured Boer War appeals, Mid-Winter Sales, and advertisements offering 'New Year Cards' from the 'Gazette Office'. No public celebrations appear to have taken place to welcome the new century, contrasting with the preparations 100 years later.

Broad Street in 1897 celebrating Queen Victoria's Diamond Jubilee. (Courtesy Hereford Library)

F. Whittle, vice-chairman of Ross-on-Wye Urban District Council

In 1905 the town was described as 'much modernised of late by the erection of new buildings, and by the numerous handsome plate-glass fronts which have been put in several shops and places of business', adding that Ross 'still has a somewhat antiquated and old-world appearance and presents in this respect, a great contrast to the melancholy uniformity of many modern towns' probably due to the developments made after the Improvement Acts.[1] The population in 1901 stood at 4,912, which, after a mid-century decline, rose to 9,074 by 2004.

Before the Local Government Act of 1888, the Courts of Quarter Sessions were the most influential authority within each county. Their varied duties included compelling Boards to fulfil their obligations, the valuing and assessing of properties, making the rates, disbursement of all money, and holding the final power of Judicial authority.[2]

After the Act of 1888 the administrative functions of Quarter Sessions and Turnpike Trusts were transferred to the newly created county councils. Later the work of the Ross Town Commissioners and other local boards was undertaken by Ross Urban District Council following a further Act in 1894. By 1902 Ross Urban District Council were holding their monthly meetings in the Town Hall (Market House) under the chairmanship of Henry Purchas, a wine and spirit merchant. The Vice Chairman was Frederick Wintle, secretary of the Alton Court Brewery Company, and the other members were Francis Adams, a solicitor; William Barrass, a hairdresser, tobacconist and cycle agent; Frederick Cooper, an auctioneer with Cooper and Preece; John Davies, an accountant; Richard Drew, from the Railway Inn; James Meredith, a draper; and Edmund Turner, a boot manufacturer.[3]

After the upheaval of two World Wars with its tragic loss of life, destruction, deprivation and rationing, a Post-War 'Planning Survey of Herefordshire' was published in 1946. Forward thinking and optimism continued into the 1950s. This atmosphere was reflected when a Coat of Arms was granted by the College of Arms to Ross-on-Wye Urban District Council in 1953. It was designed by the President of the Fylde Heraldic Society and included the motto 'Porta Vagae' — 'Gateway to the Wye'. The name 'Ross-on-Wye' had been given

Coat of arms for Ross-on-Wye Urban District Council

Ross-on-Wye Council Chambers in 1999

official recognition in 1931, a change meant to help attract tourism, and to distinguish the town from others named simply Ross, even though these lay in northern Britain.[4]

Major changes were made to local government in 1974. Despite opposition, Herefordshire became part of the new county of Hereford and Worcester, and district councils were merged into larger authorities, which placed Ross-on-Wye in South Herefordshire District Council. The Act also created Ross-on-Wye Town Council with the powers of a parish council, although the chairman now took the title of Mayor. With plenty of advance publicity, Herefordians were delighted when in 1998 Herefordshire split from Worcestershire and the district councils were disbanded, leaving the new Herefordshire Council 'the sole providers of local government services in the county'.[5]

With the passing of the first Local Government Act in 1888, radical and sweeping changes were set in place which have significantly altered the face of Ross and the life-style of its inhabitants. After 50 years in existence Herefordshire County Council reported 'It is

Community Hospital opened in 1997

difficult as yet to estimate fully what country people owe to the Local Government Act of 1888. By giving each County a freely elected governing body to manage its own affairs, and to interpret Acts of Parliament in accordance with its special needs, the principle of self-government may be said to have been brought to the very door of every cottage dweller.'[6]

The county councils had always intended to bring the administration of Poor Law under their control, but political difficulties delayed this happening until 1930. One effect of this was the closing of workhouses which changed their names and functions. From 1930 the Ross Workhouse became the Poor Law Institution, and subsequently, the Public Assistance Institution and the Ross Social Welfare Institution, and it ended its days as Dean Hill Hospital. During the 1970s the hospital cared for long stay Age Care residents and those with learning difficulties, but with changes in styles of care introduced in the 1980s the hospital was eventually closed.[7] The site was re-used for the Ross Community Hospital which was opened on 15th July 1997 by the Princess Royal, 'who made local history ... as the first member of the Royal Family to visit Ross in 40 years. The last time Royalty came to the town was in 1957, when the Queen, accompanied by the Duke of Edinburgh, visited Herefordshire.'[8] The Community Hospital replaced and extended the facilities of the former Cottage Hospital, which has since been redeveloped.

The Education Act of 1944 introduced eleven-plus entry to Ross Grammar School in Ryefield Road, and enabled a secondary modern school to be built at Overross in 1953. In 1979 these two schools combined to form the John Kyrle High School at the secondary modern school site. In 1998 the High School with 1,000 pupils aimed 'to provide quality education to enable all members of the school community to achieve their potential and be valued members of society.'[9] The primary school, which had remained at Cantilupe Road, outgrew the school buildings, and moved to new premises at Ashfield Park in 1970. The old grammar school was converted into the Larruperz Community Centre, and the Cantilupe Road School was demolished to make space for Ross Library. A group of men under the odd name of 'Larruperz' had raised money from their musical performances throughout the 1920s and 1930s with which to build a community hall. A site was purchased, but the Second World War intervened and the project was delayed. Finally, after an exchange of property in 1990 the Larruperz Centre was opened in

John Kyrle High School

part of the former grammar school.[10] The remaining part of the school was passed to Social Services and used as the Ryefield Centre, initially run by the local Enterprise Centres for the Handicapped, and then by Social Services itself, to provide day care for people with learning difficulties as part of the Dean Hill Hospital closure programme.

None of the Private Schools in Ross survived to the end of the twentieth century. St. Joseph's Convent started as a private establishment in 1934 on the Walford Road at Thomas Blake's former house 'Lebanon'. For financial reasons the school was taken into the state system in 1975. In 1999 it catered for 135 pupils.[11]

Herefordshire Council is now responsible for Ross-on-Wye Library, but the origins of a library in Ross date back much earlier. In 1818 a 'Permanent Library' was established by the Ross Permanent Reading Society 'in order that a lasting collection may be made'. This was short-lived, as in 1823 T.D. Fosbroke, as chairman, for some unknown reason 'resolved to break it up and sell the books among the members.' By 1830 there were 'four reading societies, which by 1840 were 'supplied with a choice collection of books, periodicals, etc.' From the mid-nineteenth century circulating libraries were run by booksellers, including John Counsell and William Hill. 'The Ross Free Library, Reading Room, and Recreation Grounds, in Broad Street, were generously presented to the inhabitants of the town by their fellow townsman, Thomas Blake Esq., the present M.P. for the borough of Leominster. The institution was formerly handed over to the trustees on the 31st of July 1873.'[12]

The former Ross Free Library

The Public Libraries Act of 1919 empowered county councils to run their own libraries. Grants from the Carnegie Trust enabled them to set up a county library service, but could only be used 'on condition that the ultimate responsibility for the library should be borne by the Local Authority, and that a qualified librarian should be appointed at a minimum salary.'[13] It was not until 1937 that a council run library was opened at Ross-on-Wye, with J.R. Colcombe acting as librarian, in Broad Street at the prop-

149

*One of the last vestiges of the railway —
the static display mounted at Five Ways*

erty donated by Thomas Blake. After
the Second World War, the library
moved into the Market House, where
it remained until 3rd March 1988
when the Minister of Arts opened 'the
first purpose-built library ... in the old
County of Herefordshire for over one
hundred years.'[14]

Apparently, in 1939 the 'most
popular committee among members
of every County Council is that which
deals with the highways and bridges of
the County', and it was reported that
'Many people can still remember the
time when motors were regarded as
terrifying monsters reeking of oil and

raising clouds of dust which covered the neighbouring hedges with a shroud.'[15]

Before the railway closed in 1964, Ross-on-
Wye had already been linked to the motorway
system via the new Spur Road built in 1960. Since
the 1980s various schemes were suggested to
improve traffic conditions within the town. This
led to the construction of a relief road in 1985,
and the introduction of a one-way system in 1997.
Although this is not entirely satisfactory, it has
reduced the amount of traffic through the town
centre, where the Enhancement Scheme of 1997
has improved conditions for pedestrians. Without
a train service, Ross-on-Wye relies for public
transport upon a bus and coach service, which
has been improved by Herefordshire Council.

In 1937 the Ross Water Undertaking utilised
water from the Alton Court Pumping Station, and
used river water from the 'Dock' for industrial
purposes. In the County Planning Survey of 1946
it was reported that 'The Ross water authority
utilises as its source of supply four boreholes in

Early garage in Ross, c.1920

the Old Red Sandstone. It is believed that these are together capable of yielding more than the normal requirements of the Authority's area of supply, although, even now, water for some industrial purposes is obtained from the Wye. It is doubtful, however, whether the combined yield of these boreholes would be sufficient to meet the demand from a population much increased above the present if such increase were attended by any considerable industrial development. In fact, it is felt in some quarters of Ross that the success of any housing and industrial development depends upon a greatly improved and augmented water supply.'[16]

In the early 1960s the pumping station at the 'Dock' ceased, and the site was re-used as a sewerage pumping station under the ownership of Hyder in 1999. The water supply was outlined by Welsh Water: 'Ross-on-Wye is served by the Alton Court water treatment works which treats water abstracted from an underground aquifer. The town's water supply is also augmented by importing water from the Severn Trent water treatment works at Mitcheldean. The blended waters are stored in a service reservoir located on the hill above the Alton Court works. Fully treated potable water leaves this reservoir for subsequent distribution in Ross-on-Wye to domestic and industrial customers.'[17]

Coach services to Ross, c.1950s

The gas works established in the nineteenth century were run by the Ross Gas Company Ltd. in 1902. Its gasometers in Kyrle Street continued to function until North Sea gas was introduced. Electric Lighting Acts were passed in 1882 and 1888, but Ross did not apply to the Board of Trade for authorisation to 'produce, store and supply electricity' until 1901.[18] The application was made by John Parker of Hereford, an engineer who intended to carry out the works, initially supplying a very limited area based upon the High Street and Market Place. For example,

Above: Alton Court Pumping Station in 1985
Below: Electricity advertisement placed c.1920.
(Courtesy Ross Library)

it was proposed to only lay lines for 140 yards along Gloucester Road from the Market Place; 66 yards along Copse Cross Street from the Market Place; and in Edde Cross Street only as far as New Street. The following year Edwards and Armstrong from Hereford were appointed as electrical contractors to the Ross Electric Light Company and H. Pengelly and Co. Electrical Engineers, were offering to install electric lighting and transmit power from a branch in Ross.[19] By 1941 electricity was supplied by the Shropshire, Worcestershire and Staffordshire Electric Power Co. with an office at Brookend, and Edward Rowbery & Co were the electrical engineers in Ross-on-Wye. They bought and sold new and secondhand lighting plants and carried out all classes of electrical installations. Today there is an increased demand for power, which is obtained from the Midlands Electricity Board.

With the spread of telecommunications, most businesses and a few private residents had installed telephones by 1914. 'Tel. No. 1', was the Post Office in Gloucester Road, which presumably housed the telephone exchange. The Ross Year Book of 1930 included a 'Telephone Directory', but since 1941 ''phone directories' have replaced the trade directories, though the latter now serve as a useful source for local historians.

By the start of the twentieth century Ross was already established as a tourist town. *Burrow's Guide* of 1905 described Ross as 'one of the finest tourist centres in England', offering 'excellent accommodation', 'magnificent scenery', 'delightful walks', 'a good supply of boats', and places of interest 'to which drives may be made'. With the development of tourism in Ross and the Wye Valley, various associations and boards were set up over the years to maximise its potential, including the Wyedean Tourist Board founded in 1946. The Ross Chamber of Commerce, the Ross Hoteliers and Caterers Association, and more recently the

Association for the Promotion of Herefordshire and the Tourist Information Centre promote Ross-on-Wye as the 'Gateway to the Wye Valley'.[20]

With shorter hours, better pay and equal opportunities introduced throughout the century, both women and men from all backgrounds began to have more time and money to spend on leisure. In Ross many clubs, societies and places of entertainment which had their roots in the nineteenth century flourished in the twentieth century.[21] During the 1940s the town boasted two cinemas — the Kyrle Picture Palace in Gloucester Road and the Roxy Luxury Cinema in Broad Street which gave way to the Maltings shopping arcade in the 1980s. Although Ross, no longer boasts a cinema, the Phoenix Theatre and Ross Choral Society are thriving. A cultural change took place in 1996 when the annual Ross-on-Wye International Festival started, which featured 'the very best in International Music, Theatre, Opera, Dance, Film, set on the banks of the River Wye.' There was also a Festival of the Arts held on a smaller scale, every other year.[22]

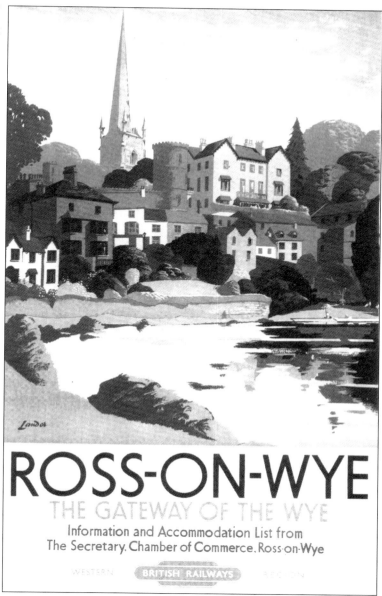

Railway poster, c.1940s

The traditional field sports of hunting, shooting and fishing still continue, but golfing, walking, canoeing and swimming have become increasingly popular. Apart from the Ross-on-Wye Golf Club, other courses have been opened to cope with the demand. Walking is now encouraged as a healthy exercise, and ramblers may enjoy a selection of delightful routes chosen from numerous walking guides. Swimming had always been enjoyed in the River Wye despite its dangers and a tradition that the Wye took a victim each year. So demands

ROSS-ON-WYE

TABULATED INFORMATION

Population : 4,920 (approx.).
Early Closing Day : Wednesday.
General Post Office : Gloucester Road.
Food Office : Market House.
Information Bureau : 27 Gloucester Road.

Places of Worship
CHURCH OF ENGLAND : St. Mary's, Church Street.
ROMAN CATHOLIC : Walford Road.
BAPTIST : Broad Street.
CONGREGATIONAL : Gloucester Road.
FRIENDS MEETING HOUSE : Brampton Street.
METHODIST : Edde Cross Street.

Sport and Recreation
BATHING : Near boat house. Enquire before plunging.
BOATING : Wye Street.
CRICKET : The Park.
FISHING : Near Wilton Bridge. By ticket at Symond's Yat (Royal Hotel).
GOLF : The Park, Rudhall, 1 mile north-east of Ross.
TENNIS : Near Wilton Bridge. Hard Courts at Ashfield.

Entertainment
CINEMAS : Roxy, Broad Street. Kyrle, Gloucester Road.

Tourist Information issued in the 1940s

for a safe place to swim began in the 1930s, but the provision of a swimming pool was delayed until 1973 when the Ross-on-Wye Swimming Pool was opened, and now caters for all abilities. Although there has been a decline in boating, canoeing is fashionable, and the Ross Regatta has been held every August Bank Holiday since it was founded in 1874.

During the 1990s an effort was made 'in regenerating the town and its environment' to give a boost to tourism, which 'produces jobs and investment benefiting everyone in Ross-on-Wye.'[23] Attractions recently established include the Market House Heritage Centre, the Heritage Trail and the Wye Valley Walk. The John Kyrle Walk was improved and enhanced by the Countryside Service and the Ross Civic Society in 1999. Although written 30 years ago, an observation written by Martin Morris, then editor of the *Ross Gazette*, still encapsulates Ross-on-Wye, 'The tourist of today rarely has the opportunity of travelling by water, but whether on footpath or on tarmac road he still finds a valley wrapped in tranquillity and beauty.'[24]

The twentieth century saw a dramatic change in the occupations and employment of the inhabitants of Ross. The traditional industries of milling, tanning, brewing and iron-working ceased, and were eventually replaced by light manufacturing industry on trading estates situated on the outskirts of the town. The interruption of two World Wars, advances in technology, changes in agricultural practice and a revolutionised transport system have all contributed to a shift in manufacturing and retailing.

A few establishments that were listed at the start of the twentieth century managed to keep pace with modern developments, although some have changed their name and owner-ship. They included the 'Ross and District Sanitary Steam Laundry' trading as 'Paragon Ross Laundry' in Ledbury Road , 'J. B. Kemp and Sons, steam and saw mills' known as 'Kemps of Ross' in Alton Street, 'William Bevan, builder, joiner and undertaker' in Old Gloucester Road retained the same name and address in 1999, together with 'Ursells of Ross-on-Wye' listed in 1902 as 'A.W. Ursell, Waterloo Monumental Works' in Cantilupe Road. Their 'headstones and monuments' ornament the county's churchyards and their 'Stone Drinking Fountains and Troughs' were supplied to the Herefordshire and Worcestershire R.S.P.C.A. in 1905.

After the Second World War, unemployment in the town became a serious issue, worsened in 1956 with the closure of the Alton Court Brewery which had been one of the biggest employers in Ross. To tackle this problem the Alton Court Industrial Estate was established, followed by the Ashburton Industrial Estate, officially opened in 1979.[25] In 1988 the district council planners reported that 'the past can be preserved hand-in-hand with the advantages of contemporary technology' in the 'delightful small town' of Ross-on-Wye, by 'the encouragement of industry and commerce in areas which, although, immediately convenient to the town centre, do not intrude upon its antiquity.'[26]

In 1946 better housing conditions were planned by Herefordshire County Council, who prepared schemes to provide separate dwellings for each family so as to eliminate overcrowding. Many properties in the town were condemned as insanitary under the 1936 Housing Act, although those of architectural or historic interest were exempt.[27] Decisions taken at the time probably led to the demolition of Markye's Almshouses in Edde Cross Street, the closure of the Game Cock Inn in Brampton Street, and the replacement of the George Inn with a line of shops, which all took place in the early 1960s.

YOU ARE LOOKING AT THE

Leading Luxury Cinema of Herefordshire

"THE ROXY"
ROSS-ON-WYE
PHONE 198

The finest chosen Programmes are presented with perfect Sound and Comfort

DAILY   -   -   -   5.0 until 10.30 Continuous
SATURDAY   -   -   2.0 until 10.30 Continuous
BOOKING DAILY. OFFICE HOURS 10.30 to 12.0

Proprietors ROSS CINEMA & THEATRE CO., LTD.

Above: Advertisement for the Roxy Cinema, and Right: for the Ross Sanitary Laundry both c.1940/50

HIGH-CLASS LAUNDERERS and DRY CLEANERS

IT is important, from so many points of view, to choose the Laundry that exercises the most scrupulous care.

IF you entrust us with your Washing and Dry Cleaning you are assured of each article receiving that individual attention which ensures the best possible results.

WE make a great feature of

OUR SERVICE

Our Van visits All Districts. Collections are prompt and the work is punctually returned.

Send a Post Card and our Van will call

Depôt: No. 2, Broad St., Ross
Telephone : Ross No. 82.

From this date there was a growth of employment opportunities in Ross and the Forest of Dean, which together with a motorway link made the town an attractive place to live both for those in employment and those seeking a rural retirement. Housing estates spread rapidly over Lincoln Hill, Chase Side and Overross to cope with a population which leapt from 5,641 in 1961 to just under 10,000 in 1999. A further sweep of buildings was made during the 1980s including Wallace Hall's old home, 'Springfield' which was promptly covered with houses hitting the skyline. Even in the 1990s the heritage of Ross was being lost when the Alton Court Brewery was unexpectedly demolished.

People in the 1990s were more aware and concerned about planning applications, which were available for inspection at Swan House. One application provoked considerable controversy, that for the erection of a modern dwelling on the former Lerego Garage site in Wilton Road, which would block a view of the Wye from the foot of the Gazebo tower. Despite enormous publicity, both locally and nationally, an inappropriate building was constructed on this narrow strip of land which probably originated from a piece of roadside waste dating from the construction of the Wilton Road in the 1830s.

Many of the shops of Ross have not weathered the changes of shopping patterns. Barnwell and Son, grocers; Blake Bros., ironmongers; T.W. Bailey, saddler; and George Eltome, gentlemen's outfitters, were amongst those who served their customers into the mid-twentieth century, but all no longer exist. 'Benjamin', the chemist, supplies pharmaceutical goods, but the dispensary is at the Community Hospital. The drapery business of Henry Southall appears to have become 'H.W. Raynor' by 1930, which continued to trade until the 1970s.

A glimpse into the past of businesses has been recorded at the Market House Heritage Centre. Mr. Geoff Williams recalls his memories of 'Williams Central Bakery and Café in the Market Place'. He describes the changes that have taken place since the 1920s, including

Advertisement for Eltome & Son in Broad Street, c.1920. (Courtesy Ross Library)

the largest of all, that caused by the arrival of the supermarkets. George Eltome of G. Eltome and Son, gentlemen's outfitters, remembers how 'in the 1930s, most of the shops around the Market Place were occupied by whole families. When they married, they moved into flats above the shop. It was a close knit community with all the different families trading with each other.'[28]

George Nicholls outside his shop in 1999

At the end of Brookend, where the industry of Ross first began, there was an old fashioned ironmongers run by George E. Nicholls. At nearly 90, he had 74 years experience in the hardware trade, which qualified him as the oldest working ironmonger in the country. His store was 'stacked from floor to ceiling and hangs down from the ceiling. It includes just about every type of kettle from copper to enamel and those with whistling spouts; a range of different size and style tea pots above the neat displays of traditional china; there is brass hearth furniture on display and brass coal scuttles hanging from the ceiling; boot polish and paint brushes on the counter and hand brushes hanging from the front of the counter.'[29]

Unlike George Nicholls, the supermarkets sell packaged goods, but modern shoppers demand easy access, good parking and goods available under one roof. Apart from supermarkets, the shops in the town centre tend to specialise in supplying unusual, luxury and antique items. Many former shops are now estate agents, building societies or charity shops, but a new row of shops have been erected opposite the library, and a grubby corner in the Crofts has been transformed into a pleasant shopping square. With the completion of the Enhancement Scheme, it was hoped that the programme would 'provide a vibrant town centre, assist in strengthening and diversifying the local economy and help provide long lasting regeneration for Ross-on-Wye.'[30]

Notables associated with Ross during the twentieth century include a range of personalities. In the 1920s and 30s Lloyd George often stopped at Ross while travelling from London to North Wales.[31] Sir Frederick Burrows lived at Thrushes Nest on the Rope Walk. He began his working life as a railway porter, became president of the National Union of Railwaymen, went to India and was appointed the last Governor of Bengal in 1945.[32] Dennis Potter, the talented and controversial playwright came from the Forest of Dean to live in Ross, but tragically died in 1994.[33] The only female writer of note was Margiad Evans, who lived in and around Ross during the 1930s and 40s. Her writings showed unfulfilled promise before her untimely death in 1958.[34] The popular television actress, Noele Gordon, lived across the Wye from Ross and was buried in the graveyard in 1985.[35]

At the beginning of the twentieth century homes in Ross were lit by oil lamps, baths taken in tubs, with the sound of horse drawn vehicles in the streets. At the end of the century most householders expected modern conveniences, the benefits of advanced technology, and the use of a car, but this led to other problems, such as light, noise and air pollution. The impact of social change throughout the twentieth century has been reflected in Ross-on-Wye. For example, individual buildings have outlived their usefulness, and have either been converted, demolished, or rebuilt. Unforeseen changes are taking place in the twenty-first century, but will be left for future historians to record.

The sign of times gone

Appendix

Houses, Histories and Inventories

The appeal of the town of Ross has been first in its situation and then in the interest provided by its streets and buildings. In spite of this interest very little detailed work has been done on the buildings of the town. When, in the course of this research, we came upon two seventeenth century inventories which could be identified with houses in the town, we felt it appropriate to use these documents to investigate the buildings and gain some insight into their layout and the lives of their inhabitants.

Alton Court

March ye 28th 1667

A true and perfect Inventory of all the goods chassels and Cattle of John Marky late of Alton In the parish of Ross in the Countye of Hereford gent, then taken & indifferrently prized by us whose names are subscribed

		£	s	d
	Imprimis all his weareing Apparell prized at	20	0	0
Item	In the Hall one table, one chayre, one foorme and two stilltopps at	0	9	0
Item	In ye Parlour 2 table boardes with carpets, one Cupboarde, eleaven chayres, one Couch, 1 paire of Andirons, 1 Iron grate, 1 fire shoule, 6 cusshins at	1	13	8
Item	In ye Kitchen 1 old table, 1 old chest, 2 wooden Chayres, 1 Jacke, 1 foorme, 4 Kottles, 3 potts, 4 posnetts, 3 drippin panns, 3 Spitts, 3 dozen of pewter, 1 payre of toungs, 1 payer of cobbins, 1 pan, 1 Grate, 1 payre of dogges, and 1 chafre with one crane, 1 Iron Backe pothookes & linkes at	5	14	0

Its	In the celler 3 wheeles, 16 vessels	1	0	0
Item	In ye Buttery a cheese press, 1 churne, safe, 2 pewter gunns, 1 flagon, 4 Candlesticks, 1 Peece of tinn, 2 pewter tancards at	0	10	6
Its	ffire Coale and wood at	5	10	0
Its	At the Stayres heade 1 old chest and 1 press prized att	0	5	0
It	In ye study Bookes and trenchers att 2 deskes & 1 table boord	2	16	0
It:	In ye great chamber 2 beddsteeds, 2 feather bedds, 2 boulsters, 2 payre of blanketts, 2 Ruggs, 2 paire of pillows, 1 table, 1 Chest, 1 skreen, 1 paire of brasse Andirons, 3 chaires, fower stooles, 1 bellowes, 2 shute of curtaines wth vallens & 1 twiggen chaire prized att	5	18	4
It:	In the middle chamber 2 beddsteeds, 2 feather bedds, 2 boulsters, 2 blanketts, 2 ruggs & old curtains att	1	10	8
It:	In ye chamber over ye Kitchen 1 high & 2 low beddsteed, 3 feather-bedds, 3 boulsters, three blanketts, 3 Ruggs, 1 presse, 3 chairs, 1 suite of curtaines, 1 Round table, 1 presse (deleted), 2 stools, 1 warming pann, 1 paire of toungs 1 paire of Andirons, 1 fire-shovell, and 6 stools, prized att (deleted) wth 1 trunck att	3	0	0
It:	In ye garretts 2 truckell beddsteeds, two feather bedds, 2 boulsters, 2 blanketts, 2 old Ruggs, 1 table, 1 paire of old Andirons att	1	0	0
It:	In the backhouse chamber 1 beddsteed, 1 flock bedd, 1 floc(deleted) blankett, and 1 old couching att	0	8	0

It:	Silver plate of all sorts	7	5	0
It:	Linnen of all sorts for bedd & boord	5	6	8
It:	One mare prized att	2	6	8
It:	3 Cows, 1 heyfor, & 1 bullocke att	5	10	0
It:	All ye sheep young & old att	24	0	0
It:	Piggs of all sorts att	1	14	0
It:	Bacon & beefe in the house att	3	12	0
It:	Butter & cheese prized att		16	6
It:	1 fouling gunn, & 2 decaied pistolls att	0	9	0
It:	Corn growing of all sorts att	7	0	0
It:	Corn in houses thrashed, & not thrashed, and Malt prized att	4	13	4
It:	Lumber, potts, sadles, bridles and all tack [deleted] tack afor ye mare, with all Utensills, and trumpery of all sorts not yet prized	1	13	4
	Summa Cat:	114	01	08

The names of prizers
John Mason
John Griffiths[1]

There has been a house at Alton since at least the thirteenth century, but it is likely that the present house, or at least the north range, was constructed after the site came into the hands of the Markye family in 1602.[2]

The present house appears as a 'half H' plan with two wings projecting from a central range and with the main door placed in the north wing. This last is of two storeys, timber-

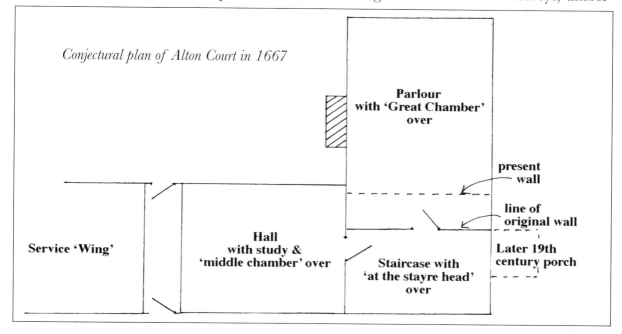

Conjectural plan of Alton Court in 1667

Parlour with 'Great Chamber' over

present wall

line of original wall

Service 'Wing'

Hall with study & 'middle chamber' over

Staircase with 'at the stayre head' over

Later 19th century porch

framed and close-studded, with herring-bone timbering in the gable end. At the end of the last century unconvincing gables were inserted in the roof and the windows on the front were replaced, though the latter may occupy a similar space to the original windows. Although much altered this would appear to be the oldest part of the building.

In the late seventeenth century the central range was either rebuilt or cased in stone and all trace of any earlier building has been obliterated. The south-east wing has been added to the house at some subsequent date. It is therefore possible that, at the beginning of the seventeenth century, when William Markye bought the house, the central range comprised a mediaeval type hall, with or without chambers over.

The inventory taken for probate on the death in 1667 of John Markye, the second Markye to live in the house, provides some insight into the way the house was used in the seventeenth century and which features have survived to the present day. It also lends credence to the suggested design of the house. It must, however, be said that any reconstruction of the building is, at best, tentative.

The RCHM report implies that the east façade was the main front and that there were two wings to north and south, making the timbered range with its large windows, the parlour range.[3] If this is the case, the hall would have occupied much of the south-east range with the kitchen behind. At this time, in the seventeenth century, the hall was going out of use as a main living room and this hall was no exception. All it contained was 'one table one chayre one foorme and two stilltopps'. The table and form would have been designed to be placed along one wall and may even have been 'built in'. The 'stilltopps' sound like distilling equipment, dumped in the hall for convenience, but it is interesting to find that Alice Kyrle's inventory for no. 34-36 High Street (see below) also cites a still in the hall. No hearth furniture is listed.

If the layout suggested above is correct, the parlour would have been in the timber wing and the great chamber, a sort of grand bed-sitting room, above the parlour. A large masonry stack, which served both lower and upper rooms, is still incorporated into this wing. The presence of '1 paire of Andirons 1 Iron grate 1 fire shoule', in the parlour inventory shows that this room was heated and it was comfortably furnished with eleven chairs, six cushions and a cupboard. The chairs would have been arranged round the walls in the formal manner expected in seventeenth and eighteenth century interiors. The two tables

Inside the roof space over the timber wing at Alton Court

were each provided with a 'carpet', a heavy patterned covering which was often woven to fit the table. There was also a couch, a type of upholstered settle.[4]

The inventory then leaves this wing and, returning through the hall, starts at the other end of the house with the kitchen, buttery and cellar. All the main cooking would have been done in the kitchen on the open fire, so there were spits to take the great

The late seventeenth century staircase at Alton Court

roasting joints, a 'jacke' to turn the spit and pans to catch the fat and juices. For boiling and stewing there were 'linkes' suspended from a bar in the chimney. To these 'kettles', large open pans with handles were attached by pothooks. A 'crane', a bar on swivel, could also hold a kettle. Baking would have been carried out in a separate bakehouse, which for some reason is not listed, although the room over the 'backhouse' does appear at the end of the inventory. The buttery held equipment, like the cheese press and churn, which in some houses was kept in the dairy, and the cellar held 'vessels', possibly brewing utensils or barrels for storing the finished product.

After assessing the service wing the valuers went upstairs. The small annexe to the parlour was originally even smaller than it is today — the mortise holes for the partition are apparent in the ceiling beams. It now contains the grand staircase and may have accommodated the original staircase. This staircase only reached to the first floor, to 'the stayres head', where an 'old chest' and a 'press' would have been placed to guard the stair opening. From this 'stayres head' room there must have been access to the study, a small unheated room with the owner's books, a table and two desks. It was probably sited over part of the hall.

Also reached from the 'stayres head' was the great chamber, which lay over the parlour. This, like the parlour, was a heated room, since hearths would have been placed one above the other so as to make the best use of the stack. The hearth furniture is listed as '1 paire of brasse Andirons' and '1 bellowes'. There were two bedsteads, each with a 'shute' (suite) of curtains and a valence, and bedclothes, a feather bed, pillows, bolsters, blankets and rugs (shaggy woven coverings) for both. There was a chest for holding clothes, a table, a screen — perhaps for privacy — three chairs, four stools and a 'twiggen' (basket) chair.

The 'middle chamber' was probably over the hall and was also unheated. Here there were only two bedsteads with bedding, and the bed-curtains were described as old. The 'chamber over ye Kitchen', on the other hand, must have been the most comfortable room in the house.

Not only was it over the kitchen, which provided background heating, but it also shared the kitchen stack and had its own fire-place. There were three beds, two low beds and one a grander affair with curtains, and three chairs and a round table. A press (cupboard) and a trunk took care of clothes storage and a warming pan ensured that the beds were properly aired. It is likely that this was a family bedroom, while the 'great chamber' was used for guests.

The 'garrets', with their truckle beds were used for the servants and there is no indication how they were accessed. One puzzling entry is the 'old andirons'. If they indicate a hearth in the attic, this would make the fifth hearth of the five recorded for the house in the hearth tax of 1665.[5] On the other hand they may merely have been stored in the attic and the fifth hearth may have been in the unlisted bakehouse.

John Markye was followed at the Court by his son William who died in 1689, leaving his property first to his widow, Lydia, and then, after her death, to his nephew, Markye Abrahall, his sister's son. Lydia Markye did not remain in the house but moved into Walford parish. From that time onward the property must have been let, for the Abrahalls had their own estates at Foy.[6]

The late seventeenth century alterations to the central range were probably carried out by William shortly before his death, since such far reaching modifications were surely the work of the owner rather than a tenant. He built in stone, with the drip-mouldings and plat band typical of the period, butting the new masonry up to the timber wing. The 'bodged' construction in the roof, where the purlins of the new building meet the rafters of the earlier wing, can clearly be seen in the roof space. As part of this project he also inserted a grand staircase, which was taken right up to attic level. This necessitated the re-siting of the partition between parlour and staircase. The staircase has been dated on stylistic grounds to the last years of the seventeenth century and resembles those in the Market House and in Palace Pound, although the balusters are slenderer.

The later documentation for Alton Court is very sketchy. It is known that in the middle of the eighteenth century the property was let to Enoch Evans, who styled himself yeoman. He seems to have been a well-to-do farmer, who lived at the house with his wife, Hannah and three sons and two daughters. On his death in 1767, he left to Hannah, my 'dwellinghouses with Yards, Gardens and appurtenances'. Hannah's own will, dated 1779, adds an intriguing twist to the story. She refers to items in her 'new house at Alton' and it is at least possible that this phrase refers to the south-east wing. This wing was certainly added after the central range, as the plat band of this range, the stone moulding above the ground floor windows, runs behind the newer structure. Unfortunately, only the stone cellar of south-east wing is accessible and although this is probably an eighteenth century construction, the remainder of the wing is so heavily cased, on the outside in render and on the inside in plaster, that there is no way of telling its date.

Enoch and Hannah's eldest son John died a bachelor in 1779, at the same time as his mother. His brother Robert inherited and farmed there until 1794.[7] Between them the Evans family must have been responsible for most of the eighteenth century farm buildings surrounding the Court. It was during this time that the name Alton or Olton Court, which dates from the early mediaeval period, was rationalised to Old Town Court.[8]

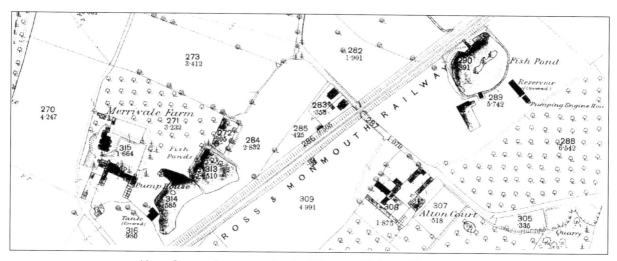

Alton Court after restoration by Thomas Blake (1887 OS map)

Although there is little nineteenth century information about the house it appears to have been occupied by a series of successful men. The occupant entered on the terrier for the Wakeman map (1823) is Richard Addis, who styled himself 'gent.' and lived at the Court from before 1813 to his death in 1835.[9] The Tithe Map recorded Elizabeth Addis, presumably his widow, there in 1840-43.[10] In 1847, Hunt & Co.'s Directory placed Francis Hamp Adams, another farmer, at Alton Court; Adams was no ordinary farmer for two years later he was part of the banking firm of Morgan and Morgan. The occupant in 1867 was Captain Frederick Allen who was listed among the Gentry in Littlebury's Directory.

Sometime before 1880 the Alton Court property came into the hands of a Mr. Ephraim Hallam. Thomas Blake, the Ross philanthropist, anxious to obtain a satisfactory water supply for the town, had his eye on the estate, which, he was certain, could provide suitable sites for artesian wells. Mr. Hallam refused to sell the estate without the house and eventually Blake bought the land, house and farm for £11,000. During the 1880s he not only set up his water-works, but also turned his attention to the house which needed money spent on it; £2,000 was laid out in repairs to this house and another on the estate. In addition, just west of the house, he built four new cottages dated 1885 for workers on the estate. It seems highly likely that some of the money expended on the Court went towards the new roof on the north wing, with its overtones of Victorian mediaeval, the heavy restoration of the north front and the re-siting of the main door in the north façade. The presence on the 1887 O.S. map of the new north porch shows that the work on this wing had been completed by this date. More money was probably spent on refurbishing the inside of the house and providing modern plumbing.[11]

Thomas Blake continued to make his home at the house he had built on the Walford Road, but his son Gordon Blake took over Alton Court. Gordon's widow continued to live there after his death and was still there in 1920, when the house was put up for sale. The description of the house given in the sale catalogue is still recognisable to-day, although some of the larger rooms have been subdivided and fire-places removed.[12]

John Kyrle's House

A true and perfect Inventory of the Goods Chattles and Cattles of Alice Kyrle, of Rosse, in the County of Hereford Widdow deceased taken and apprised the third day of Aprill one Thousand six Hundred sixty and three: by us, whose names are underwritten

Inprimis her wearing apparell		£13	13s	4d

Item	Plate at	£12		
Item	in Gold	£42	16s	
Item	Ringes at		20s	
Item	in ready money	£18		
Item	in arrears of rent	£42	12s	

In the Hall

One Table board & frame one forme and Chaire one still and a payre of andirons		12s	8d

In the Parlour

	Inprimis two Table boards and frames and one Cupboard		33s	4d
Item	seven old chaires covered with Cloth six old stooles covered with leather, and five joyned stooles		20s	
Item	five turkie old cushions, and three old carpetts		12s	
Item	one payer of andirons, a payre of tongues, a grate an iron backe, one picture, three curtaines & curtaine roddes to ye windowes		13s	4d

In the Buttery

One Table board & frame one Chaire one old Chest one safe eight dozen of trenchers one buttery basket and a voider		15s

In the Kitchen

	Inprimis on Table board & frame one dresser, one Chaire, foure low stooles, one linnen wheele & three pailes		6s
Item	five old brasse Potts & three posnetts		30s

Item	five old brasse Panns, six old kettles, two chafing dishes, two brasse Candlestickes, a morter and pestle and two skimers	£2		
Item	Twenty two pewter dishes, small and great, five saucers, one great plate and three little plates, two basons one cullender, and one Cesterne all of Pewter		26s	8d
Item	four pewter candlesticks, one flagon, one pewter canne, three chamber potts and two counterfet dishes		6s	8d
Item	foure spitts, two old iron dripping pans one iron barre to the chimney, one fish pike one gridiron, three pott hookes, three linckes to the chimney & one old frying panne		8s	
Item	one old Jacke & leaden weights, one payre of rackes one andiron, one payre of tongues and fire shoule		12s	
Item	one chopping knife & chopping board one old rollingbill, one old hatchett & axe and one barre to the drippingpan		1s	6d

In the Brewhouse

One brewing skeele, a brewing fate and some other vessels of small value	5s	

In the Studie

One case of boxes, one writing table and one chaire and one little trunke	16s	

In the Sellar

	Inprimis foure hoggsheads of syder and one hoggshead & barrell of beere and halfe a barrell of vinegar	£2	10s
Item	eleven caske of hoggshead barrells and firkins		30s
Item	one board, one bench, and trames for the vessells and one salting stone		5s
Item	Bacon & beefe, butter, butter tubbs cheese and other household provision	£2	10s

In the Chamber over ye Hall

One little table board & frame, one side
Cupboard, three chaires, foure stooles and
one great chest, one bedsteed wth curtains
& valians, one feather bedde, two boulsters
two pillows, one counterpane, and one
payre of blanketts, and hangings to the
roome, one closestoole & pan, one payre
of andirons, a fireshoule, tongues, bellowes
and a warming panne   £6

In the Chamber over ye entrie

Two bedsteeds, two feather bedds, one flock
bedde, one sette of curtaines & valians, three
coverletts, three blanketts, foure boulsters
and one pillow, a little table and frame
one chaire & one trunke   £3   10s

In the Upper Chamber over ye entrie

One bedsteede, one flocke bedde, two flocke
boulsters, two old coverletts, and one Table
board and frame   12s

In the uper Chamber over ye Hall

One Bedsteede, one truckle bedde, one little
table board and frame, one old trunke,
one old fether bedde upon one strawe bedde,
one sette of curtaines, one flock bed, two
feather boulsters, and two flocke boulsters
one pillow, two payre of old blanketts and
two coverletts, one presse, & a payre of andirons   £2   10s

In the Chamber over ye Parlour

Inpr One bedsteede, one side cupboard, one little table
and frame, two chaires, one trunke, one feather
bedde two boulsters, two pillowes, a payre of
blanketts, one Rugge, curtaines valiance and
counterpan, and a looking glasse, a payre of
andirons, a payre of bellowes, a pr of tonges
& fireshoule   £4   5s

Item   Twelve payre of flaxen sheetes, one old holland
sheete, & three old holland pillow beares,

foure payre of flaxen pillow beares, foure
payres of hurden sheets, five payre of overworn
hurden sheets, three payre of hurden pillow
beeres, and two paire of old worne hurden
pillow beeres, and three old boulster cases
one suite of old damaske, seven old flaxen
table cloathes, seven hurden over worn Table
cloathes, foure dosen of flaxen napkins
foure dosen of old hurden napkins, seven old
flaxen cupboard cloathes halfe a dosen of
flaxen towels, halfe a dosen of course hurden
towels, and more old wore linnen of
small value £8

In the Chamber over ye Kitchen

Molt, five males, one old table board and
chest, old tubbs, and other small lumbar
and some hurden yearne £4   10s

In the uper Chamber over ye Kitchen

Pease barley, Rye and wheate £3

In ye Backside and Stable

Inprimis, wood and coles		20s		
Item	two small piggs	13s	4d
Item	one Nagge, and old saddle packsaddle and bridle	£8		
Item	hay over the Stable	20s		
Item	two ladders & a wetting fate	6s	8d

Debts owing by Specialtie

Inprimis from Richard Parsons by Bond	£100		
Item	from Mr Richard Barlow by Bond	£40		
Item	from Mr John Butler by Bond	£40		
Item	from Mr John Keise by Bond	£50		
Item	from Mr John Merwicke by Bond	£5		
Item	from Mr. John Walwyn by Bill		40s	
		£450	6s	6d

Will. Baker

Ben Bulkeley

Tho Rodd
James Fisher[13]

169

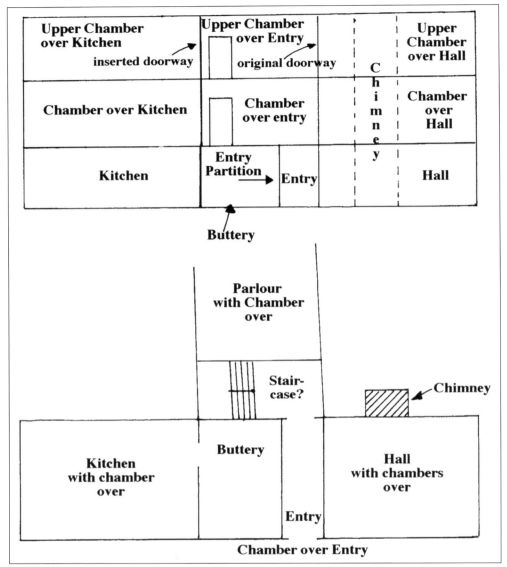

Plan and diagram showing conjectural lay-out of Alice Kyrle's house in 1664

Like Alton Court, the 'Man of Ross' house has been subject to many alterations over the years. The discovery of Alice Kyrle's inventory is an invaluable tool in studying the house, but the change, some years after John Kyrle's death, from private house to inn, together with the later division into three separate houses, make it difficult to be certain how it was used either in John Kyrle's or in his mother's time. Despite the problems, by carefully comparing the probate inventory with the physical structure of the building, certain deductions have been made which fit both the documentary and the structural evidence, without doing violence to either.

At the same time it must be said that any reconstruction is, inevitably, conjectural, and, although the placing of the hall and entry rests on solid evidence, the position of kitchen and parlour are less certain. The presence, throughout the ground floor of both 35 and 36, of moulded ceiling beams which apparently continue into the putative service area, might be thought to preclude the kitchen being in the front range, since such mouldings are more often confined to the 'upper' end of the house. The lack of visible structural evidence in no. 34 is a further complication, but there is some indication that the ground floor of this part of the house was cut up into smaller units, which perhaps included the study and brewhouse.

Since other evidence lends credence to the service wing occupying this end of the building, the kitchen has been placed at the west end corresponding with part of the ground floor of no. 34. According to the inventory, next to the kitchen

Engraving showing John Kyrle's house, on the right of the Market Hall, in 1797. The entrance to the house corresponds with the entrance suggested in the reconstruction and with the evidence of the partition within no. 35. (Samuel Ireland, Picturesque Views on the River Wye, *1792)*

was a buttery and then an entry through the house to the back premises. This entry is depicted on the engraving by Samuel Ireland, and, despite the oddity of Ireland's perspective, its position can be established by comparison with the upper windows and the 'quoins' marking the division of the property. The position is confirmed by the presence of mortises for the entry partition in the cross-beam above the shop door in no. 35. On the other side of the entry, there would have been a two bay hall, now no. 36, reached from the entry. This contained a large chimney which also served the hearths on the floors above and these hearths are both noted in the inventory.

It is suggested that a two storeyed parlour wing was sited in no. 35 in the back portion of the shop, a theory that would explain the lack of weathering of the timbers on the rear frame. These timbers can be seen from within the shop, where the lower part of the frame has been removed to enlarge the ground floor space, leaving an odd, open area with the 'outside' wall of the two upper chambers exposed. A possible explanation is that this is a stairwell and that a staircase against this wall served the two existing doorways on the upper two floors, and linked the front of the house with the parlour wing. This would also explain the absence of any evidence for floors in this bay of the wing.

On this assumption the stone built wing behind the shop, which now houses the offices of the *Ross Gazette*, would be a later addition to or extension of the parlour range. The structural evidence of this part of the building is confusing, and alterations and subdivisions in the nineteenth and twentieth centuries have made interpretation particularly difficult.

On the upper floor the framing, visible in the first floor front room of no. 35, shows that from 'the chamber over the entry', an original door led through to the 'chamber over the hall', in no. 36. This room was later sub-divided using panelling from elsewhere in the house. Another door cut through the opposite wall in no. 35 at a later date, led to the 'chamber over the kitchen', a servant's room, which must originally have had its own separate access.

As was often the case in the second half of the seventeenth century, the hall, by now something of an anachronism, was sparsely furnished, with an old fashioned table-board and frame, a form, a chair and a pair of andirons. The parlour, however, made up for this lack; here there were two table boards and frames, and a cupboard, with three carpets to cover them — carpets and cupboards were nearly always draped; there were seven chairs with cloth covered seats, six stools with leather seats and five joined or jointed stools. To soften these seats there were five turkey work cushions. Most of this furniture was described as 'old'. There was also a picture and three window curtains and rods, implying three windows.

The kitchen contained table and dresser, a chair and stools. There were large quantities of pots and pans and the standard links and pot hooks, with four spits, and a jack to turn the spits driven by weights. There was a well-equipped brewhouse. This may have adjoined the kitchen, within the front range or it may have been outside. There was also a study, with a writing table and case of boxes.

The doors showing the Kyrle coat of arms

The chamber above the hall was well furnished with hangings on the walls, a curtained bed with valance and counterpane, a cupboard, three chairs, four stools and one great chest. It was probably Alice Kyrle's own room, for it was fitted out for comfort with its own close-stool, and a warming pan. There was a hearth equipped with andirons, tongues, shovel and bellows. Evidently coal, rather than wood, was being burnt.

The room above and the chamber over the parlour were equally well furnished. The chamber over the entry had two beds, but only one had curtains and the room was unheated. The upper chamber over the entry was obviously a servants' room with a flock bed and two flock bolsters.

Behind the house was a 'backside', where wood and coal was stored and where 'two small piggs' were kept. There was a stable for the 'Nagge', with a hayloft over.

Most of the fittings in the building have gone. Some panelling remains together with three doors each with the Kyrle coat of arms set out in nails. Two doors, which originally flanked a panelled over-mantel, are in the lino-type machine room at the *Ross Gazette*. One has been altered to fit an odd little outhouse behind no. 34 High Street. All these doors are dated to 1689 and it is likely that the house was renovated in that year.[14]

John Kyrle's devotion to his garden is legendary and a small summer house in the garden behind the house was attributed to him. This summerhouse has been demolished and only the relieving arch for the plinth has survived among the rubble and weeds at the edge of the car park behind the house.

After the death of John Kyrle in 1724, the house descended to a relative, Vandervort Kyrle, and after his death his son, Walter, turned the building into an inn, the King's Arms. Part of the garden behind became a bowling green.[15] At some time before 1797, when Samuel Ireland drew the house, no. 36 was divided off and became a separate house. The eighteenth century occupant of no. 36 distinguished his property from the rest of the building by plastering the front and finishing it with mock quoins made of wood, which are depicted on Ireland's engraving. A side entrance was made by blocking off the end of the 'hall' and a tiny staircase constructed in the south-west corner of the building. The large room over the 'hall' was subdivided, using some of the panelling already in the house. Also during this period the roof lost its line of gables and the windows were altered from casements with side lights to sashes. In 1805 the inn was closed and the property divided up. It seems that nos. 34 and 35 were bought by Samuel Philpot Brookes, surgeon apothecary.[16] He lived at no. 34 and on an upper window of no. 35 there is scratched:

S.P. Brookes let this House to Messrs Jones and Love Bankers May 29th 1824.

Amor nummi crescit quantum ipse pecunia crescit[17]

In 1835 no. 34, was bought by William Cary Cocks, also an apothecary, and he began to develop the ground at the back of the building, erecting stables and other premises. The next plot, no. 35, was taken by Benjamin Powle, who was a printer. No. 34 became Thomas Roper, chemist in 1851, and then Matthews the chemist in 1876. The last chemist to occupy the site was J.F. Hart in the 1980s. The printer's shop is now the premises of the *Ross Gazette*.[18]

References

Chapter 1

1. Trevor Rowley, *The Landscape of the Welsh Marches*, Michael Joseph 1986, p.7
2. S.C Stanford, *The Archaeology of the Welsh Marches*, Collins 1980, p.35
3. *Herefordshire Archaeological News*, 1995, and No 68, 1997
4. Rosamund Skelton, *HAN*, 1995
5. Stanford, p.35
6. Bryan Walters, *The Archaeology and History of Ancient Dean and the Wye Valley*, Thornhill, 1992, p.16
7. Rosamund Skelton, *HAN*, 1995
8. Walters, p.24
9. *Herefordshire Archaeological News*, 1995
10. Walters, p.23
11. Thomas Bonner, *10 Picturesque Views*, 1798 p.34
12. *Hereford Times*, July 29, 1999

Chapter 2

1. *Guide to Some Sites of Early History Near Ross-on-Wye*, The Market House Heritage Centre (pamphlet), 1998
2. S.C Stanford, *The Archaeology of the Welsh Marches*, Collins 1980, p.102
3. Tacitus, *The Annals of Imperial Rome*, Penguin Classics, biographical note and Book XII, 30
4. Stanford, p.120
5. Bryan Walters, *The Archaeology and History of Ancient Dean and the Wye Valley*, Thornhill, 1992, p.60
6. Tacitus XII, 33
7. Walters, p.77ff, p.72, p.75
8. Walters, p.82
9. Elizabeth Taylor, 'Report on the excavation of Huntsham Romano British Villa and Iron Age Enclosure 1959-1970', *Transactions of the Woolhope Club* Volume XLVIII, 1995. See especially p.280ff
10. Walters, p.90
11. Walters, p.91
12. Rev. T.D. Fosbroke, *The Wye Tour*, 1833, p.1
13. As quoted by Walters, pp.120-121
14. Elizabeth Taylor, *Kings Caple in Archenfield*, Elizabeth Taylor/ Logaston Press 1997, p.13
15. *Book of Llandaff*, quoted by Elizabeth Taylor, *Kings Caple in Archenfield*, p.13
16. As quoted by Walters, p.128
17. Walters, p.129
18. The document is at Corpus Christi, Cambridge (MSS382), quoted by Walters, p.132ff; Taylor, p.16
19. Rosamund Skelton, *HAN*, no. 70, 1999, p.10
20. Stanford, p.181

Chapter 3

1. *Charters and Records of Hereford Cathedral*, p.8
2. Hillaby J., *Ledbury, A Mediaeval Borough*, (Logaston 1997) p.11
3. Cal. Close R. 1227-31 556
4. HRO AL 2/23 Calendar of Charter Rolls I (Typescript) p.12
5. Morris, M. *Book of Ross*, (Barracuda 1980) p.27
6. Cal. Pat. R. 1355-58 194

7. Berrisford, M., *History on the Ground*, (Sutton 1984) p.166; Girouard, M., *The English Town*, (1990) p.12
8. HRO HD OIL 28 *Red Book of the Bishop of Hereford* Rent Roll
9. *Ibid*
10. *Ibid*
11. HRO B71; B85/1-2; D4/61-70; A81/11/211
12. Hillaby, *Ledbury* p.20/1. In his discussion of the burgage plots of Ledbury, Dr. Hillaby points out the difficulty of estimating the size of the original plots
13. Parish Map 1823. This now belongs to Miss Elizabeth Okell who has generously made it available for research purposes
14. HRO HD O/L 28 *Red Book of the Bishop of Hereford* Rent Roll
15. Hereford City Library Pilley Collection Cuttings 183
16. Longleat Library Ross Collection Rent Roll for the Borough of Ross, 1648. Note that the Ross material in the library at Longleat has not previously been catalogued in any detail and few items have piece numbers. All the Herefordshire material is currently (1999) being fully listed.
17. Longleat Library Rent Roll 1648, Ross Collection Correspondence 1678; NA C66/1121/f.17
18. Longleat Library Ross Collection Bailiffs Account 1655
19. Deeds in the possession of Ross Old Books
20. HRO N 53 (LC1071)
21. Cal. Pat. Rolls Edward VI Vol 111, p. 159; HRO Glebe Terriers 4/18
22. HRO J 74 1-63
23. Ross Rectory Box (HRO BW14) bundle 4
24. HRO BA31/195; B 85/1; AW 44/42/3.9
25. Longleat Library Ross Collection Court Roll 1625
26. Longleat Library Ross Collection; John Eisel, 'The Tower, Bells, and Ringers of Ross-on-Wye, Herefordshire' in *The Ringing World*, (1992) p.1049, quoting Stanhope and Moffat, *The Church Plate of the County of Hereford* (1903)
27. HRO BA31/195; AW 44/42/3/9
28. HRO B 85/1
29. Parish map 1823
30. HRO HD O/L 28 *Red Book of the Bishop of Hereford* Rent Roll
31. Fred Druce, *A Good Plain Country Town* (Ross 1980) p.16
32. HRO HD O/L 28 *Red Book of the Bishop of Hereford* Rent Roll
33. Longleat Library Herefordshire Estates, Accounts and Correspondence, 1703, 1705, 1708, 1710
34. Longleat Library Ross Collection 1827; Rent Roll Ross Foreign n.d. (*c*.1628); Court Rolls
35. Longleat Library Ross Collection Court Rolls 1704
36. Longleat Library Ross Collection Leases 1604-1657; Indenture rents 1646
37. Longleat Library Ross Collection Bailiffs Account 1655
38. Longleat Library Ross Collection Court Rolls 1656, 1676
39. HRO Inventory of Richard Harris 9th April 1685
40. Reg. of Bishop Mascall p.28
41. HRO G87/33/5; W33/1,2
42. Reg. of Bishop Lacy p.28; Reg. of Bishop Stanbury p.69
43. Longleat Library Ross Collection 1832, 25th Sept. 1693
44. HRO O/L2 8 *Red Book of the Bishop of Hereford* Rent Roll
45. Camden W., *Britannia* (1610) p.621
46. Lambeth Palace Library Ms 708 223

47. HRO 068/III/52

48. Lambeth Palace Library Ms 3206 f803

49. HRO 068/1/35

50. NA C66/1137 51

51. Calendar, State Papers Domestic 1547-80 Vol VII 31, 141, 285, 440, 441

52. Calendar, State Papers Domestic 1558-60 p.285

53. Calendar, State Papers Domestic 1547-80 Vol VII p.427

Chapter 4

1. HRO HD O/L 28 *Red Book of the Bishop of Hereford* Rent Roll; 'Merchet — a fine or composition paid by inferior tenants to their Lord for liberty to dispose of their daughters in marriage', Jacob, O., *New Law Dictionary* (1782). Tol and tak were market dues

2. Wood, James G., 'Notes on the Chace and Penyard Park in Relation to the Dean Forest', in *Transactions of the Woolhope Club*, (1903), p.207, 208

3. Cal. Close R. 1227-31 16

4. Reg. of Bishop Cantelupe 108/9

5. Cal. Pat. Rolls 1313-17 (136)

6. Cal. Pat. Rolls 1343-45 (288); Gilbert p.39

7. Cal. Pat. Rolls 1266-72 (373); Cal. Pat. Rolls 1327-30 (424)

8. Register of Bishop Orleton xxvi

9. Cal. Pat. Rolls 1321-24 (452)

10. Cal. Close Rolls 1242-47 (509)

11. Reg. of Bishop Orleton p.122; Reg. of Bishop Trillek p.201/2, 206

12. Cal. Pat. Rolls 1334-37 (450)

13. Longleat Library, List of leases 1604-1657

14. Longleat Library Rent Roll Ross Foreign 1646

15. Coates and Tucker, *Water Mills of Middle Wye* (1983)

16. H.R. Schubert, *History of the British Iron and Steel Industry* (1957), references taken from Longleat Library, the Devereux Papers, vol. Iii, fols 60, 107, 127

17. Heather Hurley — discussion of the furnace at Bill Mill; Taylor Elizabeth, 'The Seventeenth Century Iron Forge at Carey Mill', in *Transactions of the Woolhope Club* (1986) pp.450-468; Baker, H.G., 'Early Iron Manufacture and an Inventory of Whitchurch Forge, Herefordshire', in *Transactions of the Woolhope Club*, (1944) pp.103-18

18. HRO 068/II/53. It has been claimed (erroneously) that it was one of the more recent forges to be built see Jenkins, R., 'Industries in Herefordshire in Bygone Times', in *Transactions of the Woolhope Club* (1937-8) p.72

19. Pers. Comm. Heather Hurley

20. Longleat Library, List of leases 1604-1657; indenture rents 1646; rent roll 1646

21. Bodleian Library Mss Seldon Supra 113 70

22. HRO E12/VI/DCf/4. I am grateful to Mr. Peter King for pointing out this collection and to Mr. A. Foley for allowing me to look at it.

23. HRO E12/Vl/DCc/7

24. HRO EI2/V1/DEf/17

25. HRO EI2/VI/DGf/21

26. Cooke W.H., *History and Antiquities of the County of Herefordshire* Vol III (1882) p.194

27. Beauties of England and Wales (Vol vi, p.527) quoted in Baker, H.G., 'Early Iron Manufacture and an Inventory of Whitchurch Forge, Herefordshire', in *Transactions of the Woolhope Club*, (1944) pp.110

Chapter 5

1. Buteux, V., Ross-on-Wye, in *General Marches Historic Towns Survey*, Hereford and Worcester County Council 1996

2. The Register of Bishop Cantelupe pp.120, 301

3. The physical evidence for the church is discussed fully in the *RCHM* vol II East (1932) pp.158-61 Ross on Wye, and is also dealt with in the forthcoming church guide. It has therefore been felt unnecessary to deal with the building in detail.

4. Cathedral register — quoted from Morris, M., *The Book of Ross* (Barracuda 1980) p.16

5. G.H. Cook, *Mediaeval Chantries* (1963) p.12

6. Reg. of Bishop Swinfield p.477

7. *Dictionary of National Biography* (1917) XVII p.216

8. Cal. Pat. Rolls Henry VI 1441-46 p.40; Reg. Gilbert p.2

9. e.g. Reg. of Bishop Stanbury p.183

10. Cal. Pat. Rolls 1548-50 II 399-400, III 156-9, 261-2, 280-1

11. Cal. Pat. Rolls 1548-50 II 399-400, III 156-9, 261-2, 280-1; Church Guide n.d.; Reg. Bishop J.Trefnant (1914) p.186

12. Cooke W.H., *History and Antiquities of the County of Herefordshire* Vol III (1882) p.123

13. RCHM II p.161

14. Reg. of Bishop Swinford p.227

15. Calender of Letters and Papers 1537 Vol 12 Pt 2, 1287

16. HRO Glebe Terriers 4/18. This damaged manuscript of 1630 has been corrected from a copy in the Rectory Box (HRO BW14), made in the early nineteenth century

17. Fosbroke, T.D., *Companion to the Wye Tour*, (Ross 1822) p. 141, 142

18. Calamy, Edward, *Nonconformist Ministers*, II (1802) p.250

19. See chapters 9 and I0 Cooke W.H., *History and Antiquities of the County of Herefordshire* Vol III (1882) p.119

20. *Dictionary of National Biography* XIV (1917) p.394. For further information on John Newton see Anthony a' Wood, ed. Philip Bliss, *Athenae Oxoniensis*, (1817) 1190

21. HRO Ross Parish Register; Cooke W.H., *History and Antiquities of the County of Herefordshire* Vol III (1882) p.118

22. HRO Ross Parish Register 1671

23. HRO Ross Parish Register 1679

24. HRO Ross Parish Register 1721

25. HRO Ross Parish Register 1728

26. Fosbroke, T.D., *Companion to the Wye Tour*, (Ross 1822) p.81

27. Cal. Close Rolls 1232-6, 1256 pp.174, 341.

28. Webb, J., *Roll of the Household Expenses of Bishop Swinfield*, (Camden Society 1854) p.cxliii, 63

29. Hillaby, J., *Ledbury, A Medieval Borough*, (Logaston 1997) p.67

30. Southall Henry, in the *Wye Valley Guide*, (1905) 'In blasting the rocks in its [the new Wilton Road] formation the old well belonging to the ancient Bishop's Palace was exposed to view.'

31. Webb, J., *Roll of the Household Expenses of Bishop Swinfield*, (Camden Society, 1854) p.cxliii, 63

32. Fosbroke, T.D., *Companion to the Wye Tour*, (Ross 1822) p.81

33. Reg. of Bishop Swinford p.85

34. Reg. of Bishop Mascall p.75

35. Webb, J., *Roll of the Household Expenses of Bishop Swinfield*, (Camden Society, 1854) p.cxlvii; a drawing of the prison, made in 1837, is reproduced in Webb, J., *The Civil War in Herefordshire*, p.345

36. J.W. Tonkin, 'The Palaces of the Bishop of Hereford', in the *Transactions of the Woolhope Club*, Vol XLII 1976-8 p.55

37. Fosbroke, T.D., *Companion to the Wye Tour*, (Ross 1822) p.81

38. Longleat Library, List of leases 1620s/30s

39. Hillaby, J., *Ledbury* p.74

40. L. Toulmin Smith, ed., *Leland's Itinerary*, (1910) part XI p.169

41. Longleat Library, from a bundle of Court Rolls 1629

42. Longleat Library, Correspondence and Court Rolls Ross Borough 1684; also Fines and amercements 1707

43. HRO BG 99/1/15 Abstract for Palace

44. Trust House Ltd, Royal Hotel, Ross-on-Wye, Title Deeds 1860

45. Longleat Library Accounts and Correspondence

46. Longleat Library Accounts and Correspondence Presentments

47. Lady Mary Cheek was the daughter of Sir William Pitt of Hartle, Southampton. She married first, John, third son of William Rudhall of Rudhall. He died in 1636 and, although she outlived him, her effigy lies beside his on his tomb in Ross Church. She then married Sir Alex (or John) Chalk of Shalbourn, Wilts, (variously spelt Chocke, Cholke, Chalke). Thirdly she married John Vaughan of Over Ross. Her will can be found at HRO 1660/1 no.100. Cooke W.H., *History and Antiquities of the County of Herefordshire* Vol III (1882) p.108, Robinson, C.J., *The Manor and Mansions of Herefordshire*, (1872) p.244; Reeves, N., ed., The 1675 Thomas Blount Manuscript History of Herefordshire (1997) p.53; HRO B56/9 14b, I5a. See also papers in Parish Box at Ross Rectory

48. Longleat Library 1648 Rent Roll; Manor Court Presentments 1689

49. The family information has been pieced together from various sources, mainly from WRO 898:2 BA 1303/9 1696, 1303/24 and from the will of William Fisher. HRO William Fisher 4th June 1709; Trust House Ltd, Royal Hotel, Ross-on-Wye, Title Deeds; HRO BG99/1/15

50. Trust House Ltd, Royal Hotel, Ross-on-Wye, Title Deeds; HRO BG99/1/15; BA 31/173

51. Longleat Library Rent Roll Ross chief rents 1687; HRO L70/10

52. HRO BG99/1/15

53. HRO Will William Fisher 4th June 1709

54. Rectory Box (HRO BW14) Charity Records Bundle 4; comparison of Land Tax and Ross Poor Rate HRO L78/5

55. Cooke W.H., *History and Antiquities of the County of Herefordshire* Vol III (1882) p.116

56. Cat. Pat. Rolls III 281-2

57. Charity Commissioners' Report for Herefordshire 1819-37 p.75

58. Cat. Pat. Rolls 1548-50 III 156-9

59. Longleat Library, List of leases 1604-1657. Blanch Hughes appears to be the same woman as the Blanch Wall who lived next door to the Church House, see Longleat Library Court Roll 1666 October

Chapter 6

1. HRO A28/68-77

2. Cal. Pat. Rolls 1441-6 40; NA C66/1121 f.17. This later grant of chantry land refers to 'All these shops or market stalls lying and being in Bucherrowe'

3. Longleat Library Court Rolls, 1625

4. Longleat Library 1828 Deed of 1690; The Charity Commissioners' Report for Herefordshire 1819-37 p.45; Longleat Library Court Rolls 1653 Jan

5. NA PROB 11/124

6. Bonner, T., *The Perspective Itinerary* (2nd number) (1799) p.18

7. HRO Registrars' Files 1665/207

8. Longleat Library Rents 1658

9. Longleat Library, Document 1828

10. Longleat Library Court Roll 1651 Jan

11. Longleat Library 1828. Quoted by Bonner, T., *The Perspective Itinerary* (2nd number) (1799) p.18

12. Longleat Library Court Roll 1653 Jan

13. HRO RI7 LC 10718

14. Longleat Library Petty Constables Returns 1655

15. Moore Nicholas, The Market House, Ross-on Wye, typescript report prepared for the Market House working party, June 1991

16. Longleat Library Court Rolls 1653

17. Longleat Library Petty Constables Returns 1655, Court Rolls 1653, 1654, 1660, 1667

18. Longleat Library Petty Constables Returns 1656, Accounts and correspondence 1707

19. Longleat Library Court Rolls 1654,1660,1667,1669

20. Longleat Library Court Rolls 1669

21. Dec. 17th 1891 in Hereford Library Pilley Collections 183 Book of Cuttings

22. Longleat Library Court Rolls 1624, 1668

23. Longleat Library Court Rolls 1677

24. WRO 898:2 BAI303/9 Ross Meeting Monthly Minute Book; Longleat Library 78H Minutes 1723/4

25. Longleat Library 78H Minutes 1723/4

26. Pers. Comm. N.A.D. Molyneux

27. HRO William Fisher's will 4th June 1709, see chapter 10

28. HRO D/4 61-3. It has been established from later rent rolls that these houses are 4-6, Broad Street

29. Longleat Library Court Roll 1625

30. Longleat Library Court Roll 1625; Court Roll 1654/5; Court Roll 1689

31. Longleat Library Court Rolls 1687,8,9; HRO William Fisher's will 4th June 1709

32. Longleat Library Court Roll 1667

Chapter 7

1. Cal. Pat. Rolls 1340-3 235; Cal. Close Rolls 1343-6 536

2. Cal. Pat. Rolls 1385-89 257

3. Cal. Pat. Rolls 1370-81 471; Cal. Pat. Rolls 1405-8 459

4. Reg. of Bishop Mascall p.75

5. Cal. Pat. Rolls 1391- 6 399, 541; Cal. Pat. Rolls 1416-22 134, 220

6. Cal. Pat. Rolls 1441-6 317

7. It is known that the Congregationalists built a chapel in Kyrle Street but there is no reference to it before 1749. See chapter 10

8. Longleat Library Ross Foreign Court Roll 1659

9. Longleat Library Court Roll 1625

10. Longleat Library Court Roll 30th Sept, Jas. 21

11. Cal. Pat. Rolls 1548-9 399

12. Hereford City Library LC942.44 Hill Mss Vol.III p.11 Ross Description and History

13. Ross Rectory Box (HRO BW14) bundle 4 — nineteenth-century copy of 1606-1653 benefactions; WRO 899:91 BA 4893/7. The information has been cross-checked with the Longleat Library rent rolls 1648 and 1687 to provide the location

14. Webb, Rev. J., *Civil War in Herefordshire*, (1879) II p.224

15. Longleat Library Rental, 1687, 1768; HRO D4/66

16. Charity Commissioner's Report for Herefordshire, (1819-1837) p.45; the Charity Commissioners state that the house was John Chest's house — no more is known about the Chest family — then belonged to John Kyrle Esq., and later to Mr. Cary Cocks

17. Stratford, J.A., *The Wye Tour*, (1896) p.41

18. History of Ross-on-Wye 1854-1954 — chronicled by W. Leeds (Women's Institute)

19. NA Will John Tarne 1658 308
20. HRO D4/64
21. HRO L 78/5. Comparison with a number of deeds, tax lists and rent rolls suggests this
22. Rectory Box (HRO BW14) charity papers
23. Hearth Tax (microfilm)
24. Cooke W.H., *History and Antiquities of the County of Herefordshire* Vol III (1882) p.113
25. Longleat Library Court Rolls 1651, 1655 May, 1666 October
26. *The Wye Tour* (1896) p.46
27. Morris, M., *The Book of Ross*, (1980) p.47
28. *Mercurius Rusticus* (1685) p.82
29. Webb II p.17
30. Webb II pp.32-4
31. Parish Box, The Rectory, Ross, bundle 2
32. Shoesmith, R., *The Civil War in Hereford*, (Logaston 1995), pp.87-108
33. Miles Hill, *A true and Impartial Account of the Plunderings, Losses, and Sufferings of the County of Hereford ...* (1645) p.6
34. Webb II p. 224
35. Shoesmith, R., *The Civil War in Hereford*, (Logaston 1995) p.119, 120
36. Quoted from *Mercurius Publicus*, June 6th, 1660, in Cooke W.H., *History and Antiquities of the County of Herefordshire* Vol III (1882) p.109
37. Longleat Library Court Rolls 1655 May
38. Longleat Library Court Rolls 1655 May
39. Quoted from *Mercurius Publicus*, June 6th, 1660, in Cooke W.H., *History and Antiquities of the County of Herefordshire* Vol III (1882) p.109
40. Hearth Tax 1665. See deeds of no. 52, High Street, in private hands
41. This is described in the 1770s as the 'House only adjoining not tenanted' in the insurance policy of the then owner, Isaac Taylor, the map maker. HRO Q/RTw/13 Window tax); Sun Life Insurance Policy 432165
42. *Memoirs of the Life of James Parry*, (1735) p.115
43. HRO Alice Kyrle probate inventory 31st March 1664; Appendix
44. *The Life of John Kyrle Esq.*, printed and published by Lawrence and Fowler, Ross (1912) p.9 This little booklet gathers together most of the stories told about John Kyrle
45. Heath, C., *Excursion down the Wye* (1828)
46. *Ibid*
47. HRO Will William Fisher 4th June 1709, G37/33/5, E12/VI/DFf/1 f.5
48. HRO BG 99/1/15. Both this lease and the one for the mill were dated 1st October 1693
49. HRO Will William Fisher 4th June 1709
50. *The Life of John Kyrle Esq.* p.6

Chapter 8

1. Calamy, Edward, *Nonconformist Ministers*, II (1802) p.250
2. HRO AN59/2
3. HRO L92/1 Towes, L.T., *A Short History of the Congregational Church meeting at Ross-on-Wye* (1962) pp.1-6
4. HRO HD4/1 Bishop of Hereford's Consistory Court Books — Office Books 1662, ff212v, 272; Ross Deanery 1674/6 ff.1-3, 25, 45/6, 88
5. HRO typescript 1665 Hearth Tax
6. Parish Box, Rectory, Ross. Vellum deed of 1709 and Rev. T. Underwood's letter 1811 bundle 5/6
7. HRO Bishop's Registrar Files Excommunication 1674/35
8. This building features in the 1749 poor rate (HRO L78/5) for Ross when Mr. Vaughan paid 2d for the meeting house. Comparison with the Land Tax of 1776 shows that this meeting house was not the same as the Quaker meeting room near the mill
9. HRO M21/1
10. Penney, Norman, ed., *The First Publishers of Truth* (Friends' Historical Society 1907) p.124
11. Nickalls John, *The Journal of George Fox* (Cambridge 1952) p.450, 517
12. cf Morris, M.H. *The Book of Ross*, (Barracuda 1980) p.51. The traditional venue for the first Quaker meeting is the house later called Friends' Place in the Market Place. The Merrick family paid tax on houses near the Market Place in 1664, but the deeds for Friends' Place (HRO D4/61-66) indicate that the Merricks did not own this house at that time. In the eighteenth century the house did, however, become the home of the Morgan family, Quaker drapers and bankers, and this connection may have given rise to the name
13. Penney, p.124
14. Longleat Library Rent Roll 1648; Penney, p.124; cf Deeds for Ross Meeting House, (3), Friends' House Library
15. *Quaker Faith and Practice*, (London Yearly Meeting 1995)
16. *A Collection of the Sufferings of the People called Quakers*, Vol I (1751) p.254
17. Penney, p.124
18. Friends' House Library, Deeds for Ross Meeting House (3,4)
19. Longleat Library Rent Roll 1648; WRO 898:2 BA 1303/9
20. HRO Bishop's Registrar Files Excommunication 1674/35
21. *A Collection of the Sufferings of the People called Quakers*, Vol I, (1751) p.261
22. Friends' House Library, Deeds for Ross Meeting House (1,2,7,8)
23. Friends' House Library, Deeds for Ross Meeting House (9)
24. Friends' House Library, Deeds for Ross Meeting House (13) See *RCHM* II p.165
25. Pevsner, N., *The Buildings of England, Herefordshire*, (1990) p.282
26. WR0 898.2 BAI303/9 1693
27. Longleat Library Rent Roll 1648; HRO BA31/194
28. HRO B31/188
29. Friends' House Library, Deeds for Ross Meeting House (9)
30. Friends' House Library, Deeds for Ross Meeting House (10, 11)
31. Friends' House Library, Deeds for Ross Meeting House (21)
32. WRO 898.2 BA1303/9 1700
33. WRO 898.2 BA1303/9 1702/3
34. WRO 898.2 BA1303/9 1729
35. HRO 069 (LC 4723)
36. See Chapter 6
37. Steel, D.J., *Sources for Nonconformist Genealogy and Family History*, (1973), p.604
38. HRO will Thomas Taylor March 26th 1707
39. WRO 898.2 BA1303/9 Ross Monthly Minute Book 1696
40. HRO will William Sparry 1st June 1717 (from copy volume); will William Grindall 7th Aug. 1733
41. WRO 898.2 BA1303/9 1715
42. WRO 898.2 BA1303/9 1715
43. HRO will William Sparry 1st June 1717 (from copy volume); Friends' House Library, Deeds for Ross Meeting House (13)
44. WRO 898.2 BA1303/9 1691

Chapter 9

1. Ross Charity Records 1810, HRO BG99/1/15
2. Ross Charity Records 1810, HRO BG99/1/15
3. Benefactions to Ross Church (1819) 5, Rectory Box (HRO BW14) bundle 16, Plaque displayed on Rudhall's Almshouses
4. Ross Charities (1848) p.61 Rectory Box (HRO BW14) bundle 16
5. Rent Roll 1648 Longleat Library & Benefactions to Ross Church (1819) p.19, Rectory Box (HRO BW14) bundle 16
6. W.H. Cooke, *Collections towards the History of Herefordshire* (1882) III p.116
7. Ross Charities Scheme 1982, Ross-on-Wye Rectory
8. Petition 1667, British Museum Addit. Mss. 11054 No.128
9. Will of Thomas Addis 1614, Rectory Box (HRO BW14) bundle 12
10. Benefactions 1606-1653, Nineteenth century copy Rectory Box (HRO BW14) bundle 16 & Will of William Mann 1705, Rectory Box (HRO BW14) bundle 4
11. Furrney Family *c.*1750, Rectory Box (HRO BW14) bundle 4. Jane Furrney in Benefactions to the Church & Poor (1819) p.9, Rectory Box (HRO BW14) bundle 16 & in Ross Charity Records 1810, HRO BG99/1/15
12. Vestry Minutes 6th Feb 1786, HRO L78/9
13. C.A.V. Morgan & J.M. Briffett, *The Ross Union Workhouse* (1998) p.7
14. Bakers Charity (1867) Rectory Box (HRO BW14) bundle 16
15. Ross Charities Scheme 1982, Ross-on-Wye Rectory
16. J.A. Stratford, *The Wye Tour* (1896) p.86
17. Information given by the Trustees in 1997
18. Ross Charities Scheme 1982, Ross-on-Wye Rectory
19. Spalding Directory (1784), Terrier, Valuation & Tax Asses *c.*1824, Rectory Box (HRO BW14) bundle 2, & Deeds 1824-1876 in the possession of Geoff Gartside
20. H. Hurley, *Ross-on-Wye Heritage Trail* (1997)
21. Lease 1803, HRO G87/33/8 & W.H. Cooke, *Collections towards the History of Herefordshire* (1882) p.128
22. H. Hurley, 'History of the Chase', unpublished mss. 1999
23. *The Ross Guide* (1827) p.44
24. Overseers Accounts 1766, HRO L78/6
25. Vestry Minutes 1844, HRO L78/11, & Mr Millard in *Lascelles Directory* 1851
26. H. Hurley, 'The Forgotten Man of Ross', *Transactions of the Woolhope Club* (1985) XLV 306
27. *Ross Gazette* 5th Oct 1995 & 17th July 1997

Chapter 10

1. Minutes of the Meeting of the Comm. of Charitable Uses 1675, HRO F44/1
2. Charles Heath, *Excursion Down the Wye* (1799) 23. Dobbs death recorded in the *Hereford Journal* 29th Aug. 1798
3. Charity Schools in G.H. Cook, *Mediaeval Chantries* (1963) 32, & K. Tullett & R Lax, *Christchurch Free School* (1993) p.1
4. Notes on The Schoolhouse, *c.*1821, Rectory Box (HRO BW14) bundle 5/6
5. Report to Thomas Cromwell, Cal. L and P. 1537 Vol 12 part 130
6. Letter, Rev. T. Underwood 1811, Rectory Box (HRO BW14) bundle 12, & DNB Vol. XIV, 394/5
7. *Athenae Oxenienis* 111 (1817) 1191
8. Vestry Minute Book, HRO L78/8-9
9. Letter, Rev. T. Underwood 1801, Rectory Box (HRO BW14) 5/6
10. Grammar School Subscription List 3rd June 1811, Rectory Box (HRO BW14) bundle 5/6
11. Letter, Rev. T. Underwood 1811, Rectory Box (HRO BW14) bundle 5/6
12. *Ross Guide* (1827) p.38
13. National School, Form of Application 1834 (courtesy Virginia Morgan)
14. *Littlebury's Directory* (1876-7)
15. Charity School Accounts 1709-1788, Rectory Box (HRO BW14) bundle 5/6
16. Vestry Minute Book 1764-1795, HRO L78/9
17. Charles Heath, *Excursion Down The Wye* (1828)
18. Abstract Walter Scott's Charity School 1823, Rectory Box (HRO BW14) bundle 16
19. Winifred Leeds notes from Minute Book of the Walter Scott Charity School 1798-1860
20. K. Brookes & C. Price, *Walter Scott's Charity School* (1993) p.9
21. Ross Urban Council Senior Mixed School Log Book 1928 (courtesy JKHS)
22. Letter, Rev. T. Underwood 1811, Rectory Box (HRO BW14) bundle 5/6
23. Winifred Leeds notes of the Lancastrian School, nd
24. Peter Thacker, *Quakers in Ross* (1996) Ch.3 & *The Life of Thomas Blake* (1904) p.3
25. *Ross Gazette* 4th May 1929
26. Brief Sketch of the British Schools 1842, Rectory Box (HRO BW14) bundle 16
27. Supplementary Digest, Charity Commissioners (1891) 12/13
28. Bird's Index to the *Hereford Journal* 1770-86, Hereford Library
29. Virginia Morgan, School Notes *c.*1970s
30. *Ross Gazette* 17th Sept 1868
31. Burrows *Wye Valley Guide* (1905)
32. Grammar School information from *The Rossian* (1916) No 12 & *The Rossian* (1912-1979), (courtesy JKHS)

Chapter 11

1. Hereford Bishop's Registers printed, Booth (1921) pp.61, 355
2. Wilton Bridge Act 1597
3. H. Hurley, *A History of the River Crossing at Wilton-on-Wye* (1993) p.6
4. Rev. J. Webb, *The Civil War in Herefordshire* (1879) Vol. I, p.7
5. F. Steer, J. Andrews etc. *Dictionary of Land Surveyors (1550-1850)* pt III 245 & Ross Parish Registers 1772-1812, HRO AG39/3
6. H. Hurley, *The Old Roads of South Herefordshire* (1992) Ch. 4
7. Quarter Sessions Trinity 1876, HRO Q/SR/164-65
8. Ron Shoesmith, *Hereford* (1992) Ch.10
9. H. Hurley, *A History of the River Crossing at Wilton-on-Wye* (1993) p.9
10. Wages to Bargemen 1828, HRO D48/47
11. A Survey of the Parish of Ross *c.*1825, Rectory Box (HRO BW14) bundle 2
12. Goods carried by barge in *The Ross Guide* (1827) p.14 & Carriers Accounts 1827, Hereford Library
13. *Hereford Journal* 23rd Mar. 1828
14. *The Annual Register* Feb. 1768, p.72
15. Charles Heath, *Excursion Down the Wye*, 1828 ed.
16. *Dictionary of National Biography* (1908) Vol. VI 576
17. From Grey's letter to William Mason 24th May 1771, & William Gilpin, *Observations on the River Wye* 1770 (1983 ed.) p.15
18. *Ross Guide* (1827) p.49
19. T. Sherwood Smith, *The Tourist's Guide to the Wye* (1855) p.26
20. J.A. Stratford, *The Wye Tour* (1896) p.19
21. Ross Turnpike Trust Minute Book 1838-54, HRO Q/RWT/33
22. Hereford, Ross, Gloucester Railway, Mins. of Comm. TNA Rail 302 Vol. 2

23. H. Rake, 'The Hereford, Ross & Gloucester Railway', *Railway Magazine* 1909, 312
24. Fiveways Enhancement, SHDC (1995) Screen 4
25. Rev. J. Webb, *The Civil War in Herefordshire* (1879) Vol II p.224, & in a stray charity record of 1606, Rectory Box (HRO BW14) bundle 4
26. The George Inn, Cal. Pat. R. 1548-49, 399 & *Hereford Journal* 21st Nov. 1771
27. Coach information in N. Herbert, *Road Travel & Transport* (1985) 47 & *Pigot's Directory* 1835
28. H. Hurley, 'Barrett's Royal Hotel', *Ross Civic Society Newsletter*, nos.26, 30
29. T. Sherwood Smith, *The Tourist's Guide to the Wye* (1855)
30. Ross Collection, Longleat Library
31. Inns from W. Camden, *Britannia* (1806 ed.), Vol. III, p.88 & Rev. J. Webb, *The Civil War in Herefordshire* (1879) Vol. II, p.224
32. J.A. Stratford, *The Wye Tour* (1896) p.25
33. D. Eagle & H. Camell, *The Oxford Literary Guide* (1977) p.288 & Hon. John Byng, *The Torrington Diaries* 1787, (1934 ed), Vol. I, p.264
34. *Hereford Journal* 28th July 1802.

30. Police details in List of Police Houses & Lock-Ups, HRO AB86/1 & Ross Div.Gen. & Routine 1857-98, HRO G56/37
31. *Ross Gazette* 16th Jan 1958
32. *Jakeman & Carver's Directory* 1902 & Mission Room 1880, Rectory Box (HRO BW14) bundle 10
33. *Herefordshire Directory* 1867, 1876, 1902
34. P. Thacker, *Quakers in Ross* (1996) p.4, & *The Life of Thomas Blake* (1904) p.16
35. Information from N. Pevsner, *The Buildings of Herefordshire* (1963) 279-80, Sale Part 1883, HRO M5/28/17, T. Sherwood Smith, *The Tourist's Guide to the Wye* (1855) p.27, & OS 1887 (courtesy E. Okell)
36. H. Hurley, 'The Developments in Ross', *Ross Civic Society Newsletter*, Dec. 1985
37. Impr. Mins. 1870-74, HRO S75/M/5
38. Mock Gothic from D of E Listing (1972) p.31 & a Lease 24th Dec. 1834 (courtesy Geoff Gartside)
39. Ross Turnpike Trust Mins. Mar. 1838, HRO Q/RWt/33
40. H. Hurley, 'Developments in Ross', *Ross Civic Society Newsletter* Dec. 1985, N. Pevsner, *The Buildings of Herefordshire* (1963) p.280 & Lease of John Kyrle 1696, HRO BG99/1/15

Chapter 12
1. *The Ross Guide* (1827) pp.11-12
2. Impr. Mins. 1831-39, HRO S75/M/3
3. Gas Works from *Pigot's Directory* 1835, Impr. Mins. 1849-62, HRO S75/M/4 & Impr. Act 1865
4. Underhill in Impr. Mins. 14th May 1861, HRO S75/M/4
5. *Lascelles Directory* 1851
6. L. Richardson, *Wells & Springs of Herefordshire* (1934) p.120
7. News cutting from the *Ross Gazette*, dated 1974
8. *The Ross Guide* (1827) p.29
9. Water Engine in Sale Part 1844, HRO L70/18 & Deeds 1820, HRO J74/43
10. *Lascelles Directory* 1851
11. Public Notice 1882, HRO BD11/3
12. *The Life of Thomas Blake* (1904) p.17
13. Joseph Turnock from Census Returns 1881 & *Ross Gazette* 18th Feb. 1892
14. J. Hurley, *Thomas Blake* (1996) p.26
15. Water Works from Agreement 30th Oct. 1891, Rectory Box (HRO BW14) bundle 14, & A.H. Waters, *Water Supply Report* (1945) p.13
16. Impr. Mins. 4th Mar. 1870, HRO S75/M/6
17. Letter to Impr. Comm. 30th July 1870, HRO BD/11/17
18. J.A. Stratford, *The Wye Tour*, (1896) p.26
19. Pounds & Prospect Plan 1833, HRO BA3/173
20. Ross Corn Exchange 1860, HRO S75/M/58 & *Littlebury's Directory* 1867
21. A List of Subscribers 1811, Rectory Box (HRO BW14) bundle 11
22. Churchwarden's Accounts 1772-1814, HRO L78/3
23. Fire Brigade in Littlebury Dir. 1867, General Statement 1869, HRO G42 bundle 40 (11) & Impr. Mins. 1868-9, HRO S75/M/5
24. Fire Brigade, *Ross Gazette* 5th Oct 1899, 30th Jan. 1969
25. Rev. T.D. Fosbroke, *The Wye Tour* (1822) p.195
26. Vestry Mins. 1820-34 HRO L78/10
27. Impr. Act 1830 & Impr. Mins. 1838, HRO S75/M/3
28. Rules for Ross Police 1838, HRO AP72/5
29. Impr. Mins. 1842-4, HRO S75/M/4

Chapter 13
1. *The Ross Guide* (1827) p.13
2. Nail Making from Deed 1693, HRO AJ89/3, Dr. G. Strong, *Handbook to Ross & Archenfield* (1863) p.10, Militia Tax 1813, Rectory Box (HRO BW14) bundle 11 & *Lascelles Directory* 1851
3. *Littlebury's Directory* 1876
4. Wilton Bridge Act 1597
5. Woollen Industry - Abstract of Title 1696, Royal Hotel c.1955, K. Wood, *A Lancashire Gentleman* (1992) p.88, *Littlebury's Directory* 1867, Ross Foreign Rent Roll c.1628, Longleat Lib & Militia Tax 1813, Rectory Box (HRO BW14) bundle 11
6. Barge Book 1790-1805, HRO BH58/4
7. Ross Foreign Church Rate 1794, Rectory Box (HRO BW14) bundle 7/8
8. OS 1887 (courtesy Elizabeth Okell)
9. H. Hurley, *HAN* No 52 Sept 1987, pp.28-30
10. Overross Tannery — Terriers, Valuation & Tax Assess. c.1824/5, Rectory Box (HRO BW14) bundle 2, *Littlebury's Directory* 1867 & OS 1887 (courtesy E. Okell)
11. Leather Workers in Benefactions to Ross Church (1819) pp.10, 24, Rectory Box (HRO BW14) bundle 16, *Spalding's Directory* 1784 & Assign. of Mort. 1806, HRO J74/34
12. T.D. Fosbroke, *The Wye Tour* (1822) pp.192-4
13. G. Liscomb, *A Journey into South Wales* (1799) p.66
14. Terriers, Valuation & Tax Assess. C1824/5, Rectory Box (HRO BW14) bundle 2
15. H. Hurley, 'The Alton Court Brewery', *HRO Friends Newsletter* 1997 No. 48
16. ACBC - The Brewery Trade Rev. Feb 1st 1893, Apr 17th 1897, Advert 1890, Whitbread Archive 164, and *Jakeman & Carver Directory* 1902
17. Deeds of Black Lion Inn 1833, HRO AJ89/14-15
18. T. Sherwood Smith, *The Tourist's Guide to the Wye* (1855) p.5
19. Industries from Tax Assess. 1794, Rectory Box (HRO BW14) bundle 7/8 and *Hunt & Co's Directory* 1847
20. H. Hurley, *The Story of Bill Mills*, (Logaston Press)
21. Coal & Lime in Walford Land Tax 1747 and *Hereford Journal* 5th May 1824
22. Ross Turnpike Trust Mins. 1839, HRO Q/RWT/33

23. E. Kennard, *Changing Industries in Herefordshire*, HRO AM55/163
24. A. Sanctuary, *Rope Twine & Net Making* (1988) p.9
25. Sun Fire Insur. Policies 1779-87, Guildhall Library
26. Newton family Ass. of Lease 1820, HRO J74/43 & Sale Notice 1847, HRO L70/18
27. Overseers Accounts 1767, HRO L78/6
28. Boat Building — G.E. Farr, *Chepstow Ships* (1954) p.140 and *Herefordshire Directory* 1880-1929
29. K. Woods, *A Lancashire Gentleman 1763-1847* (1992) p.80
30. Terrier, Valuation & Tax Assess. C1824/5, Rectory Box (HRO BW14) bundle 2
31. Palace Pound Sale Part. 1906, HRO M5/28/27
32. Wallace Hall — H.Hurley, 'The Forgotten Man of Ross', *Transactions Woolhope Club* XLV (1985) 305-311 & Shawcross & Co, Genealogical Table 1970
33. K. Woods, *A Lancashire Gentleman, 1763-1847* (1992) p.79
34. C.A.V. Morgan, *Nathaniel Morgan* (1995) pp.2-3
35. Savings Bank — Regs. of the Savings Bank 1817, Rectory Box (HRO BW14) bundle 14 & *Littlebury's Directory* 1876
36. *Littlebury's Directory* 1876.
37. J. Hurley, *Thomas Blake* (1966)
38. F. Druce, *A Good Plain Country Town* (1980) Ch.1&2
39. W. Leeds, 'Herefs. Postal History', *Transactions Woolhope Club* XXXVI (1960) p.275.
40. Newspapers — *Littlebury's Herefordshire Directory* 1867 and M. Morris, *The Book of Ross* (1980) p.31
41. *Littlebury's Herefordshire Directory* 1867
42. *The Ross Gazette* 2nd July 1998

Chapter 14

1. Burrows *Wye Valley Guide* (1905) p.50
2. The Jubilee of County Councils 1889-1939, p.11
3. *Jakeman & Carver's Herefordshire Directory* 1902
4. Armorial Bearings of Ross-on-Wye U.D.C., 1953 HRO AP72/8 & M. Morris, *The Book of Ross* (1980) p.132
5. Local Government — Devel. of District Councils 1997, HRO S75/M, M. Morris, *The Book of Ross* (1980) p.32, & A to Z of Herefs. Services 1998/9
6. The Jubilee of County Councils 1889-1939, p.66
7. C.V.A. Morgan, & J.M. Briffett, *The Ross Union Workhouse* (1998) p.7
8. *The Ross Gazette* 17th July 1997.
9. JKHS, Mission Statement 1998
10. H. & J. Hurley, *The Wye Valley Walk* (1994) p.49
11. M. Morris, *The Book of Ross* (1980) p.78 & pers. contact St. Joseph's Convent 1999
12. Ross Library — Ross Permanent Reading Soc. 1818, Rectory Box (HRO BW14) bundle 14, T.D. Fosbroke, Letter 3rd Apr. 1823, Gloucester Library, & *Littlebury's Herefordshire Directory* 1876

13. The Jubilee of County Councils 1889-1939, p.71
14. Ross Library Inaugural Festival Prog. 1988
15. The Jubilee of County Councils 1889-39, pp.21, 68
16. English County Planning Survey (1946) p.163
17. Welsh Water, letter 3rd Feb 1999
18. Ross Electric Lighting 1901, HRO AL6/35
19. *The Ross Gazette* 9th Oct 1902
20. *Herefordshire & the Wye Valley Guide* (1999) p.4
21. M. Morris, *The Book of Ross* (1980) pp.87-9
22. *Herefordshire & the Wye Valley Guide* (1999) pp.16, 21
23. SHDC, A Town with a Future 1997
24. M. Morris, *The Book of Ross* (1980) p.133
25. *Ibid* pp.102-103
26. South Herefordshire Official Guide 1987/8, p.22
27. English County Planning Survey (1946) pp.146-63
28. Market House Heritage Centre, Recalling Memories 1998
29. *Hardware Today*, Dec. 1998, p.7
30. Ross Town Centre Enhancement Scheme, Funding Partners 1997
31. M. Morris, *The Book of Ross* (1980) p.135
32. H. Hurley, *Ross-on-Wye Heritage Trail* 1997
33. Dennis Potter, leaflet from Ross Library, nd
34. H. & J. Hurley, *The Wye Valley Walk* (1994) p.50
35. Who's Who on T.V. 1990-91, 5th ed, p.210

Appendix

1. HRO Inventory of John Marky, 28th March 1667
2. Cooke W.H., *History and Antiquities of the County of Herefordshire* Vol III (1882) p.113
3. *RHCM* vol.II (East) p.166
4. Chinnery, Victor, *Oak Furniture, the British Tradition* (Antique Collectors' Club 1990) pp.275, 276
5. HRO Hearth Tax 1665 (typescript)
6. HRO N53/1277; AB43/7
7. HRO Enoch Evans will 28th Nov 1767; Hannah Evans will 12th June, 1779; John Evans administration 12th June, 1779
8. HRO L78/5 & 6
9. Wakeman map, Miss Okell; HRO AL39/25
10. HRO Ross Tithe Map and Apportionment
11. In Memoriam (1904)
12. HRO M5/28/12
13. HRO Alice Kyrle will and Inventory 1663/147
14. Morris, M., *Book of Ross* (Barracuda 1980) p.24 and 25
15. Heath, C., *Excursion down the Wye*, (1828)
16. Fosbroke T.D., *Wye Tour* (1822) directory
17. 'The love of money increases as one's property increases'
18. Deeds for the plot at the rear, courtesy of Mr. G. Gartside

Index

Page numbers in italics relate to illustrations

182